the art of STAIRCASES

Author: Pilar Chueca

© Carles Broto i Comerma
Jonqueres, 10, 1-5
08003 Barcelona, Spain
Tel.: +34 93 301 21 99
Fax: +34-93-301 00 21
E-mail: info@linksbooks.net
www. linksbooks.net

the art of STAIRCASES

contents

introduction

Architectural design requires techniques and systems that allow for safe and functional construction. Like all the elements that form part of an architectural project, stairs have technical requirements and must be subjected to a detailed study. To ensure a good vertical communication between the floors of a building in accordance with its use, standards and set calculations must be used.

On the understanding that stairs are a building element that represents more than merely going up and down, this book attempts to analyse all the aspects of stairs, illustrating the main types through examples taken from some of the most important architects in the world. This study of the "world of stairs" allows us to discover the different systems of support that they use, the construction possibilities, the different types of materials that can be used in their structures, the proportions they must have, how to calculate their width, and types of banisters and handrails. Everything is perfectly laid out with drawings, diagrams and many photographs that explain and help to understand this element which is so mundane and complex at the same time.

Stairs, often seen as something secondary, are also loaded with symbolism. Through them one can reach the expressiveness that is necessary for a dialogue with the space in which they are located to become a reference point for the understanding of the whole work. Though stairs used to be a clear reference to the financial status of their owners, today the references tend to be more technical and aesthetic. Because of this, stairs are becoming an increasingly important feature in buildings by contemporary architects who are seeking a given aesthetic, provinding the people who use them with new sensations. This tendency is shown in the careful selection of stairs offered in this book.

types of stairs

types of stairs

Straight-run stairs

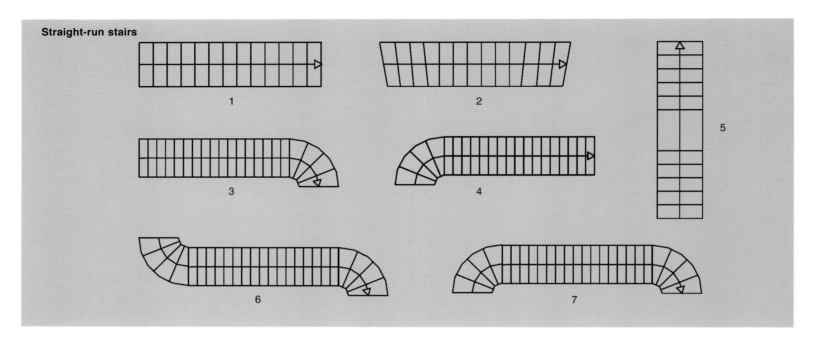

1. Straight-run
2. With oblique steps
3. With quarter-turn at top
4. With quarter-turn at bottom
5. With landing
6. With quarter-turn at top and bottom in opposite directions
7. With quarter-turn at top and bottom

8. Quarter-turn stair
9. Half-turn stair
10. Dog-leg stair with winders
11. Open newel stairs with quarter-space landings
12. Imperial stairs
13. Three straight flights with a single quarter-turn landing
14. Tour-flights stairs

Straight-run stairs with several flights

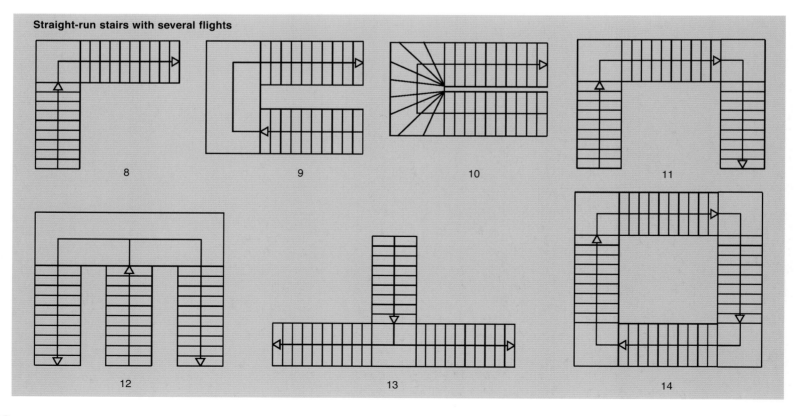

Curved stairs

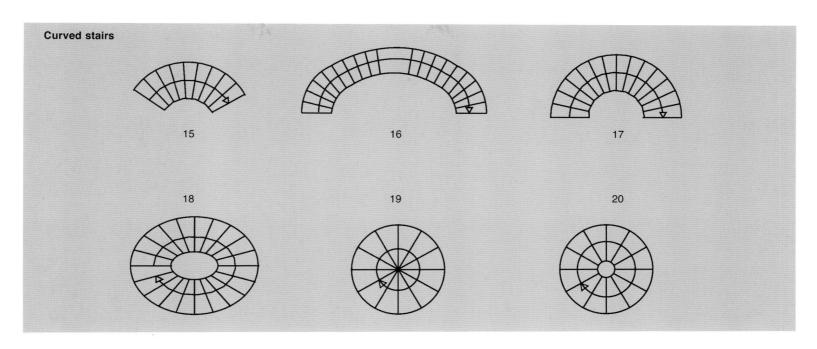

15   16   17

18   19   20

15. Arched
16. Basket arch with landing
17. Half-round stair

18. Elliptical stair
19. Spiral stair
20. Geometrical stair

Taku Sakaushi / O.F.D.A. Zigzag Rooms. Tokyo. Japan. Photographs: Hiroshi Ueda

Koichiro Ishiguro. White Woods. Tokyo. Japan. Photographs: K. Takada

Benson & Forsyth. Marico House. London. UK. Photographs: Helene Binet

11

Traut Architekten. Single Family House. Bad Camberg, Germany. Photographs: Thomas Balzer

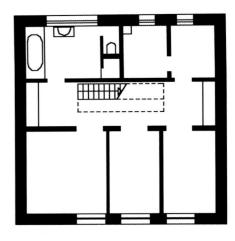

Basement floor plan

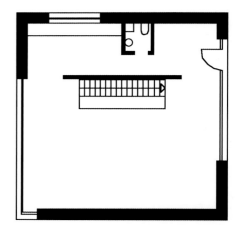

Ground floor plan

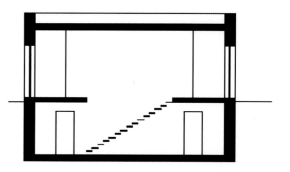

Longitudinal section

In dwellings, the most common solution is to use straight-run stairs of a single flight, because they are easy to build. The staircase can be semi-concealed behind a partition or set against one of the walls, thus maintaining order in the space. The final result will depend on the materials used, the type of steps and the type of banister or handrail.

John Pawson. Walsh House. Telluride, California, USA. Photographs: Undine Pröhl

AV 62 arquitectos. Plentzia, two single-family homes. Biscay, Spain. Photographs: AV 62 arquitectos

Behnisch & Partner. Social Housing in Ingolstadt-Hollerstauden. Ingolstadt, Germany. Photographs: Behnisch & Partner, Christian Kandzia

Böge Lindner Architeckten. Extension of the Wilhelmsburg School. Hamburg, Germany. Photographs: Heiner Leiska

Straight-run stairs with landings are the most suitable for great heights. The landings allow the users to rest without breaking the rhytthm of their ascent. In long staircases it is advisable to use several landings to break the climb.

Pica Ciamarra Associati. Napoli Shopping Centre San Paolo. Napoli, Italy. Photographs: Pica Ciamarra Associati

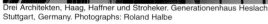
Drei Architekten, Haag, Haffner und Stroheker. Generationenhaus Heslach. Stuttgart, Germany. Photographs: Roland Halbe

Kada + Wittfeld. St. Niklaus senior citizens home. Neumarkt, Austria. Photographs: Margueritta Spiluttini, Fritz Lorber

Procter:Rihl. Slice House. Porto Alegre, Brasil. Photographs: Marcelo Nunes, Sue Barr

Georges Maurios. Montenegro House. Paris, France. Photographs: Gaston & Jean-Marie Monthiers

Carlos Ferrater, Alberto de Salas. Hotel Tryp Aeropuerto. Barcelona, Spain. Photographs: Alejo Bagué

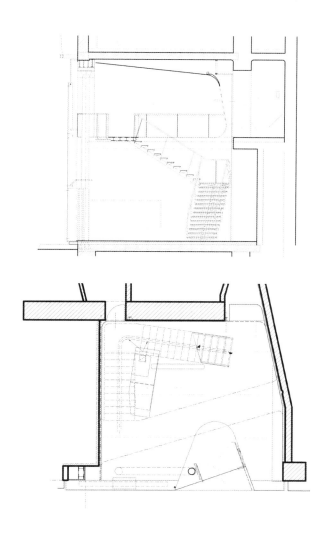

Propeller Z. GIL fashion area 1. Wien, Austria. Photographs: Margherita Spiluttini

Jürg Steiner. The Coking Plant / Exhibition space. Essen, Germany. Photographs: Steiner Architectural Office

Jean-Michel Wilmotte. University Technological. Auxerre, France. Photograph: Christophe Demonfaucon

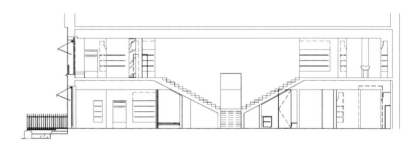

The way the space is organized tends to emphasize the long and unbroken perspectives while leaving other views to be revealed gradually. The layout of the store rotates around a T-shaped staircase, sheathed in a narrow, double-height volume, at the center.

John Pawson. Calvin Klein. Paris, France. Photographs: Vincent Knapp

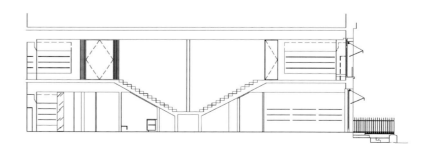

gmp - von Gerkan, Marg und Partner - Architects. Private tennis court in Jurmala. Riga, Latvia. Photographs: Klaus Frahm

19

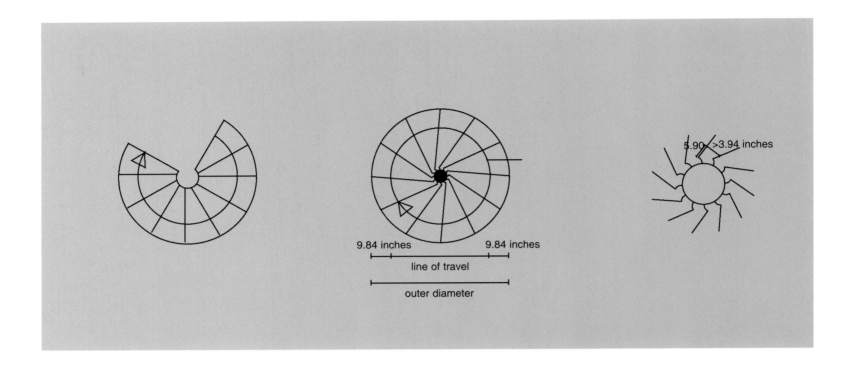

9.84 inches   9.84 inches

line of travel

outer diameter

5.90 / >3.94 inches

Circular stairs

The steps of circular stairs with a large diameter are designed according to the radius that Start from the centre of the circumference. If the tread is less than 3.94 inches, winders must be used.

Winding stairs

Winding stairs are probably the most suitable solution for linking two levels using the minimum space.

With the helicoidal system the stairs are no longer based on straight sloping flights but are of a vertical nature. Although this solution occupies less space, it requires greater physical effort for the persons using the stair, and is less comfortable and safe. Therefore, winding stairs should not be used for heights of over 13.12 feet.

Winding stairs are compoed of a series of easily assembled elements. The steps are placed one above the other on a central axis, and the balusters of the banister are connected to the outer edges of the steps.

The steps are wedge-shaped and have braces or ribs that support and secure them.

For spiral stairs with a central newel, the inner edges are placed at a tangent to the newel. If one wishes their line to be more precise and attractive, the edge of the step is cut at the newel.

The width for small stairs is 31.49 to 35.43 inches, though it may be as little as 19.68 inches. The outer diameter may be greater than 3.28 feet. If the diameter is greater than 8.2 to 9.84 feet it is preferable to install geometrical stairs rather than spiral stairs.

The pitch line may be steeper than for straight stairs, with risers of 7.02 to 7.8 inches.

The line of travel is not in the middle of the step, but 9.84 inches from its outer edge, parallel to the line of the banister. 15.90 feet from the axis, the tread must have a width of 3.94 centimetres.

Winding stairs may be right-hand or left-hand, but it must be taken into account that a winding stair is more dangerous going down than up, so it is recommended for the line of travel to go in a clockwise direction, so that the right hand can hold the banister during the descent.

The vertical clearance should be 7.22 feet and never less than 6.56 feet.

The materials used for winding stairs are normally Wood and steel because they are lighter, though reinforced concrete may also be used. If the stairs have a newel, the load-bearing structure may be made with prefabricated concrete elements.

Gaëlle Hamonic et Jean-Christophe Masson. House in a garage Abbadie. Paris, France. Photographs: Hervé

SCDA Architects. Teng Residence. Singapore. Photographs: Peter Mealin

Atelier Tekuto. Cell Brick House. Tokyo, Japan. Photographs: Makoto Yoshida

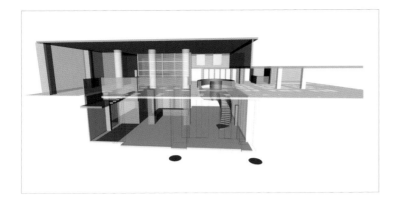

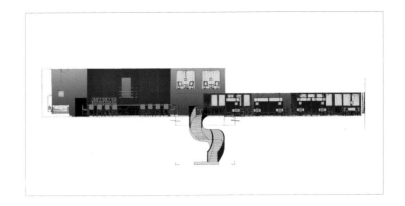

A grand spiral stair links the reception with the first floor, and represents a modern interpretation of the showpiece staircases in nineteenth century French chateaux.

Perkins Eastman Architects. Sun City Takatsuki. Takatsuki, Japan. Photographs: Chuck Choi

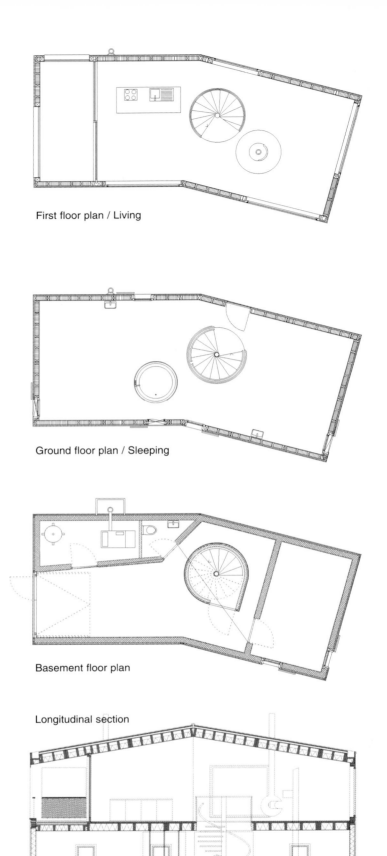

EM2N Architects. Holiday Cottage in the Swiss Alps. Flumserberg, Switzerland. Photographs: Hannes Henz

First floor plan / Living

Ground floor plan / Sleeping

Basement floor plan

Longitudinal section

Tommila Architects. Iso Omena. Helsinki. Finland. Photographs: Jussi Tiainen, Voitto Niemelä

ARX Portugal. House Extension. Portugal. Photographs: Fernando Guerra, Sérgio Guerra

Pei Cobb Freed & Partners. Eurostars Grand Marina Hotel. Barcelona, Spain. Photographs: Joan Mundó

Anne Bugugnani + Mònica Pascual. Loft in Lloret. Girona, Spain. Photographs: Eugeni Pons

Sugiura Office. House H. Nagoya, Japan. Photographs: Tamoutsu Kurumada

winding stairs

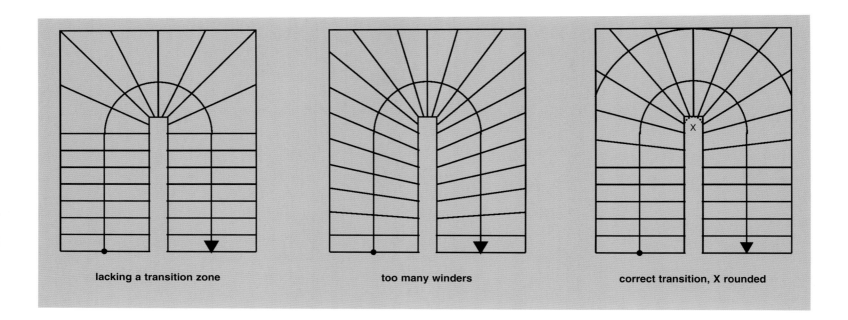

lacking a transition zone   too many winders   correct transition, X rounded

Straight-run stairs sometimes have the drawback that the height between floors is great, so they would occupy a great deal of floor space. To avoid this problem steps are placed on the landings. The steps on the landings are adjusted. The riser/tread ratio must be invariable for all stairs, even in the turns. In each case the aim is to find a form for the steps that ensuring that the structural string and the bnister are built correctly, without interruptions, maintaining the dimensions of the tread in the line of travel.

The steps are wide on the outside and very narrow on the inside, i.e. they are trapezoidal. The regulations require a minimum tread width of 3.94 to 5.90 inches at the inner ends of the steps.

To equal the width of the treads, the steps located befote and after the turn are winders. It is preferable not to use too many winders to facilitate the comfort of transit. In rectangular stairs no step edge must coincide with the corner. Stairs with winders must not be built outdoors.

Also, like winding stairs, these stairs must go straight up, because they are more dangerous for going down than up. Thus, a person going down will find the widest part of the steps on their right.

The turns must provide a gradual transition from one direction to another. A differentiation is normally made between quarter-turn and half-turn stairs. This transition is made by using winders.

The procedures for designing winders include the following:

- Rounded winders
- Development method
- Semicircle method
- Proportional division

Thinking Space Architects. House on Club Row. London, UK. Photographs: Edmund Sumner

Alexander McQueen + William Russell. Alexander McQueen. London, UK. Photographs: Alexander McQueen

29

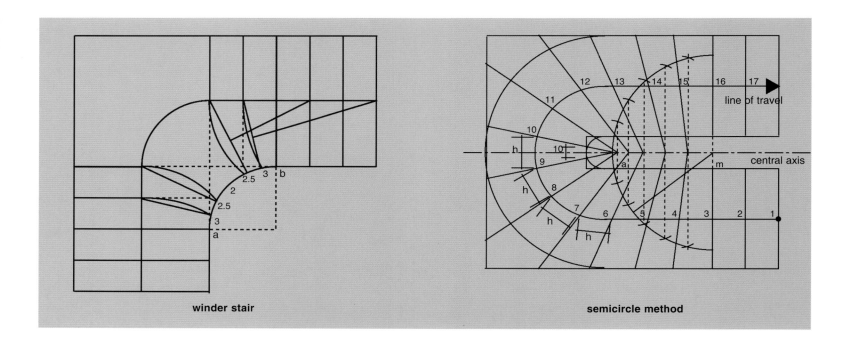

winder stair

semicircle method

Rounded winders

This is a solution for avoiding the problem in stairs with quarter-space landings, the step of the lower flight falls exactly below the first step of the that upper flight.

The winders start a few steps before and after the landing.

In this method the section of the string between "a" and "b" is curved and is divided into as many parts as stairs meeded, from the centre of the curvature. The drawing shows the division in the proportion 3, 2.5, 2, 2.5, 3. The front edges of the steps may be square or semicircular.

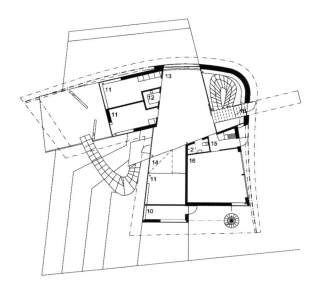

The semicircle method

This method varies according to whether the number of steps is odd or even.

When the stair has an odd number of steps, their width must be drawn horizontally over the line of travel so that the surface of a landing is in the centre of the curvature, i.e. a tread in the centre of the stair.

The last straight steps may be chosen freely (for example 3 and 15). In the curvature the central tread must be drawn, situated in the axis of the stair, with the desired width, which must be at least 3.94 inches. These points are joined with the corresponding points on the line of travel. The point where they meet corresponding to the front edges of the steps.

The front edges of the steps are extended at "a". Then the last two straight steps are joined and an arc is traced from the point of intersection in the central axis "m" witha radius of between "m" and "a". The lenght of the circle is divided by the number of winder steps to be used. This should be checked. From the corresponding points of division of the semicircle a line is drawn perpendicular to the central axis of the stair: the front edges of the steps are then obtained by joining the points of tread on the travel line to the points of intersection obtained at the central axis.

When the stair has an even number of steps, the pitch is located in the middle axis. Point "a" is obtained in the same way as in the previous procedure. We thus establish the minimum width of the treads of the steps, which are directly before or after the middle axis.

Jyrki Tasa. Moby Dick House. Espoo, Finland. Photographs: Jyrki Tasa, Jussi Tianen

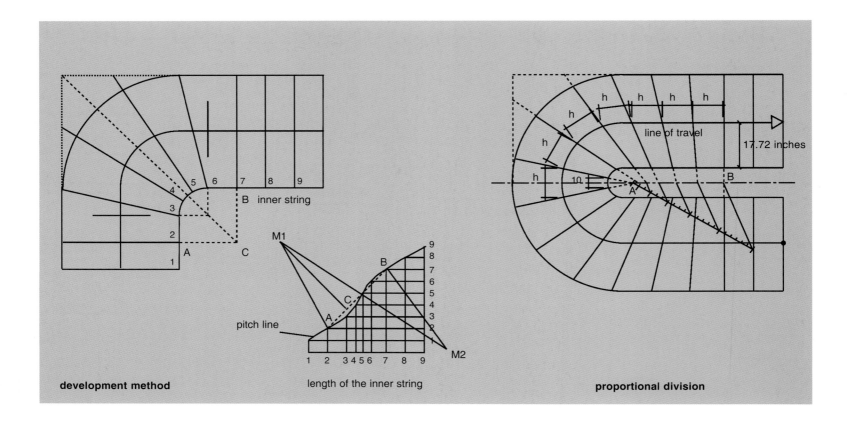

development method

length of the inner string

proportional division

Development method

A horizontal plan of the widths of the steps is drawn in equal parts on the travel line, and the rectangular steps that are required are established (for example 2 and 7). The desired ratio of the inner string is drawn. The development of the inner string is first made in the zone of straight steps. The line joining "A" and "B" is divided at the centre "C". The point of intersection of the perpendicular by the middle point at "AC", with the perpendicular at "A" on the pitch line, gives the middle point "M1" (corresponding to "M2"). The points of intersection of the arcs with their centre at "M1" and "M2" and the height of the steps gives the front edges of the steps.

Proportional division

When the stair has an odd number of steps, the steps must be divided so that a tread coincides with the axis of the stair.
The treads are distributed on the line of travel so that the edge of a step falls on the middle axis of the string. The front edges of the first winder and of the central step on the same side are extended to the middle axis, determining two points: "a" and "m".
The distance between these points is divided into parts proportional to 1, 2, 3, 4, etc., according to the number of steps included, and the points of division of the middle axis are joined to those of the line of travel. The proportional division is also normally applied in straight flights of stairs which require winders for reasons of space.
When the stair has an even number of steps, the axis of the stair goes through the tread of a step. Point "a" is established by fixing the minimum width of the tread at each side of the axis of the string (extending the front edges to the axis, which gives point "a").

Simone Micheli: Bussotti Residence. Venturina, Livorno, Italy. Photographs: Mario Corsini

33

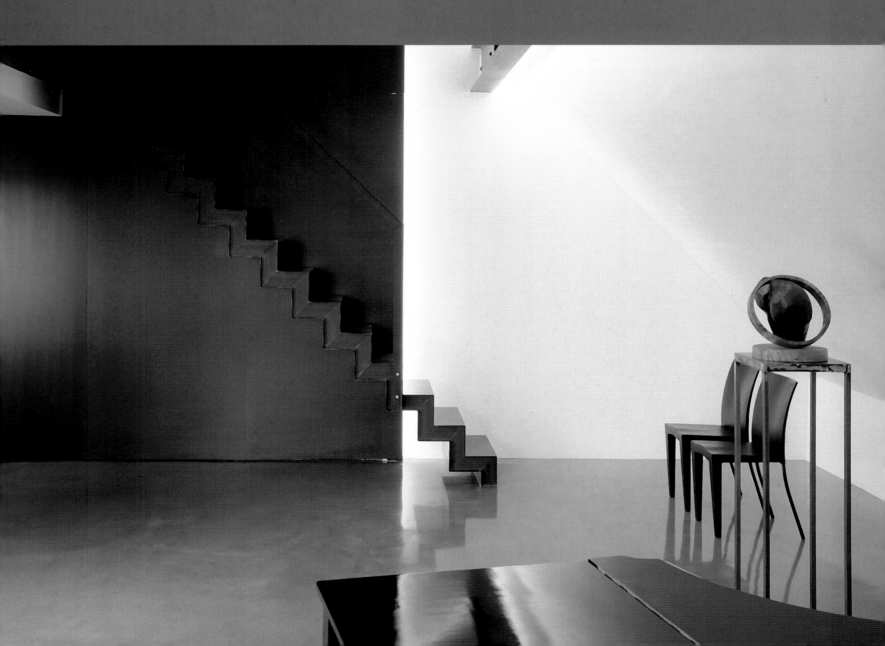

the proportions of steps

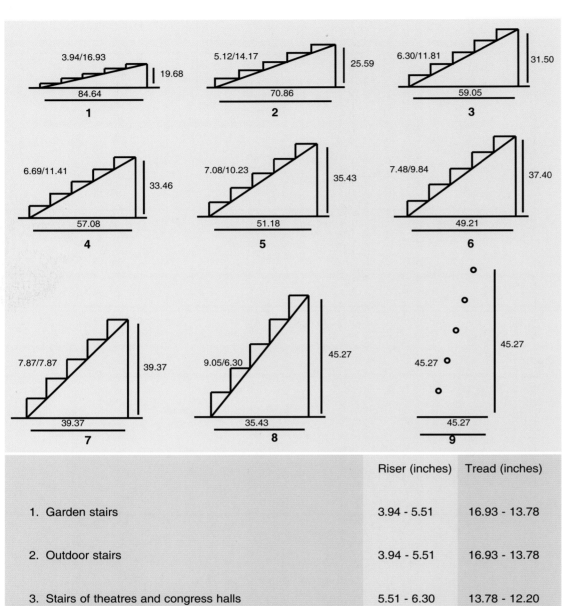

	Riser (inches)	Tread (inches)
1. Garden stairs	3.94 - 5.51	16.93 - 13.78
2. Outdoor stairs	3.94 - 5.51	16.93 - 13.78
3. Stairs of theatres and congress halls	5.51 - 6.30	13.78 - 12.20
4. Stairs of schools and public buildings	6.30 - 6.69	12.20 - 11.42
5. Stairs of residential buildings and single-family dwellings	6.69 - 7.08	10.63 - 11.81
6. Service stairs	7.48 - 7.87	9.84 - 9.05
7. Stairs of basements and attics (lofts)	7.87 - 8.66	9.05 - 7.87
8. Staircase molinera	9.05 - 9.84	6.30
9. Ladders	9.84 - 11.81	-

The riser/tread ratio is an essential factor for ease and comfort of travel on the stairs. According to the location of the stair, the following measurements are advisable:

Barclay & Crousse. Equis House. La Escondida, Cañete, Peru. Photographs: J.P. Crousse

Wulf & Partner. Adidas Factory Outlet. Herzogenaurach, Germany. Photographs: Roland Halbe

The proportions of stairs depend on the height, the space that they must occupy and the type of use. These factors determine the pitch of the stairs, though it is advisable to design stairs with a gentle slope or ramps with steps for areas of greatest transit.

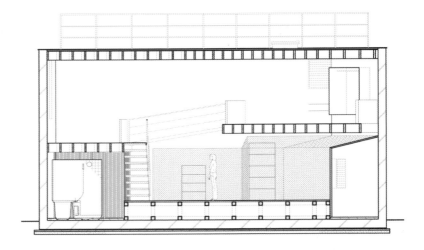

NAYA Architects (Manabu+Arata). House in Futakoshinchi. Kanagawa. Japan. Photographs: Koui Yaginuma

38

Bottega + Ehrhardt Architekten. House U. Ludwigsburg - Hoheneck, Germany. Photographs: David Franck

Catherine Furet. Housing in Rue Leblanc. Paris, France. Photographs: Jean-Marie Monthiers

DRY Design. Lengau Lodge. Limpopo Province, South Africa. Photographs: Undine Pröhl

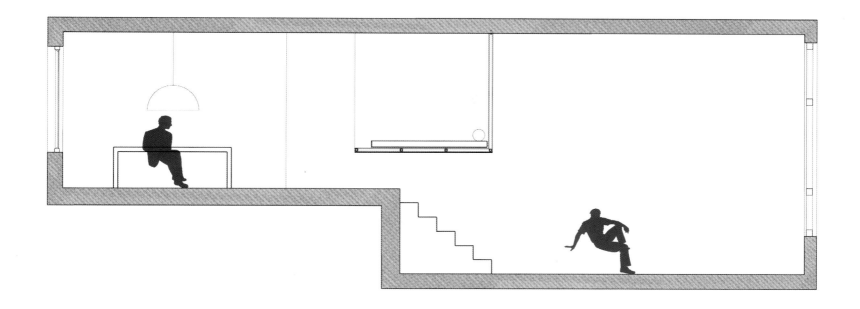

proportion of the tread

24.80

2.20

The stride of a person on horizontal ground is 23.62 to 25.59 inches long. On sloping ground, the stride is reduced by approximately half, to 12.20 inches.

For the tread and the riser of a stair to maintain a comfortable proportion there are several formulas:

The average stride rule
2C + H = 25.19 inches (24.01 - 25.59)

The safety rule
H + C = 18.11 inches

The comfort rule
H - C = 4.72 inches

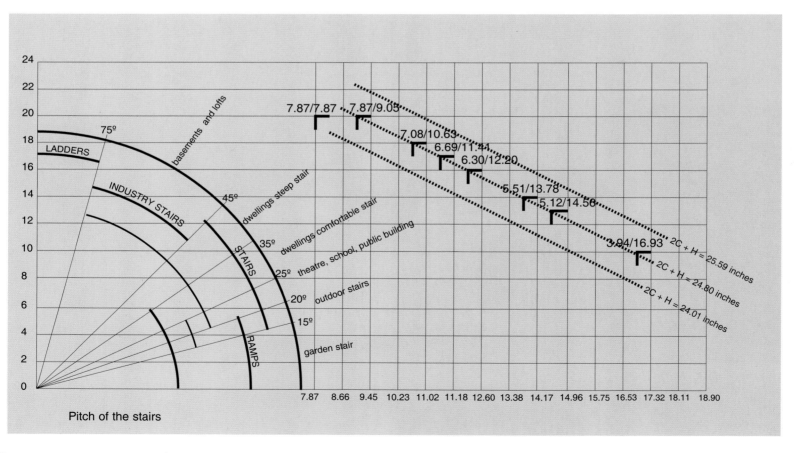

Pitch of the stairs

Stairs with a gradient of less than 45º are more comfortable and safer. The superimposition of several flights, whether in the same direction or in opposite directions, creates variety in the final structural design.

44

In order to take full advantage of the spaces without having to use a steep pitch, stairs are often located next to a wall. The interior spaces can thus be used more freely.

Waro Kishi + K. Associates. House in Karakuen II. Nishinomiya, Japan. Photographs: Waro Kishi + K. Associates

In the Zaragoza David apartment there are two separate lofts, each accessed via its own stair or ladder system. The secondary loft, set above the kitchen, features a folding ladder for easy access while a classic spiral staircase provides the elegant entry to the main loft.

David Maturen. Apartment Zaragoza David. Zaragoza. Spain. Photographs: Jordi Miralles

Mathias Klotz. Grau House. Santiago de Chile, Chile. Photographs: Estudio Mathias Klotz

Wingårdh Arkitektkontor AB. Villa Astrid. Brottkärr, Göteborg, Sweden. Photographs: James Silverman

47

stride length

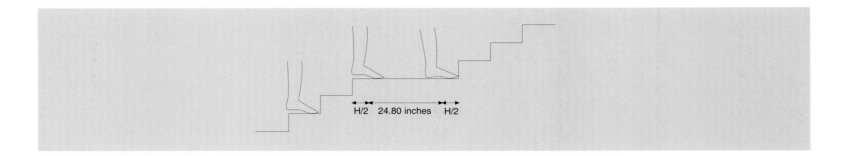

It is more difficult to go down stairs than up them. Treads of more than 12.60 inches may be uncomfortable, because one may easily catch one's heel on the edge of the steps as one goes down.

Treads of less than 9.84 inches do not provide a complete support for the foot. Also, for comfort and safety, the proportion of the step must not vary within the same flight of the stair or in a series of consecutive flights.

A set of three steps or more is considered to be a flight of stairs.

A landing is recommended for flights of 16-18 steps, and obligatory for greater numbers of steps.

The depth of the landing must not alter the rate of travel, and this distance is defined by the stride length rules.

Stride length rules $L = 2C + H$
$L = n \times 25.20 + H$

Corneille Uedingslohmann Architekten. Little Red Riding Hood GmbH. Berlin, Germany. Photographs: Joachim Wagner

A landing facilitates a change of rhythm that can involve all the elements of a stair.

Behnisch & Partner. Social Housing in Ingolstadt-Hollerstauden. Ingolstadt, Germany. Photographs: Christian Kandzia

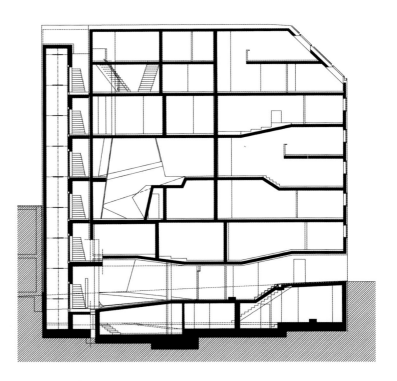

North south section

BKK-3. MISS Sargfabrik. Wien, Austria. Photographs: Hertha Hurnaus

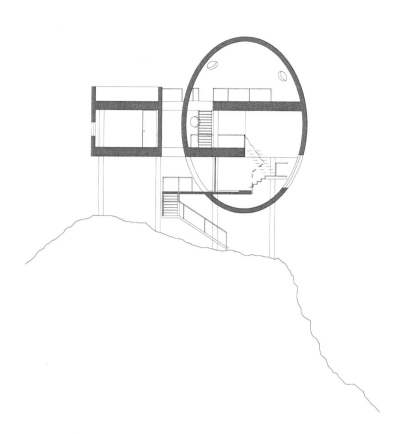

Satoshi Okada Architects. Villa Man-Bow. Atami, Japan. Photographs: Hiroyuki Hirai

51

stair width

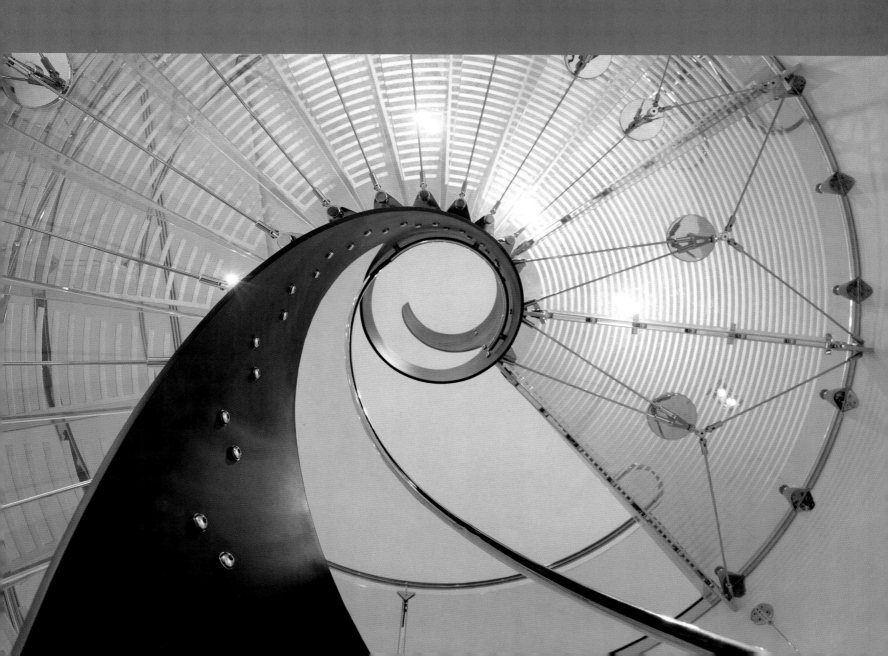

stair width

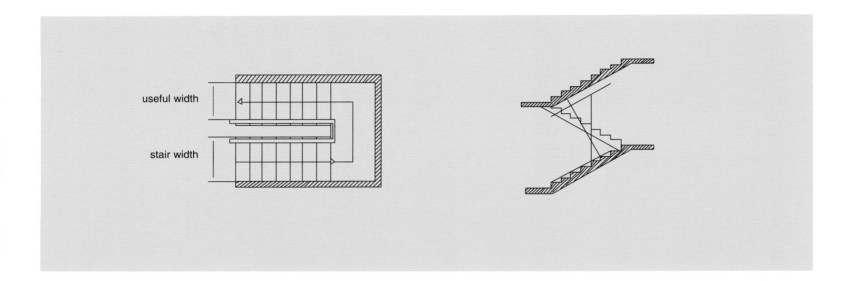

The width of a staircase is defined by its limits, but it is often re-duced at the sides by a banister or string. The useful width of a staircase is thus defined as the span between the two handrails or between the handrail and the wall.
The width of stairs is also determined by the number of persons who must circulate in both directions, by the time in which a build-ing must be evacuated and by the importance of the building in which they are located.

According to the number of persons that use the stairs, they are classified as follows:

- For 1 person .2.13 feet (minimum 1.15)
(Winding stair or narrow straight stair)
- For 1 person .3.28 feet (minimum 2.46)
- For 2 persons . . . . 4.26 feet (minimum 3.61)
- For 3 persons .6.23 feet (minimum 5.90)

According to the type of construction and the use applied to the staircase, its width is determined as follows:

- Winding stairs . . . .> 1.64 feet
- Service stairs
  (straight flight) . . . .> 2.13 feet
- Stairs for dwellings
  with up to two floors . . . .> 2.95 feet
- Stairs for dwellings with over
  two floors and one apartment per floor . . . . . .> 3.28 feet
- Stairs for dwellings with over two floors and
  more than one apartment per floor . . . .> 3.60 feet
- Free-standing stairs. . . . .> 2.95 feet
- Stairs of churches, schools and hospitals . . .> 4.26 feet
- Stairs of theatres . . . .> 4.10 -5.90 feet
- Stairs of department stores . . . .> 4.92 - 6.56 feet
- Stairs of meeting places . . . .> 4.10 - 8.20 feet

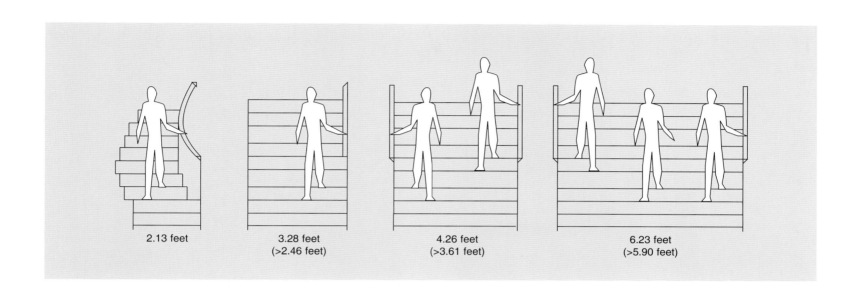

| 2.13 feet | 3.28 feet (>2.46 feet) | 4.26 feet (>3.61 feet) | 6.23 feet (>5.90 feet) |

Adrià+Broid+Rojkind. House F2. Ciudad de Mexico, Mexico. Photographs: Undine Pröhl

Jordi Garcés. House in La Fosca. Palamós, Spain. Photographs: Lluis Casals

Atelier Bow-Wow. Izu House. Shizuoka, Nishizu, Japan. Photographs: Takashi Homma

56

ADD + Manuel Bailo, Rosa Rull. Sita Murt Boutique. Barcelona, Spain. Photographs: Giovanni Zanzi

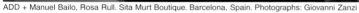

Olson Sundberg Kundig Allen Architects. Chicken Point Cabin. Northern Idaho, USA. Photographs: Benjamin Benschneider

KCAP. Homes for the Elderly in Emerald. Delftgauw, The Netherlands. Photographs: Rob't Hart & De Jong Luchtfotografie

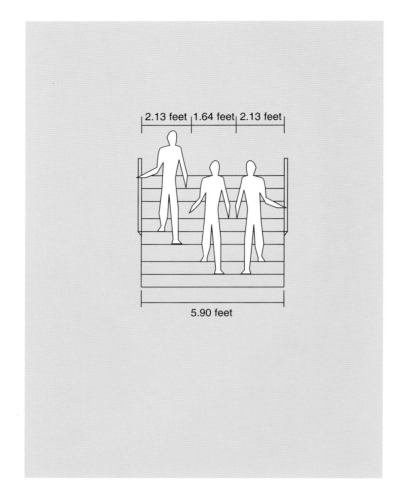

|2.13 feet| 1.64 feet |2.13 feet|

5.90 feet

For calculating the width of staircases in public buildings, the following rule may be applied:

Starting from a width of 3.28 feet, add the following supplement for every 100 persons:

- For use of 100 to 500 persons . . . . 2.30 feet
- For use of 500 to 1000 persons . . . . 1.64 feet
- For use of over 1000 persons . . . . 0.98 feet

The minimum width is 4.92 feet unless over 500 persons are to use the stair.
For example: for 700 persons
useful width = 4.92 + (5 x 2.30) + (2 x 1.64) = 19.70 m

The following rule may also be followed:
Step width = 30 + n x 50
n = number of persons circulating at the same time and the same height.

The width obtained must be divided into several zones for reasons of safety and comfort, so that the maximum width does not exceed 8.20 feet.
For widths of less than 3.94 feet the staircase must have a handrail on at least one side.
For widths of 3.94 to 6.23 feet the stairs must have a handrail on both sides.
For widths of over 6.23 feet the stairs should be divided by a banister, which is compulsory when the width of the staircase exceeds 8.20 feet.

As stairs situated in public spaces require great width to deal with heavy traffic, it is often necessary to fit banisters or handrails in the middle of the flights to give the users safety and support.

Rem Koolhaas-OMA. Prada LA. Los Angeles, USA. Photographs: Lydia Gould

Schmidt, Hammer & Lassen. Nykredit Headquarters. Copenhagen, Denmark. Photographs: Jørgen True, Søren Kuhn

line of travel

The line of travel or walking line is understood to be the virtual line followed by a person as they go up or down a staircase.

This line is considered to be parallel to the handrail or string of the staircase and is situated at a distance of 15.75 inches.

The line of travel is used to define the proportion of the steps if they are not rectangular. For curved flights it must be taken into account that if the stairs are over 3.60 feet wide, the line of travel must be considered at a distance of more than 1.64 feet from the string so that the treads next to the stairwell are not very large.

If the staircase has a width of less than 2.13 feet, the line of travel is taken 1.31 feet from the string.

Winders must have the same width at the line of travel, and become narrower towards the centre of rotation: 3.94 inches from the narrowest edge of the tread they must have a minimum width of 5.90 inches.

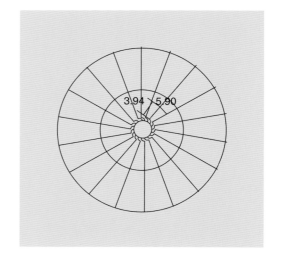

Although one goes up a spiral stair on the outer part of the steps, where the tread is wider, it is advisable to place a safety banister on the inside. In this stair, the steps are made of perforated steel plate with polished glass treads, the banister and handrail are made of steel.

Eric Raffy & Associés. Hotel des Lacs d'Halco. Hagetmau, France. Photographs: Philippe Ruault

Rahel Belatchew Lerdell. Villa RBDVD. Saltsjö-Boo, Sweden. Photographs: James Silverman

Oos Ag Open Operating System. House-Sculpture. Feldis, Switzerland. Photographs: Dominique Marc Wehrli

Schlude + Ströhle. Pflegeheim Magdalenenhof. Schönebeck, Germany. Photographs: Zooey Braun

HERTL.ARCHITEKTEN. Steinwendtner House. Steyr-Münichholz, Austria. Photographs: Paul Ott

Delugan_Meissl. Ray 1. Vienna, Austria. Photographs: Rupert Steiner

headroom

The headroom or vertical clearance is the distance from the front edge of a finished step to the lowest part of the finished ceiling. According to the building regulations, the headroom must be no lower than 6.89 feet to prevent people from banging their head.
It is recommended to measure this height in a sloping line, because on going downstairs the human body tends to lean forward slightly.

Dimensions in inches

Step		Gradient	Headroom	Height of handrail
C	H			
5.12	14.56	20º	84.64	33.46
5.90	12.99	25º	86.61	31.50
6.69	11.42	30º	88.58	31.50
7.08	10.63	35º	90.55	31.50
7.87	9.05	40º	92.52	31.50
8.26	8.27	45º	96.45	33.46
8.66	7.48	50º	98.42	33.46
7.48	9.05	50º	64.96	33.46
6.69	9.84	55º	61.02	33.46
5.90	10.63	60º	57.08	35.43
5.12	11.42	65º	53.15	35.43
4.33	12.20	70º	47.24	35.43
3.54	12.99	75º	43.30	37.40

Step	Gradient	Headroom	Height of handrail
Distance between balusters			
13.38	80º	39.37	
14.17	85º	35.43	
11.81-14.96	90º	29.53	

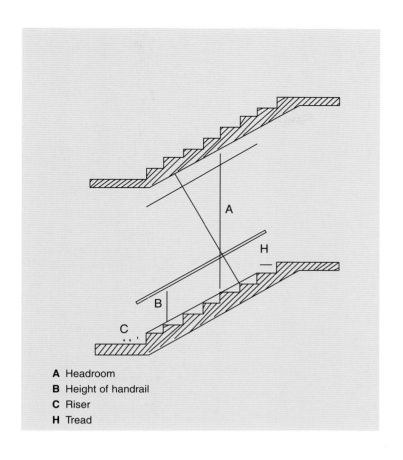

A Headroom
B Height of handrail
C Riser
H Tread

Friedrich + Partner. Altenpflegeheim Sangerhausen. Sangerhausen, Germany. Photographs: Klaus Frahm

Nieto & Sobejano. Housing Facing the SE-30. Seville, Spain. Photographs: Fernando Alda

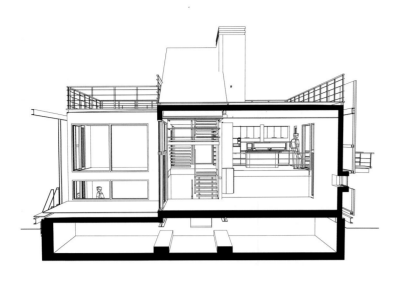

Strindberg Arkitekter AB. Villa Näckros. Kalmar, Sweden. Photographs: James Silverman

E. Cobb Architects. Lakeshore in the Cascade Mountain Range. Seattle, USA. Photographs: Steve Keating

67

Jun Aoki + Eric Carlson. Louis Vuitton. Tokyo, Japan. Photographs: Ano Daici, N. Naka

Pool. In spe-single family house. Wien, Austria. Photographs: Hertha Hurnaus

69

structural system

structural system

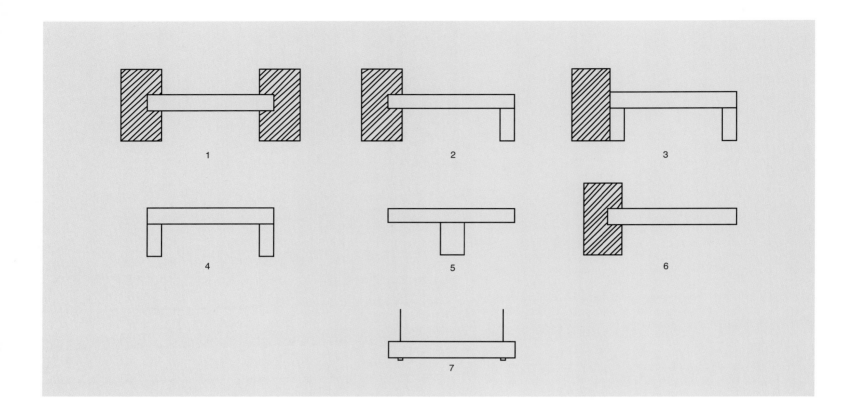

The arrangement of the steps is determined by the type of strings used to mount the structure of the staircase. The transverse structural system may be of the following types:

1. Embedded on both sides (box stair): the steps are embedded in the walls of the stairwell on both sides.

2. Embedded on one side: the steps are supported on one side by a string, and on the other side they are embedded in the wall of the stairwell.

3. Housed string: the steps are supported on both sides by strings, one of which is fixed to the wall.

4. Double string: a system derived from the previous one in which the steps are totally independent of the walls and supported by two parallel strings.

5. Central string: In this case the side strings are replaced by a single string of greater thickness, placed in the geometric centre of the steps.

6. Cantilevered or hanging step: This system has no strings, but one end of the steps is embedded in the wall.

7. Suspended stair: the steps are neither embedded nor supported by strings, but are supported by a structure of cables or ties suspended from the floor slab and give the stairs rigidity.

Manuel Herz. "Legal / Illegal". Cologne, Germany. Photographs: Boris Becker

Archi-tectonics. Gypsy Trail Residence. Kent, NY, USA. Photographs: Winka Dubbeldam

LOT - EK. Boon. Seoul, Korea. Photographs: Kyuntae Kim

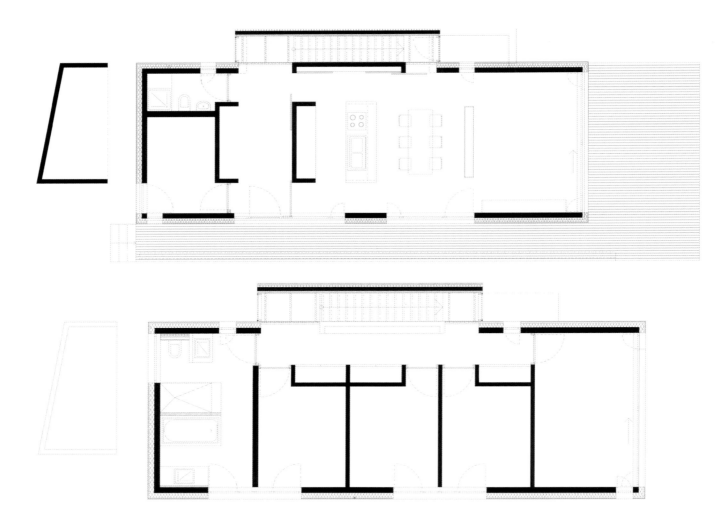

Bems Architektengemeinschaft Böwer Eith Murken. House Kaiser. Freiburg-Kappel, Germany. Photographs: Roland Halbe

Wingårdh Arkitektkontor AB. Kajplats 01. Västra hamnen, Malmö, Sweden. Photographs: Åke E: son Lindman

Werner Sobek. House R 128. Stuttgart, Germany. Photographs: Roland Halbe

Stairs supported on a central string give a particular sensation of lightness. The structure thus takes second place to the steps, which appear to be suspended in perfect equilibrium. Below, a stair with a painted iron string and wooden steps.

Buzacott Associates Architects. Hart/Picknett House. Killcare, Australia. Photographs: Adrian Boddy

Ares Fernández. Apartment in Barcelona. Barcelona, Spain. Photographs: José Luis Hausmann

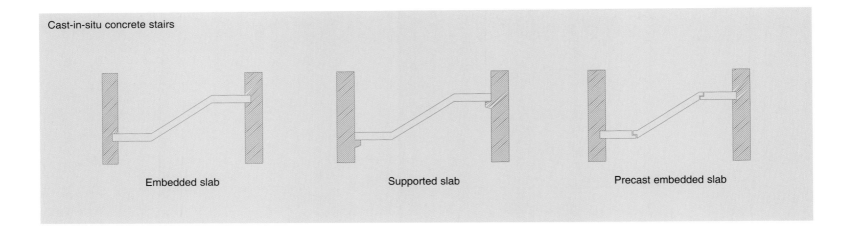

Cast-in-situ concrete stairs

Embedded slab   Supported slab   Precast embedded slab

Material used for the structure of the stair:

1. Reinforced concrete structure

These structures offer greater resistance to loads and better fire protection.

As the concrete takes the form of the formwork, it can adapt to all designs, from a straight stair to a two-flight stair —the most common type— and even a helicoidal stair.

The reinforced concrete structural support of the staircase may be of inclined slabs or joists.

The slabs and joists may be attached to the walls lengthways or in the following ways:
- embedded slab of cast-in-situ concrete
- supported slab
- precast embedded slab

The reinforced concrete slab is the most important element for stairs with this structure. By using additional reinforcement, cantilevered structures can be built. The minimum thickness of the slab at the narrowest side must be 3.94 to 4.72 inches to accommodate the steel reinforcement and provide the minimum covering.

Roy Desing. Vitra. New York, USA. Photographs: Richard Barnes

80

Massimiliano & Doriana Fuksas. Emporio Armani Chater Road. Hong Kong. Photographs: Ramón Prat

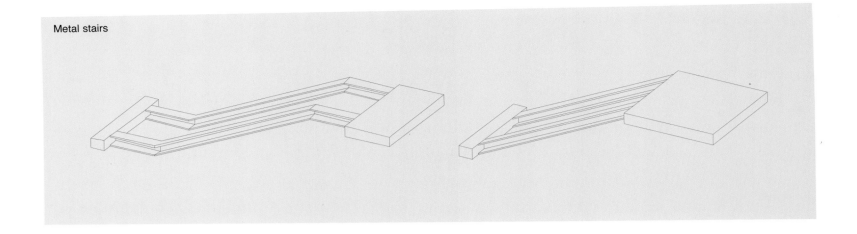

2. Steel structure

Steel structures are formed by strings made of stressed steel plate.

Steel structures tend to be used for prefabricated staircases, which are easy to assemble, and for emergency staircases. They are structures of low weight that are less of an obstacle to light than other types of stair. The fire protection regulations are particularly important for stairs of this type. As the properties of the steel (strength, maximum deformation and modulus of elasticity) vary according to the temperature, these structures must be protected with cladding or uninflammable paint.

The support is composed of string beams and brackets to support the steps, sometimes with supporting feet or posts.

The profiles most used are double T beams for the landings, and channel section beams for the strings. Finally, to join the strings and the beams, secondary steel angles are used.

AV1 Architekten. Wohnpark am Betzenberg. Kaiserslautern, Germany. Photographs: Michael Heinrich

Biselli + Katchborian. Guaecá Beach House. São Sebastião, Brazil. Photographs: Nelson Kon

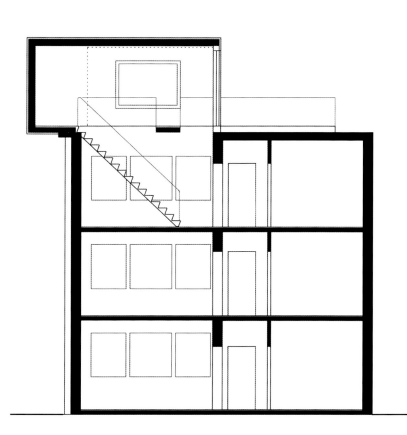

FloSundK architekten bds gbr. Symbiont Friedrich. Merzig. Germany. Photographs: G.G. Kirchner

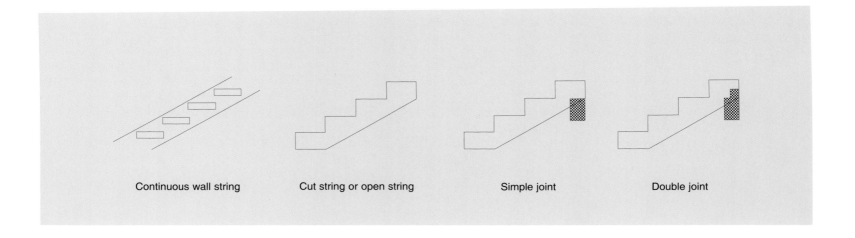

Continuous wall string   Cut string or open string   Simple joint   Double joint

3. Timber structures

This type of structure is stessed and is composed of timber joists. The drawbacks of timber structures are that they have a limited useful life and offer poor fire resistance. However, by means of complementary measures such as plastering the lower part of the stair or applying uninflammable paint, a certain degree of fire proofing can be obtained (RF 30).

- continuous wall string: a rectangular strip of wood conceals the steps.

- cut string or open string: the string is cut to fit the shape of the steps.

The strings tend to be boards 2.36 to 3.94 inches thick and 9.84 to 11.81 inches wide. They are supported on a solid floor base and at the other end, on the landing, by means of a joint with the trimmer. This joint may be simple or double.

To support the strings, which produce a thrust towards the wall, at the foot of each flight, blocks of wood are embedded in the wall to serve as additional bracing.

Gracia Studio. House GA. Tijuana B.C, Mexico. Photographs: Eduardo de Regules

Michèle & Miquel. Apartment in Virreina. Barcelona, Spain. Photographs: Josep Lluis Roig

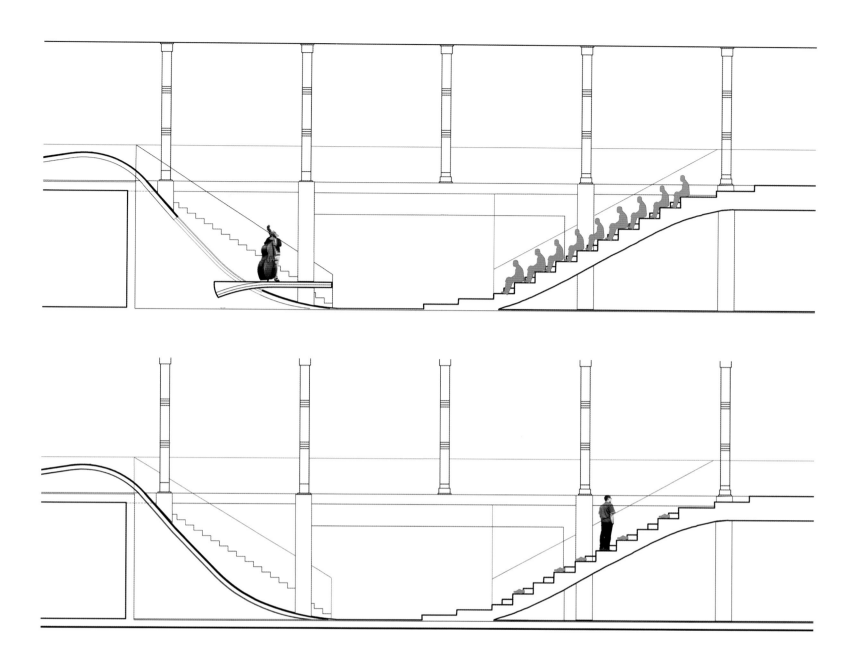

Office for Metropolitan Architecture (OMA). Prada New York Epicenter. New York, USA. Photographs: Armin Linke

José Cruz Ovalle. House in Santo Domingo. Rocas de Santo Domingo, Chile. Photographs: Juan Purcell

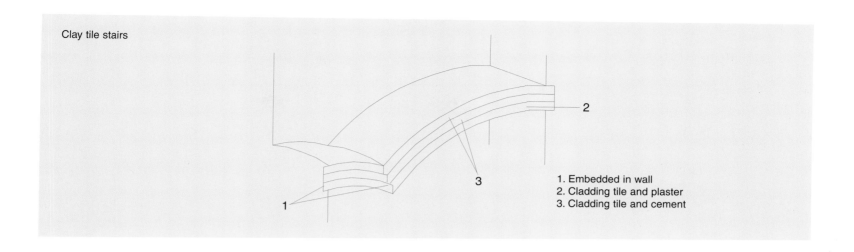

Clay tile stairs

1. Embedded in wall
2. Cladding tile and plaster
3. Cladding tile and cement

4. Clay tile structures

This is a traditional support system also known as the Catalan brickwork staircase. Its stability is obtained due to its compactness and the adherence of all the clay tiles.

Clay tile stairs are built on vaults formed by three layers of cladding tiles, the first one bonded by plaster, which sets rapidly, and the other two by Portland cement mortar.

The profile of clay tile staircases has the form of a rampant arch or basket arch, taking as a basis the inverse of the catenary resulting from joining the springs of the vault and the points of support at the end of the flight, through a string subjected to its own weight. Its length is the distance between these points increased by a tenth of the difference in height of the two points. At the base a block of solid brick is used to start the construction of the vault. The landing is usually made with a barrel vault. The end of the landing and the bottom of the flight are interlaced by interlocking the layers of clay brick.

Josep Llinàs. Teatro Metropol. Tarragona, Spain. Photographs: Lourdes Jansana

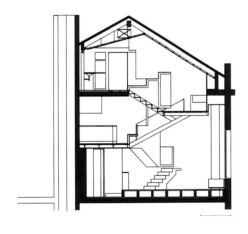

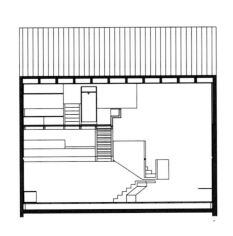

BOPBAA. Loft in Barcelona. Barcelona, Spain. Photographs: Eva Serrats

types and materials of steps

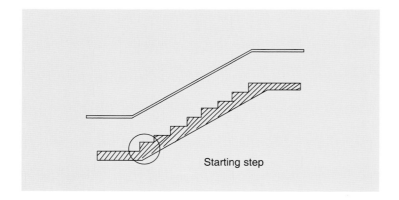

Starting step

Steps can be classified according to their situation and their section:

According to their situation:

1. Starting step: is the first (lowest) step of a flight of staircase. In general it is 0.59 to 0.78 inches higher than the other steps, to allow it to be embedded into the floor.

Jaume Bach. 4C House. Barcelona, Spain. Photographs: Lluís Casals

Iván Bercedo & Jorge Mestre. Duffy House. Sitges, Spain. Photographs: Jordi Miralles

Izquierdo + Lehmann. Vial House. Santiago de Chile, Chile. Photographs: Roland Halbe

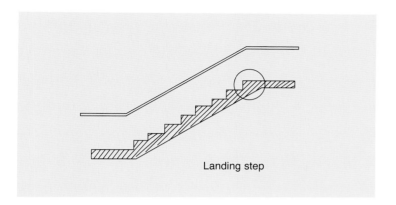

Landing step

2. Landing step: is the last (highest) step in a flight of stairs. It is at the same height of the landing, of which its tread is part of.

3. Step joining two levels: is a step connecting two levels between which there is a small difference in height. If there are more than two consecutive steps between two levels, they form a flight of stairs.

Cho Slade Architecture. Van Doren Apartment. New York, USA. Photographs: Jordi Miralles

Koh Kitayama. Plane + House. Tokyo, Japan. Photographs: Nobuaki Nakagawa

Gert & Karin Wingårdh. The Millhouse. Göteborg, Sweden. Photographs: James Silverman

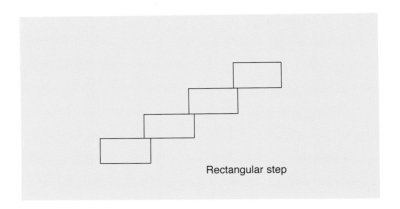

Rectangular step

According to its section:

4. Rectangular step: is a step with a rectangular or almost rectangular section. It may be solid or hollow.

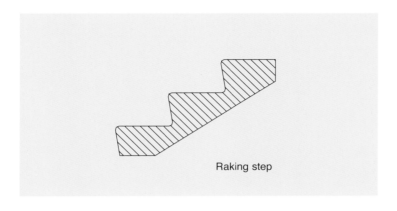

Raking step

5. Raking step: is a step with a triangular or almost triangular section. It may be solid or hollow. It saves material and weight.

Procter-Rihl. Slice House. Porto Alegre, Brazil. Photographs: Marcelo Nunes, Sue Barr

Chiba Manabu Architects. House in Black. Tokyo. Japan. Photographs: Nacása & Partners

Driendl architects. Solar Deck. Vienna, Austria. Photographs: Driendl architects

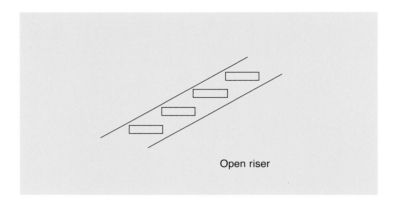

Open riser

6. Open riser: is a step composed of only a tread without a riser.

Sugiura Office. House H. Nagoya, Japan. Photographs: Tamoutsu Kurumada

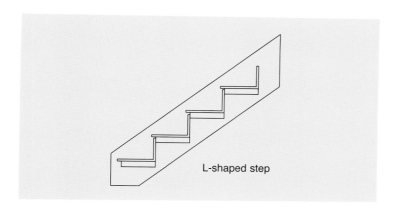

L-shaped step

7. L-shaped step: is a step composed of an L-shaped plate that may be rectangular or angular.

Takao Shiotsuka. Atu House. Ohnojo-city, Japan. Photographs: Kaori Ichikawa

Satoshi Okada architects. House in Mt. Fuji. Narusawa Village, Mt. Fuji, Japan. Photographs: Hiroyuki Hirai

Denys & von Arend + Guy Sonet. Renault Design Barcelona. Barcelona, Spain. Photographs: Joan Mundó

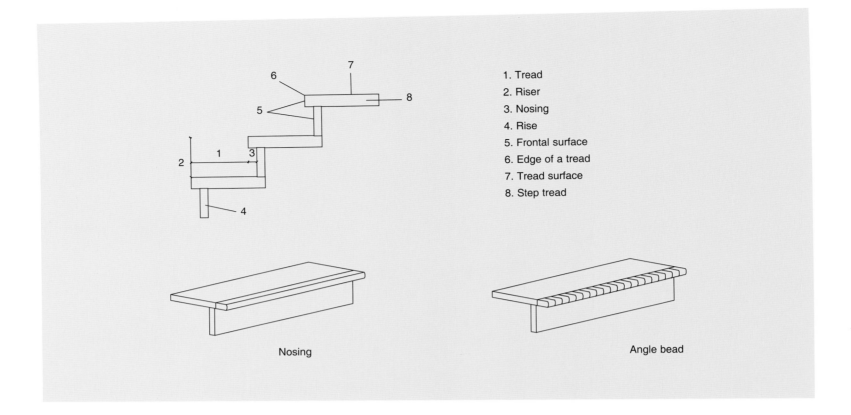

1. Tread
2. Riser
3. Nosing
4. Rise
5. Frontal surface
6. Edge of a tread
7. Tread surface
8. Step tread

Nosing

Angle bead

In some staircases the step is a structural element with a decorative finish, whereas in others it has two parts: the interior, which has a structural function, and the exterior, which serves as a decorative element.

Steps are composed of the following elements:

- **Step tread:** the horizontal part of a step.
- **Tread surface:** the horizontal surface of a step.
- **Stair tread:** the horizontal measurement from the front edge of one step to the front edge of the following step, following the direction of travel.
- **Riser:** the vertical measurement from the tread surface of one step to that of the following step.
- **Rise**: the vertical element of a step.
- **Nosing:** the horizontal measurement of the overhang of the front edge of a step above the tread surface of the lower step.

To prevent the users from hitting the riser with the tip of the foot on going up the stairs, and to increase the surface area of the steps, the tread edge overhangs slightly. The nosing is not taken into account in calculating the relation between the tread and the riser, but is added to the result obtained for the tread. The nosing must be small so that the users do not trip over it when going up the stairs. For a tread of 11.02 inches, a nosing of 1.57 inches is built, thus giving a total step width of 12.60 inches.

Steps wear out with use, and the tread edge is the part that suffers most. To protect the nosing, a reinforcement called a fillet can be placed over it. Nosings can be lined with metal or plastic, often with grooves to avoid slipping.

Jahn Associates Architects. Grant House. Sydney, Australia. Photographs: Brett Boardman and Graham Jahn

Kohki Hiranuma. MINNA no IE. Kusatsu-shi Shiga, Japan. Photographs: Hs Workshop - ASIA

Eline Strijkers. Unit 9. Amsterdam, The Netherlands. Photographs: Teo Krijgsman

Ramón Llopart Ricart. Radio Barcelona. Barcelona, Spain. Photographs: Joan Mundó

DeuxL, Vudafieri Partners. PUCCI. Ginza, Tokyo, Japan. Photographs: DeuxL, Vudafieri Partners

Ignacio Mendaro Corsini. San Marcos Cultural Center and Toledo Municipal Archives. Toledo, Spain. Photographs: Lluís Casals

Diller + Scofidio. The Brasserie. New York City, USA. Photographs: Michael Moran

material of steps

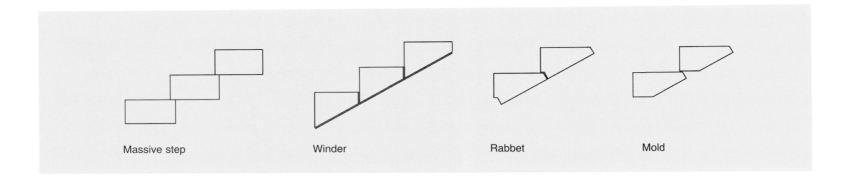

Massive step   Winder   Rabbet   Mold

The materials used to build steps range from natural and artificial stone, brick, wood, concrete, steel, aluminium and tiles to glass, cork and flexible materials such as linoleum, rubber, carpet and plastic.

Stone steps

These are normally used for outdoor staircases, since they can withstand continuous rough transit and the action of atmospheric agents. The natural stones that are most used are limestone and sandstone. Only the hardest types of sandstone are used. Among the types of stone commonly used because of its strength and resistance to wear out, are granite, basalt, slate and marble. Artificial stone made of coloured cast concrete is also used. It has a uniform composition and better properties than natural stone, so it is more resistant to wear and easier to clean. There are two types: "with finishing concrete " and "without finishing concrete".

Stone steps may have a rectangular or trapezoid section.
They may be joined together leaving a rabbet or a moulding.
The steps may be supported by a solid newel at one end and embedded in the wall of the stairwell at the other end.
However, it is more normal for them to rest on the ramp of the staircase, which is supported by joists.
The steps may also be cantilevered, though stone does not work under bending stress.
Stone may also be used as a cladding for steps. In this case the steps are built of solid concrete or brick, on which stone panels of 1.18 to 1.57 inches thickness are placed with the polished surface showing.
Steps clad with artificial stone are prefabricated in a single piece. The block formed by the tread, riser and filling materials is extracted from a mould. The tread always stands out slightly from the riser.

Kanner architects. Canyon View Office / Guesthouse. Brentwood, California, USA. Photographs: John Linden

Dominic Stevens. In-between House. Ballinamore, Leitrim, Ireland. Photographs: Ros Cavanagh

Kohki Hiranuma. MINNA no IE. Kusatsu-shi Shiga, Japan. Photographs: Hs Workshop - ASIA

Eduardo Souto de Moura. Casa Bom Jesus. Braga, Portugal. Photographs: Luis Ferreira Alves

103

| 1.18 inches | | 1.57 inches | | minimum 1.18 inches | |

Cladded step   **Finishing**

Brickwork steps

Brickwork steps are used mainly for outdoor stairs. In the interior of dwellings they are used only for short flights of steps.

Solid bricks are used in several combinations: with stretcher, header or brick on edge. A combination of natural stone for the tread and brick for the riser is also used. In staircases of reinforced concrete and vaulted brickwork, the steps are made with bricks and then cladded.

José Ramón Sierra Delgado. Housing in Polígono Aeropuerto. Seville, Spain. Photographs: Fernando Alda

Enric Sòria. House in Port d'Addaia. Menorca, Spain. Photographs: Lluís Casals

Ramón Esteve. Dwelling between party walls. Ontinyent, Spain. Photographs: Ramón Esteve

Jarmund / Vignæs Architects. Villa by the Ocean. Stavanger, Norway. Photographs: Nils Petter Dale

- Concrete steps

Concrete steps are generally used for industrial premises, due to their great weight and high construction cost, though they are also used in public buildings with reinforced concrete floor slabs, because of the finish.

The steps may be cast in the slab or rest on it. In the first case they are cast-in-situ reinforced concrete steps, which are later given a finish. In the second case prefabricated pieces that already have the finish are used.

Felipe Assadi Figueroa. Schmitz House. Calera de Tango, Chile. Photographs: Felipe Assadi Figueroa

Driendl architects. Solar Deck. Vienna, Austria. Photographs: Driendl architects

- Steps of ceramic tiles

Ceramic tiles come in a great variety of forms, colours and designs, and are strong and durable.

Michele Bonino. "One meter above". House in Torino. Turin, Italy. Photographs: Beppe Giardino

Shell Architects - D3A Studio. Andel's Hotel. Prague, Czech Republic. Photographs: Ales Jungmann

Sauerbruch hutton architects. Experimental Factory. Magdeburg. Germany. Photographs: Gerrit Engel

José Gigante. Instituto das Comunicações. Porto. Portugal. Photographs: Luis Ferreira Alves

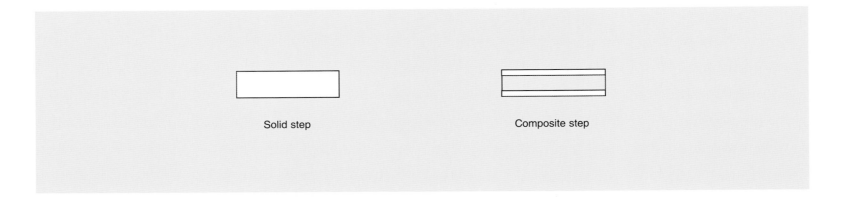

Solid step

Composite step

Cho Slade Architecture. Apartamento Van Doren. Nueva York, EE UU. Photographs: Jordi Miralles

- Timber steps

All types of commercially available timber are used to build steps. They are light and fairly economical, though their life is limited by wear and sometimes by woodworm. Therefore, they must be treated with clear polyurethane or polyester varnish to increase their strength and durability. They must also be treated with a product to protect them from insects.

Wooden steps have poor fire resistance (RF 30), so they are used in dwellings but not in public buildings.

The upper face of the steps must be protected with a protective material or an additional 0.20 inches of wood.

Wooden steps may be solid or composite; and according to this classification we have:

A) Solid steps:

- coniferous woods:
Pine, spruce, larch, fir.
The thickness of the rough wood may be 1.77, 1.96, 2.16 or 2.36 inches.

- oak and beech:
The thickness of the rough wood may be 1.77, 1.96, 2.16 or 2.36 inches.

B) Composite steps:

- composite steps BTI / BFU.
These are composed of a central layer of thick board with outer layers of veneer.

- composite steps BTI, veneered.
These are composed of a central layer of thick board with outer layers of hardwood veneer.

- steps composed of chipboard and veneer.
These are composed of a central layer of chipboard and outer layers of veneer.

- steps composed of chipboard.
Both the central layer and the outer layers are composed of chipboard.

Jahn Associates Architects. Grant House. Sydney, Australia. Photographs: Brett Boardman

Francisco Mangado Beloqui. Indoor pool in La Coruña. La Coruña, Spain. Photographs: Roland Halbe

SCDA Architects. Teng Residence. Singapore. Photographs: Peter Mealin

- Metal steps

Metal steps may be divided into:

1. Simple surface
2. Folded steel plate
3. Simple flat sheets with a lower structure
4. Metal steps combined with wood or natural/artificial stone
5. Hollow steps

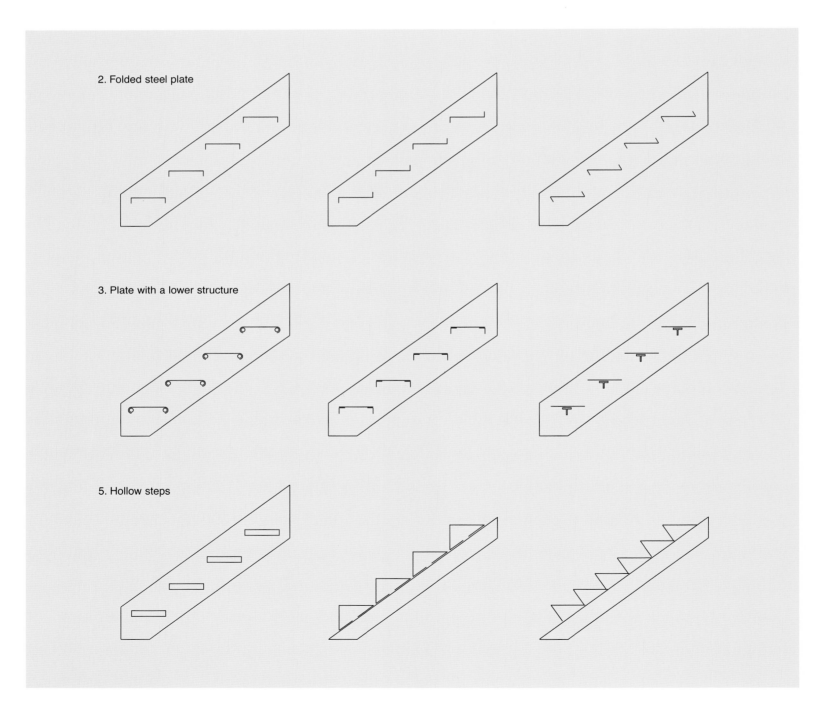

2. Folded steel plate

3. Plate with a lower structure

5. Hollow steps

Kunihide Oshinomi, Takeshi Semba. Timber Frame House with a Curtain Wall. Shinagawa-ku, Tokyo, Japan. Photographs: Van Structural Design

Marin-Trottin (Périphériques Architectes). MR House. Pompone, France. Photographs: H. Abadie

Atelier Tekuto. Cell Brick House. Tokyo, Japan. Photographs: Makoto Yoshida

Strindberg Arkitekter AB. The Red House. Drag, Kalmar, Sweden. Photographs: Gudrun Thielemann

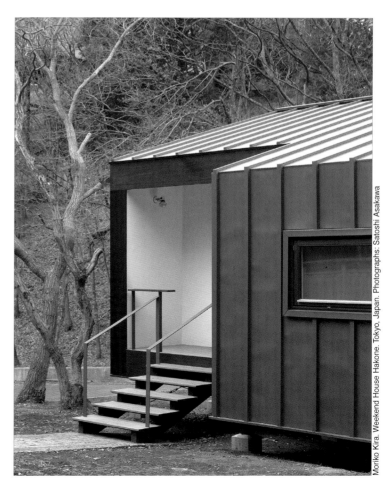

Moriko Kira. Weekend House Hakone. Tokyo, Japan. Photographs: Satoshi Asakawa

115

- Glass steps

The glass used to make the steps allows light to pass through, making the staircase seem less heavy and allowing more brightness into the space.

Most types of glass used are laminated, which prevents the glass from splintering and provides safety and protection in case of breakage.

The steps are usually made from glass between 0.59 and 1.18 inches thick, set in a steel frame that rests on the vertical supports, with a metallic plate or angle protecting the free edge.

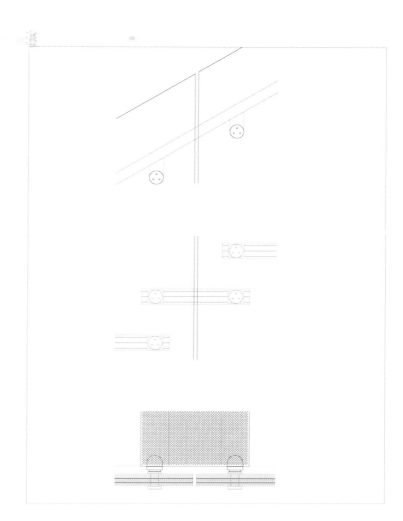

Bohlin Cywinski Jackson & Ronnette Riley. Apple SoHo Retail Store. Shinagawa-ku, New York, USA. Photographs: Peter Aaron

banisters and handrails

banisters and handrail

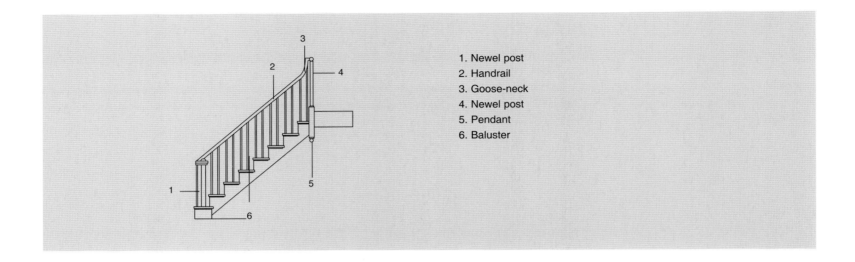

1. Newel post
2. Handrail
3. Goose-neck
4. Newel post
5. Pendant
6. Baluster

All banisters are composed of two essential elements: The vertical elements (normally balusters), and the handrail. However, the parts of the banister (handrail, posts, balusters) sometimes form a single element.

When the banisters are formed exclusively by balusters, they are called balustrades. These are mainly used for exterior staircases, since they give greater importance and majesty.

When there are openings or drops that may involve a risk of persons falling, it is recommended to protect the staircase with banisters or equivalent safety systems. These may be mobile if access to the opening is necessary.

If the staircase has fewer than five steps, or a height of less than one metre, a banister is not necessary, though it is advisable.

A banister is also unnecessary when the slope is less than 1:4.

For stairs with a useful width of less than 4.10 feet, a handrail must be placed on only one of the two sides. In work areas the handrail must be on the right side going up.

If the stair width is between 4.10 feet and 8.20 feet, handrails must be placed on both sides.

A handrail must also be placed on both sides when the stairs are curved. When the stair width is greater than 8.20 feet, middle banisters must be fitted.

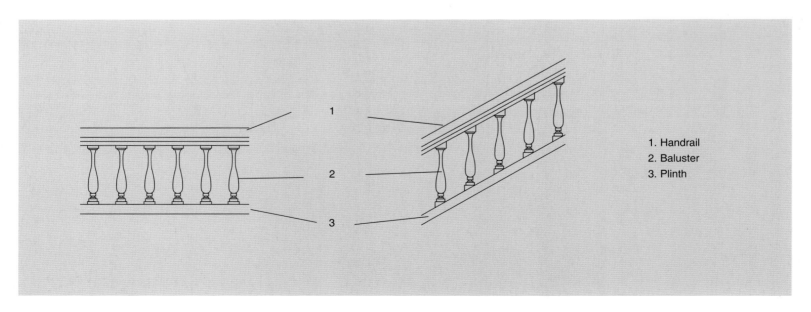

1. Handrail
2. Baluster
3. Plinth

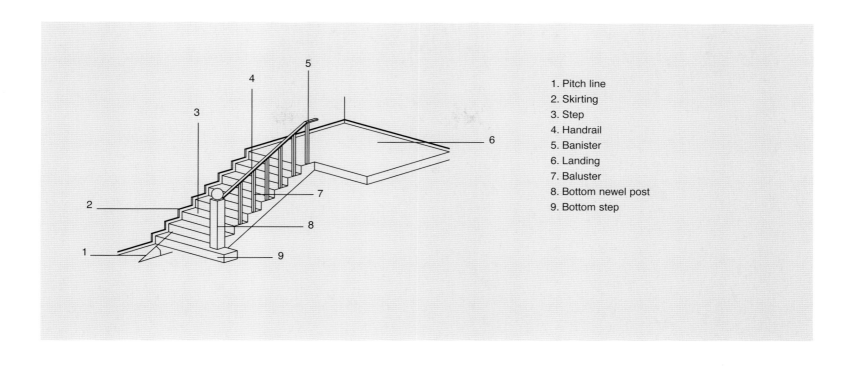

1. Pitch line
2. Skirting
3. Step
4. Handrail
5. Banister
6. Landing
7. Baluster
8. Bottom newel post
9. Bottom step

Henning Stummel Architects. Extension to Georgian Town House. London, UK. Photographs: Nigel Rigden

GAD architecture. A House with Three Eras. Istanbul, Turkey. Photographs: Yavuz Draman

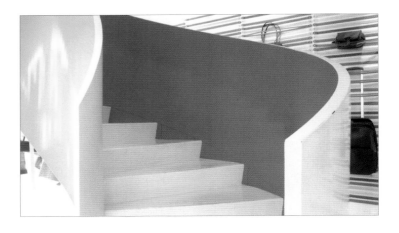

NL Architects for Droog Design. Mandarina Duck. Paris, France. Photographs: Ralph Kämena

Ackermann & Raff, architects BDA. Kindergarten in Reutlingen. Reutlingen, Germany. Photographs: Andreas Keller

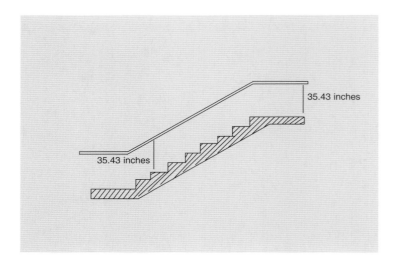

35.43 inches

35.43 inches

Stair banisters must have a minimum height of 35.43 inches from the front edge of the step to the upper edge of the handrail.
If the free fall height is greater than 39.37 feet, the banister must have a minimum height of 3.60 feet.

HERTL.ARCHITEKTEN. Casa Steinwendtner. Steyr-Münichholz, Austria. Photographs: Paul Ott

Carlo Donati. Loft A. Milan, Italy. Photographs: Matteo Piazza

Banisters are designed as follows:

- Take the difference in level between the first and last step of the flight in which the banister is to be placed.

- Take the horizontal distance between the risers of the steps, and add the number of treads without counting that of the last step, which forms the landing.

- With these figures construct a right-angle triangle in which the sides are these measurements and the hypotenuse is the slope of the banister.

- The handrail follows a line parallel to this slope at the corresponding height.

- Then the landing, the junction and the bottom of the banister are designed.

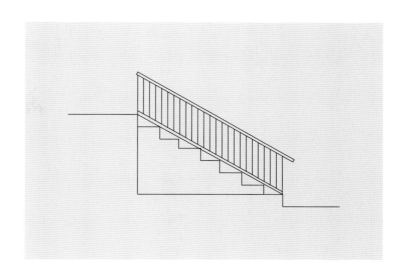

Kisho Kurokawa. Fujinomiya Golf Club Clubhouse. Shizuoka, Japan. Photographs: Tomio Ohashi

Glen Irani. Casa Hover. Venice, California, EE UU. Photographs: Undine Pröhl

Detlef Sacker. Multi-use pavilion in the Erich-Kästner-Schule. Donaueschingen, Germany. Photographs: Roland Halbe

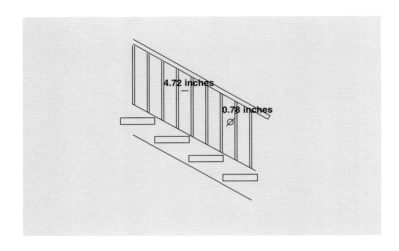

4.72 inches

0.78 inches Ø

The handrail is designed to withstand a horizontal load of 0.071 lb/in². The banister must be made of stiff material and have protective elements to prevent persons from slipping under them and objects from falling onto persons below.

Proplaning Architekten. Obere Widen. Arlesheim, Switzerland. Photographs: Naas & Bisig

Lorcan O'Herlihy Architects. Casa Jai. California, EE UU. Photographs: Michael Weschler

The banister must have no vertical or horizontal openings that allow a 4.72 inches sphere to pass through. The balusters must have a diameter of at least 0.78 inches.

Children should not be able to climb through the horizontal divisions.

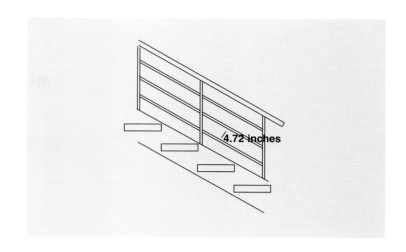

4.72 inches

Àlex Serra. Numància Apartment. Barcelona, Spain. Photographs: José Luis Hausmann

Black Kosloff Knott Pty Ltd Architects. Wrap House. Telluride, California, USA. Photographs: John Gollings

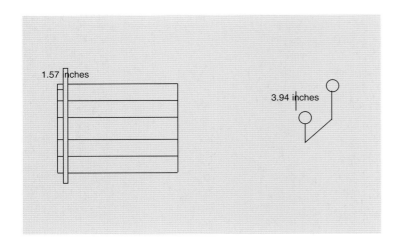

1.57 inches

3.94 inches

The handrail must be shaped to give a comfortable hand grip, with a section equal, or functionally equivalent, to that of a round tube with a diameter of between 1.18 and 1.97 inches. The separation between the handrail and the wall must be at least 1.57 inches. If the handrail is double there must be a separation of at least 3.94 inches between the two elements.

Bayer Uhrig Architekten BDA. Fellner House. Großnöbach, Germany. Photographs: Michael Heinrich

Dominic Stevens. In-between House. Ballinamore, Ireland. Photographs: Ros Cavanagh

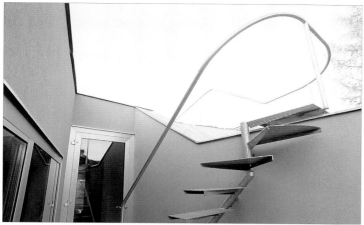

Pool. In spe-single family house. Wien, Austria. Photographs: Hertha Hurnaus

KRD. Michel Guillon. London, UK. Photographs: Dan Stevens

The banister must extend 17.71 inches from the start of the ramp or of the staircase, and must be continuous between flights.

If the handrail is continued without a curve, the break must be made on the line between the last and first riser of the steps, on the plan of the landing.

These are some of the solutions for horizontal banister sections:

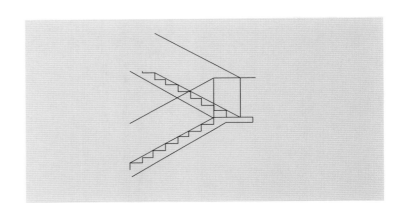

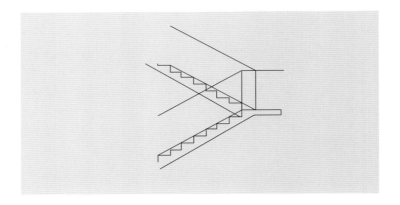

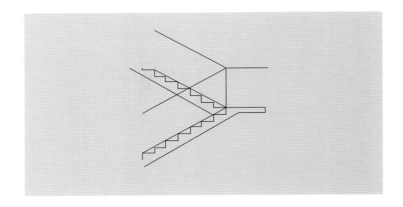

Wingårdh Arkitektkontor AB. Villa Astrid. Brottkärr, Göteborg, Sweden. Photographs: James Silverman

Mario Corea + Francisco Gallardo. Swimming Pool in Vilafranca. Vilafranca del Penedès, Spain. Photographs: Jordi Miralles

Koichiro Ishiguro. White Woods. Tokyo, Japan. Photographs: K. Takada

131

Carlos Ferrater - Alberto de Salas. Hotel Tryp Aeropuerto. Barcelona, Spain. Photographs: Alejo Bagué

Eulàlia Sardà. Apartment Sant Vicenç. Sant Vicenç de Castellet, Spain. Photographs: José Luis Hausmann

Mark Cigolle & Kim Coleman. TR-I House and Studio. California, USA. Photographs: Undine Pröhl

Eugeen Liebaut. Verhaeghe House. Sint Pieters Leeuw, Belgium. Photographs: Saskia Vanderstichele

Boije Design AB. Stem to Stern Perfection. Skåne, Sweden. Photographs: James Silverman

other types of staircases

In addition to the stairs presented above, there are other types for particular uses. The most important types are the following.

1. Folding stairs:

Folding stairs are composed of a small number of sections that fold up. They occupy little space and are concealed by a trapdoor when they are not in use.

These stairs are fixed at the top and free at the bottom. They are very light and easy to install.

The materials used range from wood (beech, pine, oak) to aluminium and plastic-coated steel.

The concertina-type folding staircase is composed of a series of hinged metal elements forming X-shapes that can be opened and closed like scissors.

These stairs must be firmly secured to the support using sturdy hinges and springs.

Cast and pressed aluminium is the material most commonly used.

2. Provisional staircases:

These can normally be assembled and taken apart easily and are generally used for access to buildings during construction or restoration work. They always have a wide banister to counteract the sensation of insecurity caused by their mobile structure.

3. Built-in ladder:

Built-in ladders are composed of round iron bars bent in a wide U-shape that are embedded in the wall at both ends. They are commonly used for access to the upper part of the chimneys, terraces and roofs.

4. Ladders:

Ladders can be carried on the shoulder and are used for gaining access in certain jobs. The most typical ones are simple ladders, stepladders and rolling ladders.

5. Rookery staircase :

This is a staircase formed by two parallel risers of wood into which steps of the same material are nailed. The treads are very wide but not very long, so they only have room for one foot.

Measurements of the opening length x width	Number of steps	Height from floor to ceiling
35.43 x 27.55	11	106.30 / 118.11
39.37 x 27.55	11	106.30 / 118.11
51.18 x 27.55	11	106.30 / 118.11

Dimensions in inches

Rolf Åsberg. House Boat. Gothenbourg, Sweden. Photographs: James Silverman

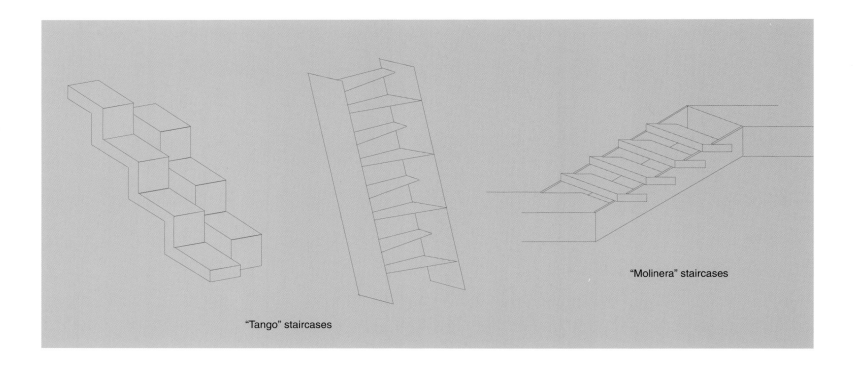

"Molinera" staircases

"Tango" staircases

6. Peg ladder:

This is a staircase formed by a thick vertical pole with perpendicular crosspieces to support the feet when one climbs up and down it.

7. "Tango" staircases:

These are very steep stairs in which the treads for each foot are alternated to save horizontal space.

They are only permitted in interiors and to access subordinate spaces such as attics and lofts.

8. Escalators or moving staircases:

These are stairs with articulated steps mounted on an endless chain, which is operated mechanically to transport persons from one floor to the next.

The movement can also be inverted to go down instead of up.

9. Exterior staircases:

Garden and terrace stairs are the most important ones. They use mainly natural materials such as stone, wood and brick.

Staircases of industrial premises or blocks of dwellings may be made of reinforced concrete or metal, with steel plate strings. The step is thus formed with metal angles and grooved plates for the tread so that the users do not slip.

There are also other staircases with different functions, such as bookcase steps or wardrobe steps. In addition to communicating two spaces at different heights, they also serve as pieces of furniture, either by lengthening the treads to form bookcases or by using the steps as wardrobe modules.

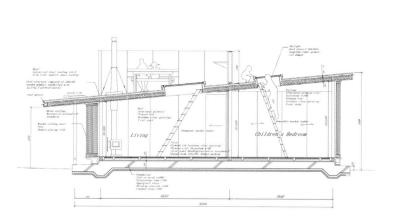

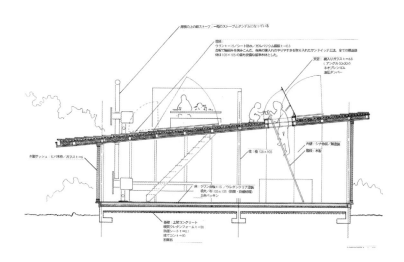

Tezuka Architects / mias. Roof House. Tokyo, Japan. Photographs: Katsuhisa Kida

Christian Pottgiesser. 24, Rue Buisson Saint Louis. Paris, France. Photographs: Luc Boegly

The shape of the stairs can be designed so that they can be used at the same time as shelves, wardrobes or desks. The space under the stairs is often left unused, and if taken advantage of, it can be a valuable asset in a small apartment.

COEX Architects. House in Via Barbaroux. Turin, Italy. Photographs: Beppe Giardino

L-Architectes. Perret House. Cully, Canton Vaud, Switzerland. Photographs: Jean-Michel Landecy

Anthony Hudson & Sarah Featherstone. Voss Street House. London, UK. Photographs: Tim Brotherton

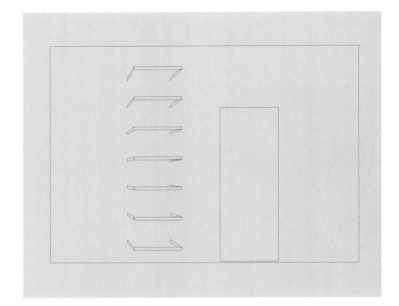

Built-in ladder

Chiba Manabu Architects. Kashima Surf Villa. Kashima, Japan. Photographs: Nácasa & Partners

Vandeventer + Carlander Architects. Camano Island Cabin. Camano Island, WA, USA. Photographs: Steve Keating

Deadline. Slender / Bender. Berlin, Germany. Photographs: Matthew Griffin

Aase Kari Kvalvik. Verven. Stavanger, Norway. Photographs: Nils Petter Dale

The weeHouse team / Warner + Asmus. weeHouse. Minnesota, USA. Photographs: Warner + Asmus

Koh Kitayama. Plane + House. Tokyo. Japan. Photographs: Nobuaki Nakagawa

DRY design, inc. 3773 Studio. Los Angeles, USA. Photographs: Undine Pröhl

David Maturen. Apartment Zaragoza David. Zaragoza, Spain. Photographs: Jordi Miralles

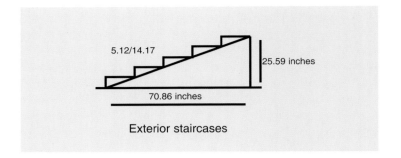

5.12/14.17

25.59 inches

70.86 inches

Exterior staircases

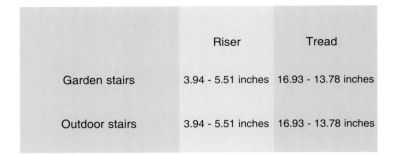

	Riser	Tread
Garden stairs	3.94 - 5.51 inches	16.93 - 13.78 inches
Outdoor stairs	3.94 - 5.51 inches	16.93 - 13.78 inches

Luisa Fontana. Square in Rosà. Vicenza, Italy.

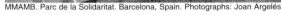

MMAMB. Parc de la Solidaritat. Barcelona, Spain. Photographs: Joan Argelés

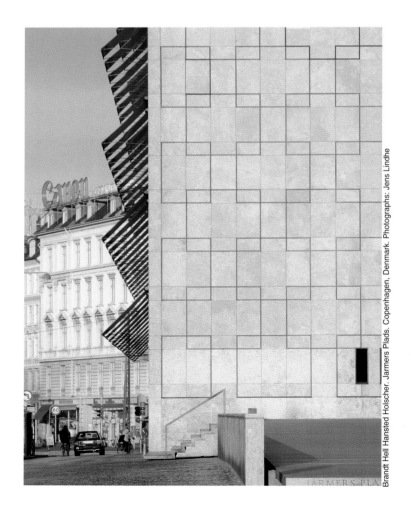

Brandt Hell Hansted Holscher. Jarmers Plads. Copenhagen, Denmark. Photographs: Jens Lindhe

148

Steven Harris Architects. House in Cabo San Lucas. Cabo San Lucas, Mexico. Photographs: Scott Frances

Hodder Associates. National Wildflower Centre. Knowsley, Liverpool, UK. Photographs: Martine Hamilton Knight

ramps, lifts and escalators

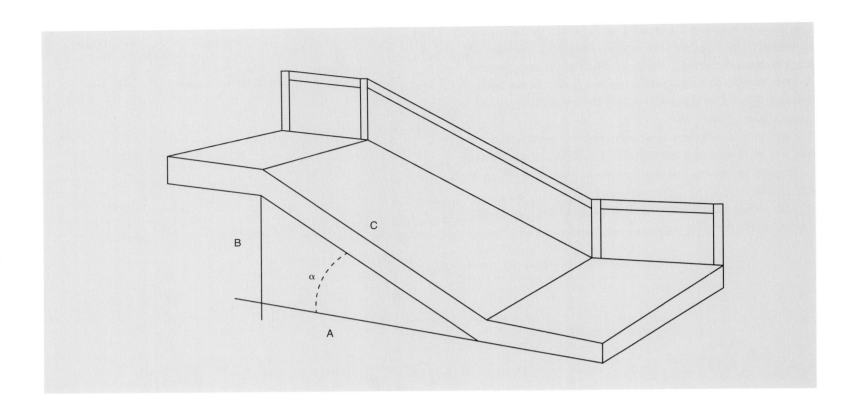

B

C

α

A

Felipe Assadi Figueroa. Schmitz House. Calera de Tango, Chile. Photographs: Felipe Assadi Figueroa

Satoshi Okada architects. House in Mt. Fuji. Narusawa Village, Mt. Fuji, Japan. Photographs: Hiroyuki Hirai

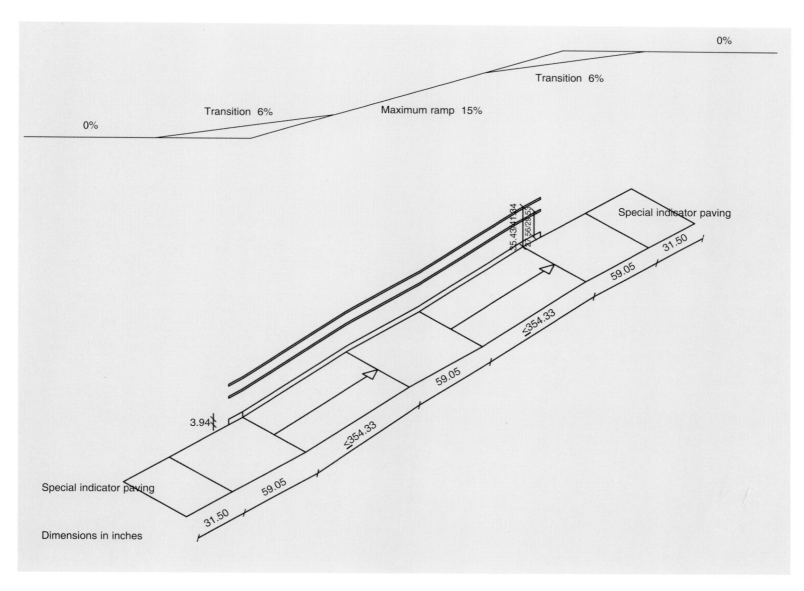

0%

Transition 6%

Maximum ramp 15%

Transition 6%

0%

Special indicator paving

31.50

59.05

≤354.33

35.43/11.81

27.56/29.53

3.94

59.05

≤354.33

Special indicator paving

31.50

59.05

Dimensions in inches

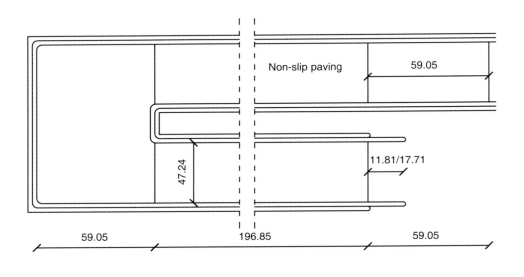

Non-slip paving

59.05

47.24

11.81/17.71

59.05   196.85   59.05

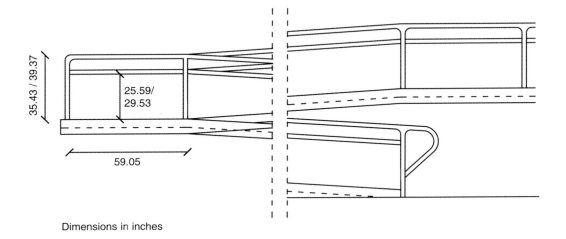

35.43 / 39.37

25.59/
29.53

59.05

Dimensions in inches

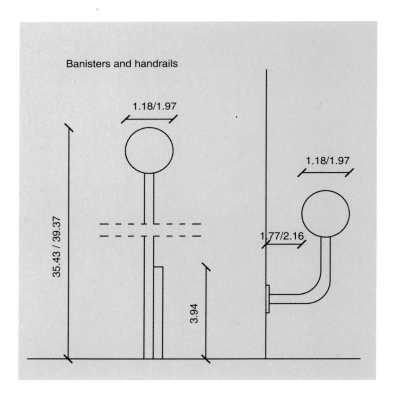

Banisters and handrails

1.18/1.97

1.18/1.97

1.77/2.16

35.43 / 39.37

3.94

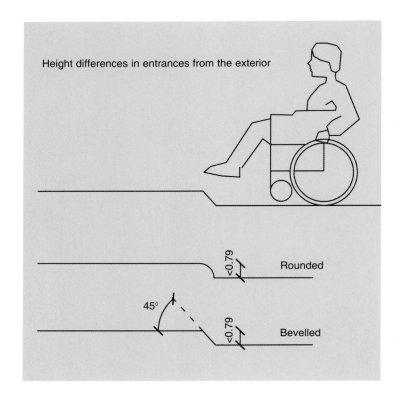

Height differences in entrances from the exterior

<0.79   Rounded

45°

<0.79   Bevelled

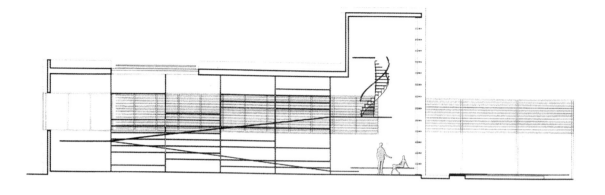

M. J. Neal. Ramp House. Austin, Texas, USA. Photographs: Barcelona Films

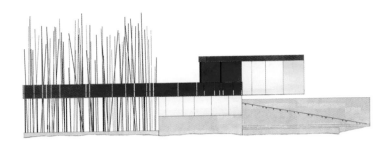

Mark Scogin Merril Elam Architects. Mountain Tree House. Dillard, Georgia, USA. Photographs: Timothy Hursley

Delugan_Meissl. Ray 1. Vienna, Austria. Photographs: Rupert Steiner

lifts

A lift is a mechanical device that carries people or people and things up and down.

A lift can be hydraulic, electric or inclined.

Hydraulic lifts are powered by the energy released by a liquid under pressure in a cylinder acting as a piston.

Electric lifts use a system of propulsion that operates through an electric lifting mechanism.

Inclined lifts have a platform or chair mounted on a guide rail, which is powered by an electric motor and allows a person or load to be carried along a staircase from one floor to the next.

When a lift carries loads rather than people from one floor to the next, it is known as a goods lift. Only the lift operator and other personnel required to load and unload goods are allowed to use these lifts.

Lifts are made up of three main elements: box, machine room and car.

The lift well is the room or space that is set aside for the lift in a building or structure. It is also called a lift shaft.

The machine room is the room that houses the motor and propelling equipment, control panels and other equipment required to manage lift operation.

The car consists of the frame, the cabin, the platform and accessories that move along the main guide rails.

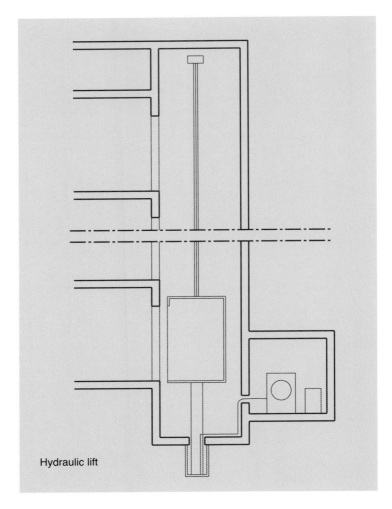

Hydraulic lift

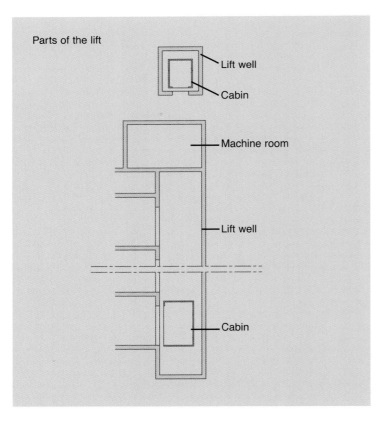

Parts of the lift

Lift well

Cabin

Machine room

Lift well

Cabin

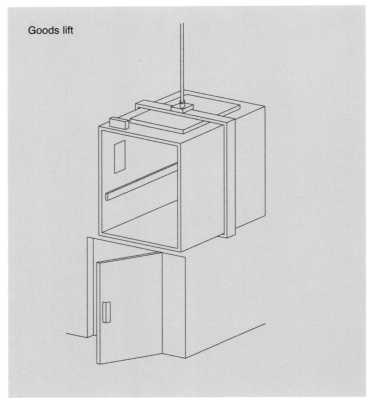

Goods lift

160

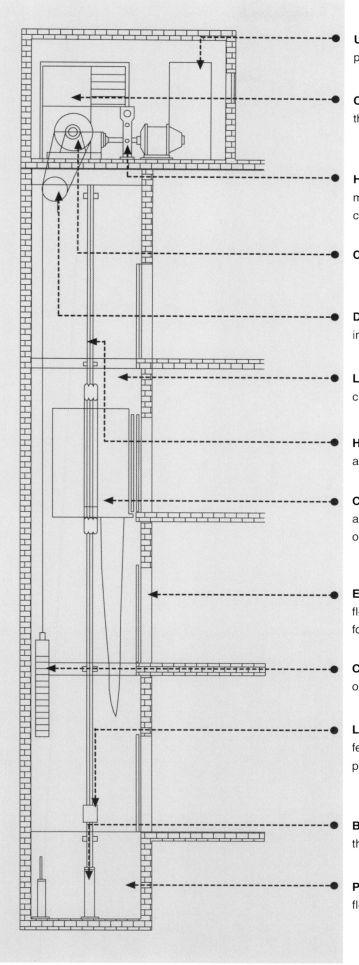

Upper hut: a structure built on the roof, which houses a water tank or provides access to a stair or lift well.

Control system: the control panel or board that allows an operator to manage the electric mechanisms through the switches and other devices it contains.

Hoisting machinery: the equipment used to lift the cabin. It consists of a motor-generator, traction machine, speed regulator, brake, sheave and control machinery.

Control sheave: sheave disc or wheel used to hoist or haul a lift cabin.

Deflection sheave: the sheave used to guide and tense the hoisting cables in an electric lift system.

Lift shaft, lift well: the enclosed vertical space that houses one or more lift cabins, including the pit.

Hoisting cable, lift wire: the cable used to raise or lower a cabin in an electric lift system.

Car safety device: the mechanical device attached to a lift cabin that allows it to reduce speed or stop, and ensures the cabin is safe in the case of excessive speed, or if the cabin falls or the cables break.

Entrance protection system: the doors that separate the lift shaft from the floor or landing. It is generally closed, except when the lift is at a stand still, for entering or exiting.

Counterweight: the weight used to keep another weight in equilibrium or offset it.

Lower stop switch: a switch that automatically turns off the power that feeds an electric motor when an object, such as a lift cabin exceeds a given point; it acts independently from the call stop floor.

Buffer: the mechanism designed to absorb the impact of the lift car at the bottom end.

Pit: the part of a lift well that is located between the lowest landing and the floor of the lift well.

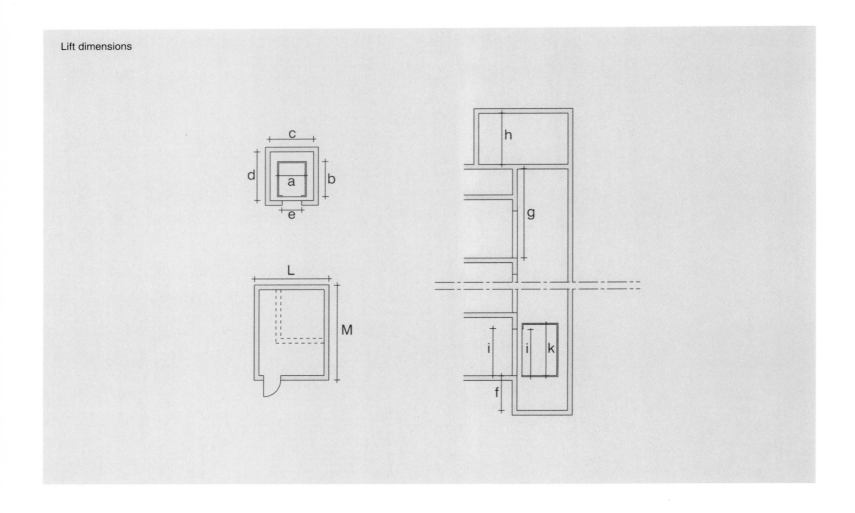

Basic lifts for people

		881.85	1388.91	2204.62
	load capacity (lb)	881.85	1388.91	2204.62
	speed (milas/h)	1.34 2.24 3.58	1.34 2.24 3.58 5.6	1.34 2.24 3.58 5.6
cabin	a. cabin width (inches)	43.30	43.30	43.30
	b. cabin depth (inches)	37.40	55.12	82.68
	k. cabin height (inches)	86.61	86.61	86.61
door	e. door width (inches)	31.50	31.50	31.50
	i. door height (inches)	78.74	78.74	78.74
lift well	c. lift well width (inches)	70.86	70.86	70.86
	d. lift well depth (inches)	59.05	82.68	102.36
	f. pit depth (inches)	55.12/59.05/66.93	55.12/59.05/66.93/110.23	55.12/59.05/66.93/110.23
	g. lift well height (inches)	145.67/149.60/157.48	145.67/149.60/157.48/196.85	145.67/149.60/157.48/196.85
machine room	L. machine room width (inches)	94.48	106.30 118.11	106.30 118.11
	M. machine room depth (inches)	125.98	145.67	165.35
	h. machine room height (inches)	78.74	78.74 102.36	78.74 102.36

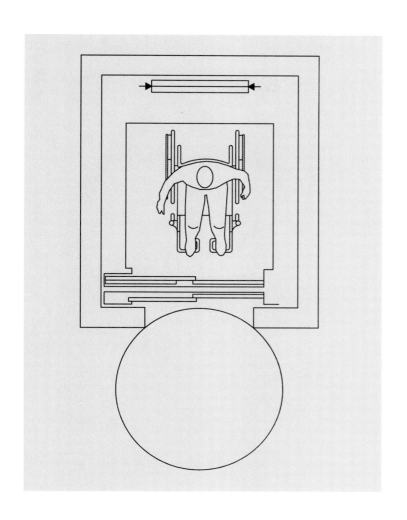
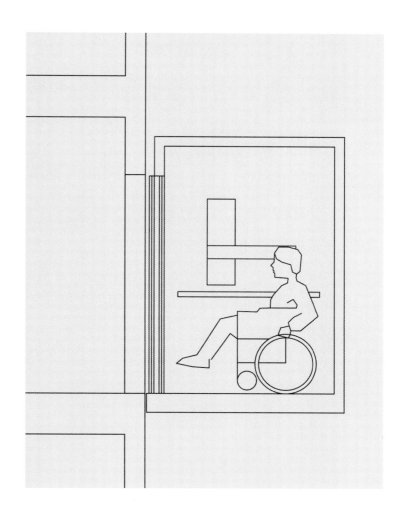

Lifts for public buildings (wheelchair access)

		1763.70 (10 pers.)	2204.62 (13 pers.)	3527.40 (21 pers.)
	load capacity (lb)	1763.70 (10 pers.)	2204.62 (13 pers.)	3527.40 (21 pers.)
	speed (milas/h)	1.34 2.24 3.58 5.6	1.34 2.24 3.58 5.6	1.34 2.24 3.58 5.6
cabin	a. cabin width (inches)	53.15	59.05	76.77
	b. cabin depth (inches)	55.12	55.12	68.90
	k. cabin height (inches)	86.61	90.55	90.55
door	e. door width (inches)	31.50	43.30	43.30
	i. door height (inches)	78.74	82.68	82.68
lift well	c. lift well width (inches)	74.80	94.49	102.36
	d. lift well height (inches)	90.55	90.55	102.36
	f. pit depth (inches)	55.12/59.05/66.93/110.23	55.12/59.05/66.93/110.23	55.12/59.05/66.93/110.23
	g. box height (inches)	149.60/157.48/196.85	165.35 204.72	173.23 212.60
machine room	L. machine room width (inches)	98.42 110.23	125.98	125.98
	M. machine room depth (inches)	145.67 192.91	192.91	216.53
	h. machine room height (inches)	86.61 110.23	94.49 110.23	110.23

The structure supporting the elevator shafts and walkways was built with vertical supports, crossbeams, profiles and steel sheeting (still to be painted). The load-bearing structure at the end of the walkway is of reinforced concrete walls clad in Llicorella stone.

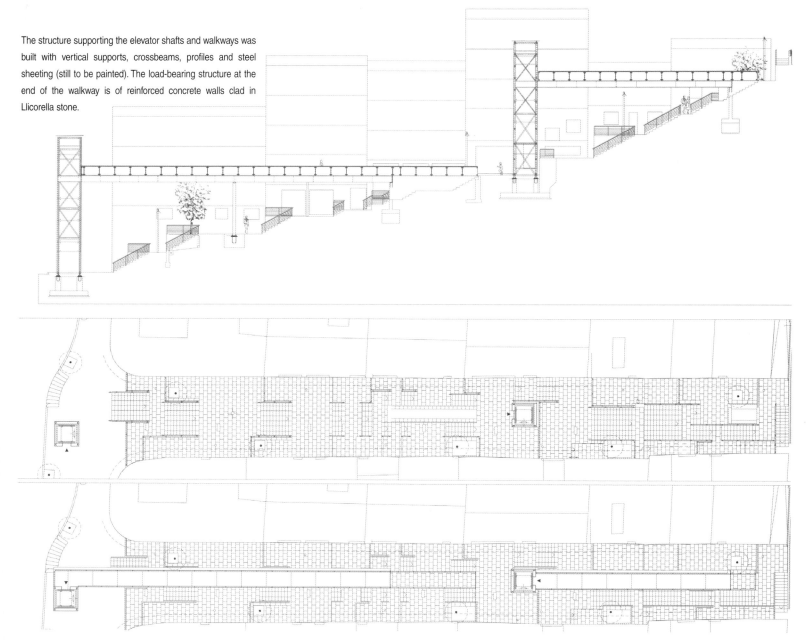

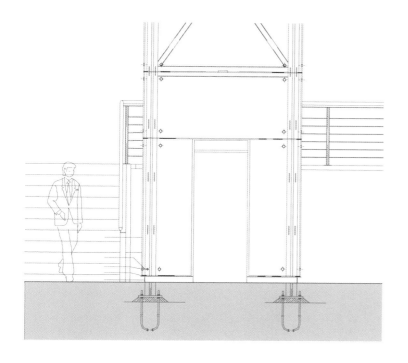

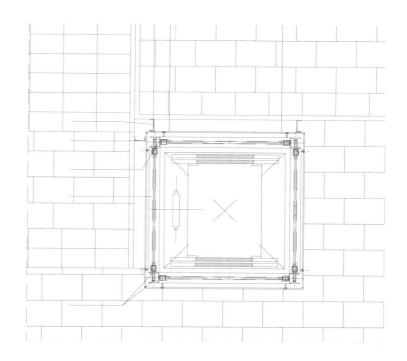

Mònica Vila. Walkways Alcántara street. Barcelona, Spain. Photographs: Joan Argelés

A lift well shall be a fire-proof construction, with no channels that are foreign to the structure, such as gas, water or heating pipes, telephone or cable TV wiring, emergency lights and so on, in the interior or built in to the walls that enclose it.

The minimum dimension of the lift well cross section shall be the same as the cabin measurements plus 13.78 inches on each side, and it will enclose the car, counterweight, guide rails and other elements required for overall operation.

The cabin shall be made from metal, and its interior height shall not be less than 6.56 feet. The facing doors of the cabin and the landing shall be separated by no more than 5.90 inches.

When the lifts are grouped in a lift well (battery), a protective element made from fireproof material and no less than 6.56 feet high shall be placed between adjacent lifts and at the bottom of the lift well.

The machine room shall be built from fireproof materials and the minimum side shall not be less than 7.22 feet.

The walls and ceiling of the machine room shall not form part of receptacles that contain liquids (water tanks) and the free height shall be at least 6.56 feet. The walls will be finished in a smooth render, plaques or acoustic render.

There shall be permanent natural ventilation, either on the side walls and placed on opposite sides, or on the side walls and overhead (skylight).

The lift may have natural and/or artificial lighting, which shall be on a different circuit independent of the power source that propels the lift. Lighting intensity shall be no lower than 15 watts per square meter, and the light source shall be overhead, with the switch on the closing side of the door.

The entrance shall be comfortable and easy to access by way of continuous steps. When access is through a staircase, the staircase shall me at least 27.56 inches wide. If the machine room access is through an uncovered roof area, there shall be a protective shelter at least 35.43 inches high for the distance to be covered.

The entrance door shall be at least 5.90 feet high and 2.30 feet wide and the panels shall be made from fireproof material and open outwards from the room over the landing. It shall be fitted with a lock with key. The steps between the different elements shall be at least 1.64 feet wide, and one of the steps shall allow manual operation of the machinery.

In front of and behind the control panel, there shall be a gap at least 2.30 feet wide. Near the entry door, on the door handle side, there shall be a fire extinguisher suitable for electric fires.

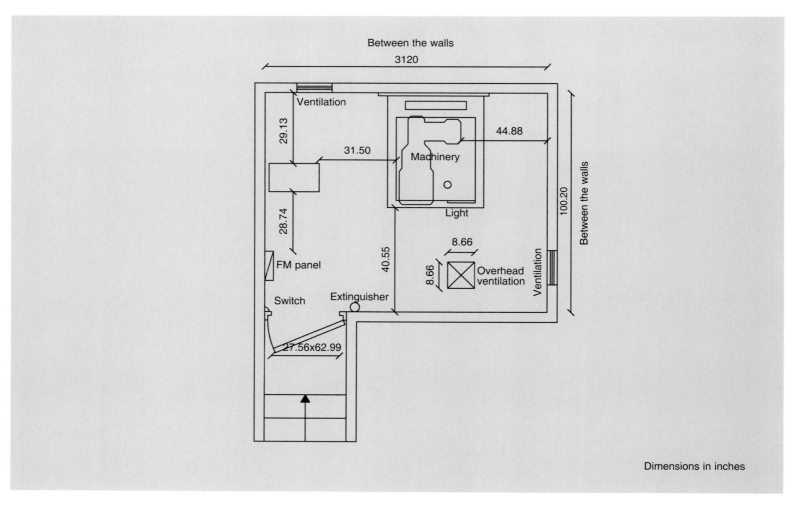

Dimensions in inches

Antonio Besso-Marcheis. Case in cooperativa. Rivarolo Canavese, Torino, Italy. Photographs: Luigi Gariglio

escalators

An escalator is a transport device consisting of an inclined staircase with its steps fixed to a conveyor belt so that they move up and down.

It is used to carry people from one level to another, without them having to move, because the treads move mechanically.

Escalators shall have the appropriate operating conditions and mechanisms required to guarantee the safety of the people who use them. The direction of their movement, either up or down, can stay the same, be controlled by an employee, or change automatically. In this case, when a person reaches the escalator from the lower level, he or she makes it operate in an up direction, while a person approaching on the upper level and standing on the platform in front of the escalator will make it operate in a down direction. This system is programmed so that the escalator direction will never be able to change while its sensors detect that there are people using the escalator. The emergency stop mechanisms shall be easy to identify and access.

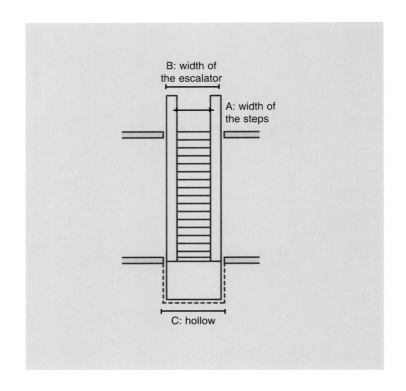

width of the steps (inches)	23.62	31.50	39.37
A	23.81 - 24.40	31.69 - 32.28	39.56 - 40.15
B	46.06 - 48.03	51.96 - 55.90	61.81 - 63.78
C	50.39	58.26	66.14
performance / h	5000 - 6000	7000 - 8000	8000 - 10000

Schmidt, Hammer & Lassen. Bruun's Galleri. Århus, Denmark. Photographs: Schmidt, Hammer

Dimensions in inches

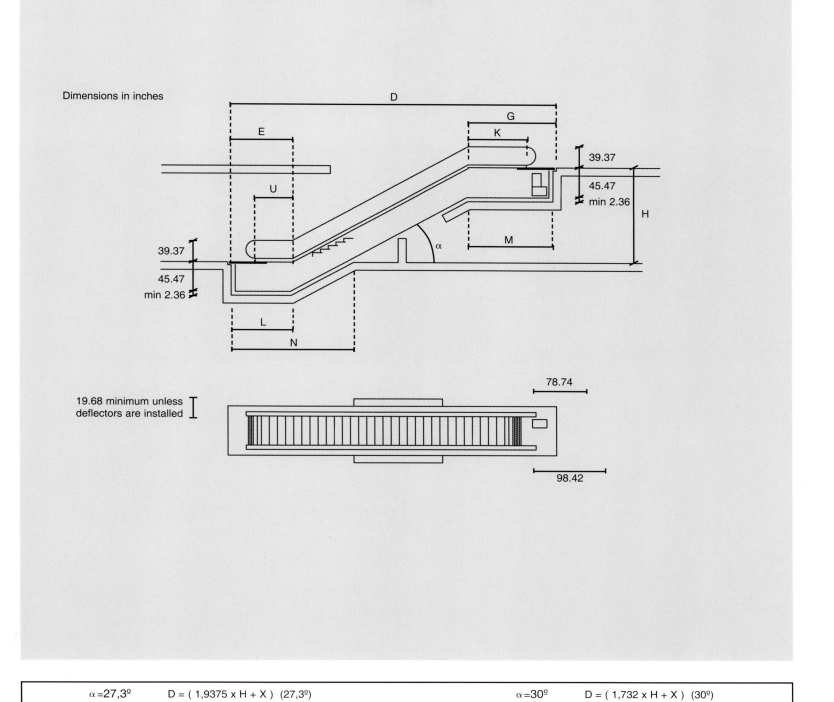

19.68 minimum unless deflectors are installed

α =27,3º	D = (1,9375 x H + X) (27,3º)			α =30º	D = (1,732 x H + X) (30º)			

α	width of the steps	horizontal steps	X	E	G	U	K	L	N	M
27,3º	31.50/39.37	2	193.62	88.46	105.16	63.50	75.04	85.23	99.17	108.35
		3	225.12	104.21	120.90	79.25	90.78	100.98	193.66	124.13
30º	31.50/39.37	2	196.26	89.33	106.93	64.37	76.81	88.54	171.37	107.71
		3	227.75	89.33	122.68	80.12	92.56	104.29	187.12	123.46

The construction and installation of escalators shall meet the following requirements:
- The horizontal angle of inclination (a) shall not be greater than 35 degrees.
- The rating speed along the inclined plane shall not exceed 1.34 milas/h.
- Each escalator shall move independently.
- The chains shall be calculated to have a safety coefficient of no less than 1.5 of the normal calculation coefficient.
- The step tracks shall be placed in such a way as to ensure that the steps and moveable elements are not displaced if the chain or the tracks were to break.

- There shall be a comb plate at the entrance and exit of the escalator, and the teeth shall fit between the cleats of the step, so that the front edges of the comb teeth are below the upper surface of the cleats.
- The balustrade shall be smooth, with no projections, and mouldings shall not project more than 1 millimetre.
- Each balustrade shall be equipped with a mobile handrail that moves at the same speed and in the same direction as the steps, and extends at least 11.81 inches beyond the line of the teeth of the comb plate at both ends of the escalator. It shall be built in such a way as to make it impossible to insert fingers or hands between the balustrade and the handrail.

José Antonio Martinez Lapeña & Elias Torres. La Granja' staircases. Toledo, Spain. Photographs: David Cardelús

Perkins Eastman. Embassy Suites Hotel New York City. New York, USA. Photographs: Chuck Choi

Foster and Partners. Canary Wharf Undergound Station. London, UK. Photographs: Nigel Young + Dennis Gilbert

TAYLOR GUITARS

Michael John Simmons

TAYLOR GUITARS

30 Years of a
New American Classic

Michael John Simmons

PPVMEDIEN

The publishing house, editor and author draw your attention to the fact that the proper names, brand names and product names mentioned in this book are as a rule registered names and trade marks protected by law. Despite the very great care that has been taken, the possibility of errors in the text cannot be discounted. The publishing house, editor and author would be grateful for suggested improvements and to be notified at once of errors as may be discovered from time to time.

© 2003
PPVMEDIEN GmbH, Bergkirchen, Germany

ISBN 3-932275-44-6

Title photos: Taylor Guitars
Title design: Saskia Kölliker
Photographs: Taylor Guitars, Pacific PreMedia, Inc.
Translation: Gerhard J. Oldiges
Typesetting and layout: Saskia Kölliker
Organisation: Alexander Schmidt
Printing: Stalling GmbH, Oldenburg, Germany

CONTENTS

CONTENTS

96 The Art of Taylor

124 Success at Last

146 New Ways of Building Guitars

Preface

This is a book about Bob Taylor, Kurt Listug, and the guitar company they founded in 1974. Like most books about guitar companies, it documents the evolution of the various models they have built over the years. It also tells the story of how Bob and Kurt bought a tiny guitar workshop in San Diego, California and over the course of three decades turned it into one of the largest and most respected guitar companies in America.

This book also documents how Bob Taylor pioneered new methods of building guitars, many of which have become standard practice for the rest of the industry; and how Bob and Kurt built a unique working relationship that allowed them to grow a company that builds more than 70,000 guitars a year. But before we get to Bob and Kurt, a brief look at the history of the steel-string guitar might help you place the importance of Taylor guitars in the larger story of American guitar building.

These days, the acoustic guitar is so ubiquitous that it's hard to believe that just a century ago it was the third most popular fretted instrument in America, after the banjo and the mandolin. But it was the popularity of those two instruments that inspired guitar makers to create what we now think of as the modern steel-string guitar. During the heyday of the banjo and the mandolin in the latter half of the 19th century, guitars tended be very small, parlor-type instruments, which were designed to be played with gut strings. Although they sounded full and rich, they just didn't have the volume to compete with banjos and mandolins.

Sometime in the 1870s, builders started making larger bodied instruments and bracing the tops for the heavier metal strings. Over the next few decades, American guitar builders started designing larger and larger guitars and by the early 1930s the guitar had evolved into what we now think of as the modern steel string flattop. No single company can lay claim to inventing the steel-string guitar, and many makers contributed to its development including famous builders like Martin, Gibson and Washburn and lesser known ones like the Larson brothers, Tilton, and Bauer.

The new, louder flattop steel-string guitars first found favor with country, folk, and blues musicians. Flattops sold fairly well throughout the 1930s and 1940s, but the most popular guitars during the swing era were the elegant archtops built by companies like Gibson and Epiphone as well as individual luthiers such as Elmer Stromberg and John D'Angelico.

In the fall of 1958 The Kingston Trio's recording of "Tom Dooley" introduced mainstream America to the folk music revival that had been percolating since the late 1940s in urban coffee houses across America. The Trio's version of the old murder ballad prominently featured a stripped down arrangement that included nothing more than a banjo and two acoustic guitars. The simplicity of their instrumental line-up inspired countless budding folkies across the nation to start groups of their own and before long the sales of flattop acoustic guitars began to rise.

By the early 1960s the flattop acoustic guitar was still the instrument of choice for folkies, but thanks to the huge cultural impact of Bob Dylan, rockers like the Beatles and the Rolling Stones were soon experimenting with unplugged sounds. By the mid 1960s the acoustic guitar had become so popular that companies like Martin, Gibson, and Guild couldn't keep up with the demand for high quality instruments, so smaller builders like Michael Gurian, Augustino LoPrinzi, Stuart Mossman, John Gallagher, and Jean Larrivée stepped in to fill the demand.

By the early 1970s there were luthiers setting up shops across America. One such shop was the American Dream Musical Instrument Company, which was started by brothers Sam and Gene Radding in 1970 in San Diego. It was at this shop, in 1973, that two aspiring luthiers named Bob Taylor and Kurt Listug met for the first time...

"This idea of making a guitar filled my mind almost every waking hour." Bob Taylor

Early Efforts

Nine-year-old Bob Taylor repairs his first guitar. Twelve-year-old Kurt Listug wants to start a band. Bob discovers vise in high school, builds three guitars before he graduates, and learns a valuable lesson about life from a broken motorcycle.

The Boy Luthier and the Budding Rock Star

In 1965, a nine-year-old boy named Bob Taylor bought his first guitar for three dollars from a neighborhood friend named Michael Broward. The guitar was an inexpensive flattop steel-string model with a red and black sunburst finish, a stamped metal tailpiece, and painted white binding. It didn't play in tune, had a poor tone, and because it had high action and a large, clubby neck, it was nearly impossible for the boy to play. But young Bob set out to learn to play it despite its shortcomings.

"Michael was a year or so older than me and had an electric guitar and amplifier," Taylor recalls. "This kid could play the Surfaris song 'Wipe Out' and the Herman's Hermits hit 'Mrs. Brown You've Got a Lovely Daughter.' He even said 'duahta' with an English accent when he sang it, just like Peter Noone did in the song. We put together a little folk singing group and we spent hours in the garage singing things like 'Michael, Row the Boat Ashore.' I also learned to play 'Green Onions' by Booker T. and the MGs from him."

A very young Bob Taylor poses with his father.

Bob Taylor struggled to learn to play the cheap guitar, but he soon became obsessed with another aspect of the instrument. The painted-on binding had become scuffed, and Taylor wanted it to look like new. So he took some white Testor's paint that he used on the models he was constantly building, and touched up the scratched binding. "I did a pretty awful job," he remembers. So he took some sandpaper and sanded off the new paint, and in the process, took off the original paint as well. Now the guitar had no binding at all. "I was in worse shape than when I started," he says. "It was time to think. What could a little kid, with a messed up guitar, some paint and a strong will do to salvage the situation? Then the answer came to me: masking tape. I'd use masking tape, and that would solve my big dilemma. So I worked patiently and masked off the area for binding, and then brushed a new coat of paint on the guitar.

Bob Taylor celebrates his second birthday.

"Of course, my excitement was blown out the window upon removing that stupid, idiotic tape, when I found that the texture of the crepe paper that it's made from allowed the paint to run underneath. So, I brought out the sandpaper, and tried it again. Eventually, I developed the skills necessary to get the job done and several attempts later I had the guitar to the point where it would have been if I had just left it alone. But with this project I learned about the limits of masking tape, how to brush paint, and how useful sandpaper was." And so Bob Taylor began his career as a luthier on Argon Street in San Diego at the age of nine.

Meanwhile, in another part of San Diego a twelve-year-old boy named Kurt Listug was learning chords on the guitar he'd gotten the previous Christmas. "When the Beatles hit in 1964, I just felt that this was my music," he says. "I kept bugging my parents for a guitar and after a year or so they bought me a cheap steel-string guitar." Listug began learning songs by the Beatles and other groups of the era and started playing in garage bands. Although the bands never made it out of the garage, his parents eventually bought him an electric guitar, which he remembers was a copy of a semi-hollow-body Vox.

Listug concentrated on learning to play the guitar instead of rebuilding them like his future partner Bob Taylor, but he was always thinking about instruments. "I was really into music gear in high school," he recalls.

Kurt Listug's high school yearbook photo from his senior year.

"When I got bored in class I would draw amplifiers and guitars instead of pay attention. I also once made a speaker cabinet in high school, which I sold to a friend."

Years later, Bob Taylor and Kurt Listug would meet at a small guitar shop called the American Dream, and discover that Bob's talent for building guitars was matched by Kurt's instinct for business. They would go on from the American Dream to start their own guitar company, but before that could happen, Bob Taylor would have to learn how to build guitars.

Bob Taylor grew up with the sort of parents who didn't mind if he spent the day after Christmas disassembling his toys to see how they worked. "I never had much fear about taking things apart," he says. "For me, playing with toys always involved a screwdriver and a wrench. I never got in trouble for taking my bike apart or ruining my Christmas presents by December 26th, but my friends did. My mom and dad knew how things worked and how to fix stuff. My father made our furniture and my mother was a seamstress, so they never gave it any thought if my bedroom floor looked like a 3-D exploded parts drawing of a skateboard, or whatever it was I was 'playing' with. To me, an electric train was fun only if it taught you something about how little electric motors worked. I didn't see the point of just watching the train go round and round."

"When the Beatles hit in 1964 I just felt that this was my music."

One day, he took apart the rear brake hub on his bicycle, and discovered he wasn't able to reassemble it. He asked his friend, Michael Broward, who had an identical brake assembly on his bike, if he could carefully take it apart. "I figured if I could just peek at the insides of his brake, I could see what parts went where," Taylor says. "Then I could calmly close his up and I'd be armed with the necessary knowledge to pick up my own pieces and put them back in the shape of a brake."

Michael was afraid that Bob wouldn't be able to reassemble the brake hub, which would get him into trouble with his parents. But Bob persisted, and eventually Michael relented. "Michael thought that since I had taken my bike apart, I should suffer the consequences. But when I pointed out that if my bike were in pieces, then he'd have to ride around by himself, he finally relented. My powers of persuasion were developing at this young age, along with my ability to shoulder responsibility and to garner trust. The bike did go back together and the peek into Michael's brake was the key. I developed a new motto from that: I'll try anything twice. We rode happily and never looked back. I learned a little bit about cautious disassembly that day, but it would take years to perfect the skill."

Bob Taylor continued to learn to play his cheap acoustic guitar, but he soon wanted an electric guitar just like Michael's. Every week, Taylor would ride his bike to a local store called Apex Music to gaze longingly at the new guitars on the wall. "I didn't know what I was looking at," he says. "Brand names of guitars were not even a thought in my ten-year-old mind, but I was drawn to the guitars. I noticed in the accessories case there was a pickguard with a pickup and two knobs all wired to it. The whole unit cost about twenty bucks. The pickup was covered with a chrome cover with holes punched in it and through the holes you could see a lay-

"I loved that pickup and thought that all I needed was a solid body guitar to put it on. I went home and 'played' with my little acoustic guitar, only this time I used a saw."

er of bumpy gold foil. I loved that pickup and thought that all I needed was a solid body guitar to put it on. I went home and 'played' with my little acoustic guitar, only this time instead of paint and sandpaper, I used a saw."

Bob sawed the neck off of his cheap guitar and unceremoniously dumped the body in the trash. He went to the Boy's Club and got a piece of one-inch thick fir plywood and cut it into a vague electric guitar shape. "I sanded the edges for hours, days, even weeks," he says. "Looking back on it, I think I did this to put off the inevitable task of figuring out how to attach the neck and, more importantly, how to pay for the pickguard. I'm not really sure what happened to that guitar, but I never finished it. I was just too young--I was only ten years old--and there were other things that were more interesting to me, such as the canyons all around my house with hills to slide down, so I had to make time for that as well. Also, I had to go to school, which I hated. I found out at an early age that you just can't fit everything in."

It was a couple of years before Bob got a new guitar, but for his twelfth birthday his parents bought him a new electric guitar at Fed Mart, a local discount store that has since gone out of business. The guitar was a cheap copy of a Fender Stratocaster with a single-coil pickup and a chrome pickguard. "I had never heard of Fender, Martin, or Gibson, and even though it was a cheap copy, that guitar was a favorite thing of mine," he says. "I spent hours trying to figure out how to play songs on it. I was never too good at it, but I still loved it."

Bob Taylor's father was an enlisted man in the Navy, so money was never plentiful. To help out with the finances, Bob's mother worked as a seamstress. "My mom worked for herself at home," he remembers. "She made clothes for all kinds of people and did alterations for the ladies at church whose bodies were changing sizes every couple of months. I think they gave their clothes to each other as well, and mom would make them fit the new owner."

Bob's mother used to send him to the store to buy thread, and it was at this time he began to suspect he was colorblind. "That means that the reds and greens get a little mixed up in my brain," he explains. "I can see red, and I can see green. But from ten feet away I can't see a red flower in a green bush. Green traffic lights look basically the same as white streetlights, and many grays can look green to me, or vice versa. I have learned to deal with my handicap and I've gotten better at naming colors, but when I was young, my seamstress mom would send me on my bike to the fabric store to buy some matching seam binding or some thread. I was too stupid to ask the clerk to match it for me, because I didn't know I had a problem, but I was always in trouble for it. I mean, you wouldn't believe the disfavor I would receive when I'd come home with brown thread to match the green seam binding that she gave me. But, I learned a lot about sewing when I was growing up, and that's not so bad. I think I was the only boy in my neighborhood who knew what it was to 'take in a dart.'"

Because money was tight, Bob Taylor's parents could only afford to get him the electric guitar. Getting the amp to plug it into became his responsibility. At first he would plug his new guitar into his father's homemade all-tube stereo. "Whenever I felt the need for volume, I would go into the family room and plug in," he recalls. "That fun was offset by my shyness at anyone actually hearing my guitar playing. I'd play pretty softly unless nobody was home and then I'd turn up pretty loud. At that point I wasn't really playing to play, per se, but rather to use the equipment. I really liked the guitar and the amp, and the idea of the two of them working together, and the fact that I was in control of the whole thing."

The combination of shyness about his ability as a guitarist and the need to share the stereo with his family drove Bob to find an amplifier of his own. One of his father's friends gave him an old stereo tube amplifier with an elegant brushed bronze face and amber knobs, but unfortunately the amp didn't work. Bob took out the tubes and checked them in the tube tester at the drug store, and was excited to find one bad tube. He brought home all the good tubes and installed them, but it still didn't work. "But I still had confidence in the future," he says. "So I embarked on the project of making a cabinet for this thing. I wanted a guitar amp that looked real, like one a regular guitar player would have, so I took plywood and built a cabinet. I had a twelve-inch Radio Shack speaker in my junk pile and placed the speaker in the lower section of the cabinet and the amp up on top, just like a real amp."

He covered the cabinet in pebbled vinyl and installed a black grille cloth over the speaker. After getting the amplifier installed in the new cabinet, he turned it on. "Of course it didn't work," he recalls. "How would a new cabinet and nice covering fix the amp? It never did work either, but I had fun building it and learned a whole lot in the process. One thing I learned was that hope springs eternal, and that the hope of something working, even without the evidence that it will, is just about the strongest stuff there is. And when I turned on the switch and the amp didn't work, I learned that reality could be even stronger than hope. I found it interesting that I could plow ahead with excitement, work on the project, and put off the real answer to how the project would turn out. Theoretically, if you work long enough and never finish anything, you would never really know how it turned out. That illusion of progress can be comforting, sometimes. At least I can say that I discovered new facts and developed new skills while working on these projects, even if they failed."

The notebook Bob Taylor used to record the various measurements for the guitars he was building during his early days. He would later use computer drawing programs to more accurately record similar information.

Industrial Arts

In 1967, Bob Taylor started the 7th grade in junior high school. One of the first classes he signed up for was drafting, which was followed the next semester by wood shop. That first year he made a simple wooden jewelry box, and in the process he learned elementary wood working techniques like cutting and fitting miter joints, shaping moldings, and basic finishing. He also learned to use power tools like the drill press and the table saw.

The next year, when he was in the 8th grade, he took classes in electronics, where he made a simple radio set, and metalworking. "I was in heaven," he now says about his days in metal shop. He learned how to cast aluminum and how the entire process of sand casting worked. "I was taught how to prepare a pattern, which is usually carved from wood, and all about things like match plates, flasks, sprue holes and risers, gateways, parting compounds, and the different types of sand. I also learned how to prepare the sand and ram up the flask, and pour the metal. And after the casting was removed, I learned how to finish and polish the metal. I loved that stuff and could have spent my whole day in metal shop."

That same year in his metal shop class, Bob Taylor met a teacher who had a major impact on his life. "His name was Ernest Labastida and you called him Mr. Labastida," he remem-

Bob Taylor poses with the lamp project he built for the California State Industrial Arts Exposition.

bers. "If you ever called him "Ernie" he'd chase you down and send you to the office, so the bad kids made sport of that information and would walk by while he was in class and yell, 'Ernie.' He'd take off and catch them. Mr. Labastida was the best teacher I ever had."

After he completed his two casting projects, Bob started on a more ambitious job. "I built a desk lamp made from sheet metal," he says. "It had a base with a drawer, all folded and seamed, with a polished copper front and a little folded copper drawer pull. Then a gooseneck came out of the base and connected the light hood, which was a rolled piece of tin with copper caps on the end. The copper caps were formed with a method called 'hydro-forming.' That's where you take a male die and rather than going to all the expense of making a female die and mounting them both in a die set, you simply put the male die, along with the sheet metal onto a block of very hard rubber, and push it in. This saves a lot of expense and makes one-off forming reasonable. When the copper came out of this form, the formed edges were wrinkled due to the limitations of a rubber female mold and the severity of the forming. The solution was to take a strap that we poured out of lead, about 1/4" thick by 1" wide and 12" long, and simply slap away at the wrinkled edges, with the male form underneath the copper. This method worked so well it shocked me. It was so fun and satisfying to

15-year-old Bob Taylor in tuxedo escorting his mother to a wedding where he will be an usher.

watch this metal, a substance that previously I had no idea you could control so effectively, conform to my wishes under my control with the aid of a few tools."

Bob Taylor entered his lamp project in the California State Industrial Arts Exposition. As part of the entry process he was required to draw a complete set of plans to go along with the lamp, and to create a "story board" which showed all the steps in making it using duplicate parts. By the time the storyboard was complete, he had made enough new parts to make three more lamps. The lamp project won first place and the prize included a plane trip to Sacramento for the awards ceremony, one hundred dollars cash, and some ribbons and medallions. "I was the first person I knew to fly on a plane," he recalls about the trip. "Part of the prize was a big dinner. They served up prime rib and baked potatoes. I'd never had anything like that before, but I knew I would like it. So after my baked potato was all buttered up and fixed with sour cream, you should have seen my face upon my first, twelve-year-old-boy bite, when I discovered that that sour cream was actually horse-radish sauce for the meat. Boy, talk about having a freight train run through your sinuses! That was my first encounter with horse-radish. And I applied what I had learned when I fixed the painted-on binding several times without the help or knowledge from any outsiders. I bore this shock on my own, stuffing my embarrassment and stupidity inside, and nobody ever knew that this incident took place. Not only that, but I ate the whole dang potato, horse-radish and all, and pretty much learned to like the stuff by the time I was done. I pile it high, given the chance, these days, and I'm not afraid to let it spill over on my potatoes."

When he returned to San Diego, Bob bought a small television set with his award money. "Now I could pretty much live in my bedroom without ever coming out," he says. "Previously, I'd have to emerge in order to watch *Then Came Bronson, The Red Skelton Show,* and *The Carol Burnett Show.* But after that, I was pretty much self-contained, which is one of the ways I like it. This allowed me to play with my chemistry set for hours in my bedroom, which really meant making fire and things that smelled really bad. I learned how to patch carpet pretty well because of that chemistry set, but I do wish that they had put a chapter in the instructions

"I was the first person I knew to fly on a plane."

The award winning vise Bob Taylor made in high school. Today, the vise sits in Taylor's office in a place of honor.

on the subject. I was lucky to have so much donor carpet in the recesses of my closet. The other thing I got from those hundred bucks was a note in my eighth-grade annual from one of the prettiest girls in school, who I heard later, became a *Playboy* playmate. (That was probably just a rumor, but she sure was cute.) She wrote, 'To the boy with a hundred bucks!' So, who said that metal shop doesn't have its advantages."

The next year of school, in the 9th grade, Bob signed up for his second year of metal shop with Mr. Labastida. "He supervised the desk lamp project that won at the state fair and then he took me to another level in the ninth grade. That year, I made a jeweler's vise on a ball swivel base. I still have it in my office and it blows me away every time we hire some 21-year-old kid who can't read a ruler and I realize that I made that thing when I was fourteen years old. I had to forge steel into curved shapes and hand file it into the final shape of the jaws. I had to turn threads on a lathe, both left and right handed threads, and make a ball to swivel the vise on. This was a challenge. Today you'd just write a program for a CNC lathe, but back then I had to use the two cross-feed handles like an Etch-a-Sketch and turn a piece of bar stock into a rough ball. Then with a little sheet metal template gauge, I filed forever to get the thing round. Mr. Labastida would come in on weekends and holidays and open the metal shop and I'd meet him there and the two of us would be the only ones at the whole school. He'd help me get my stuff done, which meant he'd point the way and then go do something on his list. His wife came in with hot dogs one weekend day and we roasted them over the forging furnace. You don't get a good teacher like Mr. Labastida too often and I'm thankful for it. Oh, yeah. I never called him Ernie." Bob entered his jeweler's vise in the California State Industrial Arts Exposition that year, and won first place again.

Musical Inspiration

Even as he began to explore the mysteries of industrial arts, Bob Taylor kept in touch with the musical arts as well. He continued to listen to some of the folk musicians he first heard as a child, like the Kingston Trio and Peter, Paul, and Mary, and he began to listen to the new singer/songwriters like Gordon Lightfoot and James Taylor. "The more acoustic side of music was beginning to interest me," he says. "I would listen to bands like Cream and Iron Butterfly when they came on the AM radio, but I didn't really get into the rock and roll scene. Instead I listened to James Taylor. By the way, not only do James and I share the same last name, we share the same birthday, only he's older. He's the first guy to come along that had a recorded acoustic guitar sound that really spoke to my heart. I could listen to his playing in 'Carolina in My Mind' or 'Sweet Baby James' for hours on end. I really think he was way ahead of his time as far as fingerstyle guitar tone and playing is concerned. He's still one of my very favorite guitarists."

Bob would listen to music for hours on end. "I remember that I'd put the two speakers on the ground about a foot apart and facing each other," he says. "Then I'd lay down with my head

"The more acoustic side of music was beginning to interest me."

in between them and listen to a song about fifty times in a row. Then I'd move on to another song. My folks would walk in and see me like that and never could figure out what I was up to, but they left me alone, which was nice. I remember sitting on my bed one day playing my guitar and singing 'The Games People Play' and my mom was in some kind of mood and wanted me to explain what kind of games I was talking about. Heck, I didn't know. I was just a kid singing a song."

Listening to music rekindled his interested in playing guitar, but instead of digging his cheap electric guitar out of the closet, he set his heart on getting an acoustic guitar. "I wanted so bad to strum those chords and sing those songs," he recalls. Like he did when he was nine years old, the now teenaged Bob would head to Apex Music, and stare at the guitars on the wall. "I was in tenth grade by now and I still hadn't heard of Martin or Gibson and any of the big name guitars," he says. "I found a guitar hanging on the wall for thirty-six dollars. It was a Coronet dreadnought with cherry stain on the back, sides, and neck. It had a fancy bridge and this big pickguard with a hummingbird and some vines engraved. It was obviously a copy of a Gibson Hummingbird model, but I didn't know that at the time. I fell in love with it but I only had about twenty-five bucks, so my sister loaned me the rest and I bought it and took it home. I was in business and I lost all interest in my little Fed Mart electric. I don't remember whatever became of that guitar."

Around this time Bob went to a talent show one night at his high school and he saw a group of kids, whom he felt were much cooler than he was, singing folk songs. The name of the group was Learned, Deering, and Prim Prim. "Those were the last names of the four guys in the band," he says. "They were great, and one of them, a big tall guy, who looked older by a year or two, played a banjo and a guitar. His name was Greg Deering, and I didn't know it at the time, but he was going to become a good friend in the future."

Bob Taylor's First Real Guitar

Sometime in 1972, perhaps because he was inspired by all of the Gordon Lightfoot records he was listening to at the time, Bob decided he wanted a 12-string guitar. Apex Music had a 12-string made by the Italian company EKO on the wall that cost $175. The EKO had a bolt-on neck that was similar to the design used by Fender on their electric guitars. "The neck was really skinny with low action," he remembers. "It also weighed a ton and had thick finish that reminded me of the varnish used on surfboards." But the guitar cost more than he could afford, so he forgot about buying it.

That same year in school he was sitting in his woodshop class wondering what to make for his next project, when he got the idea of building a 12-string guitar. His woodshop teacher had started to build a guitar, but never completed it. He had used a book called *Classic Guitar Construction* by Irving Sloane, which was one of the first generally available books on how to build a guitar. He gave the book to Bob, who pored over every page. "It was a book on building nylon-string classical guitars and I wanted to build a twelve-string flattop with steel strings," he says. "But it was sure a lot more infor-

Early 1970s EKO Ranger XII similar to the one that inspired Bob Taylor to attempt to build a 12-string as his first guitar construction project.

mation than I would have had without it. I read the book over and over, falling asleep each night with it on my chest. This idea of making a guitar filled my mind almost every waking hour and I planned and gathered materials and made things ready."

The first thing he realized he would need was a tool of some sort to bend the sides. He fell back on his metal-working experience to make a sidebender. "I went over to the metal shop, where I had a good rapport and got some four-inch steel pipe and cut a steel cap and welded it on," he recalls. "Then I welded on a piece of steel to allow it to be clamped to a bench and put an electric barbecue lighter inside. This bender is still used daily in our factory. That first heating element lasted almost 20 years."

Bob was still in the process of gathering the materials for the guitar and making the side-bender, when his teacher announced that instead of working in the wood shop, the class would spend the next two weeks learning drafting techniques so they would know how to plan their upcoming projects. "When I heard that I got frantic," he says. "I was so excited to get started on my guitar that I couldn't bear the thought of spending two weeks being taught something

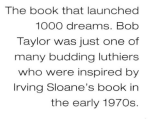

The book that launched 1000 dreams. Bob Taylor was just one of many budding luthiers who were inspired by Irving Sloane's book in the early 1970s.

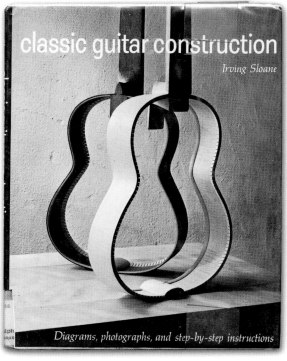

I already knew how to do. So I went home that night and drew the plans for my guitar. Front views, side views, top views, isometric views. I took them to class the next day and requested that I be excused from this activity. My teacher took one look at my plans and let me out of the drafting lessons. I spent the next two weeks out in the shop all by myself working on my first guitar. I was up and running and life was looking pretty good."

The first guitar Bob Taylor built was a 12-string dreadnought with mahogany back and sides and a four-piece spruce top. He traced the body of a friend's Yamaha FG-180 to get the shape, and he made the neck out of maple. He bought a pre-fretted ebony fingerboard at a local music shop and made his own truss rod in the metal shop. Because he was working from a book on building classical guitars, that first guitar had a few features that were unusual on a steel-string instrument. He used a Spanish foot for the neck joint, instead of the more common dovetail. The head-stock was grafted on using a scarf joint, and the heel of the neck was made of stacked blocks of wood, two styles of construction common on classical guitars, but rare on steel-strings. (Years later, Bob Taylor would return to the idea of using grafted-on headstocks and stacked heels, but with a high-tech twist.)

He also discovered that binding wasn't painted on. "Remember, re-painting the binding on that little three dollar guitar when I was nine years old was my first foray into the world of lutherie. So, because of that I carried this fixed idea along with me into my teenage years that binding was painted on. It blew my mind the day I looked closer after reading this Irving Sloane book and realized that guitar binding was a piece of plastic that was glued into a slot on the side of the body. It was like discovering Plutonium! I was on the phone in a heartbeat and found a guitar repair shop that had some."

"You'd think that making a guitar would have made me a hero or something, but in reality most people were kind of upset by the magnitude of the project," he says. "Kids would come up to me and say, 'Hey, Taylor, what are you building?' and I'd say, 'A guitar.' They'd say, 'You

Bob Taylor strums the first guitar he ever built. He later ran over this guitar with his motorcycle.

are not,' and then someone else would say, 'He thinks he's building a guitar, but he's not. He'll never get it done.' And I'd say, 'Ok, I'm not,' just to shut them up. It was pretty weird but it didn't bother me much because I was used to being a dork and doing stuff on my own."

He spent his entire year in eleventh grade working on that guitar. The process went fairly smoothly, but there was one mishap. "I remember drilling the soundhole in the top for that guitar," he says. "I used an adjustable fly-cutter, the kind with the drill bit in the center and a sliding arm with a lathe type cutting tool out on the edge. I made a backing board and fixed it to the drill press, then clamped my top in place. I got everything ready and turned on the drill press. Only problem was, I forgot to move my hand out of the way of this large diameter fly-cutter and it swung around and whacked me real hard in my fingernail. Man, that hurt! There was blood all over the place, but I was committed to that soundhole. I took a deep breath and slowly and patiently cut the soundhole. Then I unclamped it and cleaned up. Meanwhile, my finger had a completely crushed nail and blood was coming out pretty steadily, but I had a rag close by to sop it up with. I displayed an attitude kind of like, 'I meant to do that. No big deal.'"

Bob Taylor's first motorcycle.

When the guitar was completed and strung up, he invited his friends over to play it. "Everyone thought it was the best guitar they'd ever strummed," he recalls. "Like we really knew what a good guitar sounded like. Actually it was a pile, and wasn't made very well. But it wasn't too bad for a 17-year-old kid working on his own and not knowing anything about the subject."

Front view of the guitar that Bob Taylor made for himself in high school.

Around the same time he was building his first guitar, Bob Taylor bought his first motorcycle. Over the next few years he would divide his time between building guitars and riding and working on his motorbikes. "One day, after I had my license for a few months I asked if I could buy a motorcycle and my mom said yes," he remembers. "To this day I can't believe she let me buy it, but she did. She even loaned me money to get it! So I looked in the newspaper and I found a bike for sale for five hundred bucks. I didn't have a way to get there, but the guy who was selling it offered to come pick me up. So, when he showed up, he's driving a big black hearse! And I hop in and tell my mom that I'll be back in a while. So this guy drives me down 805, the newest freeway in our city, and takes me all the way to El Cajon Blvd. This is definitely NOT my neck of the woods. This was pimp town and he certainly wasn't an undertaker. It's getting dark by now and he pulls up to his place and we get out and he's got about two or three more hearses. He says you can buy them cheap. I meet his hippie wife and we go in the back and look at this motorcycle. I don't know if I fell in love with the thing or if I just didn't want him to have to drive me home, but I bought it right there. I had an Easy Rider helmet that I borrowed from my friend, you know, the stars 'n' stripes helmet? So there I was. I was seventeen and I was sitting there free as can be with a red, white, and blue helmet on in the cool of a 1972 evening on my very own motorcycle. My own fire breathin', fuel throbbin', steel machine, and I kick start it and head west toward the 805 North on-ramp and about the time I get there the engine quits. I just sort of sat there and tried to cry but it didn't happen. Well, I had to deal with the situation, so I feverishly went to work cogitating and trying to start that thing. Gas. Petcock. Yes. The gas petcock was turned off. Yes! I flipped it over and it started. I had not only escaped death by pimps, I had also avoided the embarrassment of buying a lemon. That was a sweet ride home that night with the air in my face and that engine between my long legs. I was wearing cowboy boots and I had on a canvas military jacket. Maybe I wasn't so much of a dork after all."

Lessons in Problem Solving

Eventually, Taylor succumbed to the urge to "play" with his new toy. He started by simply cleaning and waxing his bike, but soon he was taking components off to clean them more thoroughly. Before long the engine was completely disassembled and spread out across his bedroom floor. "Pistons, cams, crankshafts, gears, clutches, all laid out neatly and getting cleaned to within an inch of their lives," he says. "I polished every piece of that bike and put the engine together and in the process gained a solid understanding of how it worked. It really did amaze me to think that those pistons could go round and round, and up and down, for hours on end and never give up; until that one time I put it back together and it froze up within ten minutes of riding. I took it apart and found a melted camshaft. That meant a new cam, new rocker arms and a new cam housing. I ordered them from J.C. Whitney and put it all together and it happened again. I was stumped and depressed. I looked at it over and over until I found a flap of gasket sealer on the cam housing cover, which had an oil labyrinth cast into it. The little flap had oozed its way in front of the oil passage and acted as a one-way valve. When I'd blow air to check the passages everything was clear, but the oil flowed the other way and was stopped at that point. It took two engine rebuilds and some wrench throwing to solve that one, as it was complicated and elusive."

Because Bob Taylor's first motorcycle breakdown was caused by a complex and subtle problem, he assumed that the second time it happened, the failure would be equally complicated. "One day I started the bike, drove it into the garage, turned off the engine and took out the spark plugs to sand-blast the electrodes," he remembers. "Then I adjusted my points and put it back together. At the end of the night I went to start it and the engine wouldn't turn over. I fiddled with it for about an hour and a half and I just could not get it started. Obviously it had something to do with the spark plugs or the points since that was the only thing I played with. I decided to troubleshoot my way back to the battery. I checked the timing, the spark plugs, everything. Then, out of nowhere I decided to look in my gas tank. That was it. I had run out of gas at the precise moment that I turned off the engine. I put some gas in and it started right up. I learned from that, and have never forgotten to always check the silliest, stupidest, most minor things first, because often they are the cause of the problem. Even now, when the guys from the factory ask me about some very unusual problem that might be occurring, I'll make them switch bottles of glue or something really simple like that. I can't tell you how often it's been the solution to many of our production problems. They want the problem to be more complex. I'm just happy it's usually so easy to solve."

While he was still in eleventh grade Bob Taylor got a job working at a gas station, the only job he ever held until he became a full-time guitar maker at the age of eighteen. He started work at four in the afternoon, and closed up at ten in the evening. The job allowed him to work on his motorcycle during slow periods and he would occasionally bring a part of the guitar he was building, and work on that when he was between customers. In 1972 he began his final year of high school.

Bob Taylor was never an outstanding student, but he did get pretty good grades. And since he only needed four classes to graduate, his final year was fairly easy. He decided to devote his spare time to building two more

Back view of the guitar that Bob Taylor made for himself in high school.

guitars. "I thought I'd build two rosewood dreadnoughts," he says. "One for me and one for Mike Dwyer, who was my best buddy, and who later became my brother-in-law when he married my sister. The plan was he would pay for the wood and I would build them. Mike's a south-paw, so I had to make my first lefty in the twelfth grade. I had a little production line going and kept those two guitars moving along nicely all year long. These guitars had two-piece Sit-ka spruce tops and Indian rosewood back and sides. They had big ugly abalone rosettes and maple necks that had the peghead angle sawn rather than scarfed and the heel was laminated up with one big block. A friend of ours had a Conn guitar and I liked the peghead shape so I copied it. They were crude once again, but I am still proud to say that I made them. How many other guys can say they made three guitars before they graduated high school? That's pretty good production, given the circumstances.

Mike Dwyer didn't buy all of the parts for the two guitars Bob was building. That year Bob began riding his motorbike out to La Jolla cove, where he would dive for abalone. "It was a whole world of beauty and awe under the water," he says. "I would catch abalone and bring them home to eat. Then I'd saw up the shell and grind through the color all the way down to the white pearly part and do inlay on my guitars with it."

The American Dream

During his senior year in high school, Bob Taylor discovered a small guitar building company called the American Dream. The shop was run by Sam Radding, and he and a small crew built electric and acoustic guitars there. Bob was surprised to find that Greg Deering, the tall banjo player who had impressed him at the talent show a couple of years before worked there as a repairman. "It was at the American Dream that I discovered that you could buy shell already cut into flat pieces," Bob says. "Greg had this white oyster shell that was different from the yellow abalone shell I was using. I also bought a pattern for a banjo inlay and he showed me how to cut it. I put a 'Hearts and Flowers' Gibson banjo inlay on one of the two guitars I was building and another Gibson pattern I've since forgotten the name of on the second one."

Bob Taylor's interest in banjos extended beyond their fretboard inlays. He heard "Dueling Banjos" from the soundtrack of *Deliverance* on the radio and decided to take up the instrument. He bought a cheap banjo for fifty-nine dollars, signed up for lessons, and started learning some rudimentary fingerings and picking patterns. Within a few months he became a fairly talented banjo picker and quickly outgrew his cheap instrument. After yet another visit to Apex Music he bought a Vega Ranger, which was a much better banjo than the one he was playing. Taylor remembers that he used to stuff a pillow in the shell of his new banjo so he wouldn't wake up his family when he practiced at night. "Before you knew it, I was Mr. Blue-grass," he recalls. "And it made Greg Deering jealous. He tells the story today, and that's why I know."

Being Bob Taylor, he couldn't just learn to play an instrument, he had to learn to build it as well. "I started a new neck for my banjo and got it mostly done before I graduated," he remembers. "I had to finish it after I left school, but it was my best work yet. The shaping of the neck was really good and the inlays were well done."

Sometime during his senior year Bob announced to his parents that he wasn't planning on going to college. "I loved making guitars and wanted to do more with that," he says. "I was working at the gas station and I heard The Eagles do 'Take it Easy' for the first time. I thought, 'What was this song? Who were these guys?' There were electric guitars, acoustic guitars, banjos, harmony vocals, and drums. This song had it all. It made me think about guitars

Bob Taylor suited up in snorkeling gear and ready to go hunting for abalone.

Bob Taylor and future brother-in-law Mike Dwyer jamming on the second and third guitars Bob built.

and all the stuff you could do with a guitar. Not only could you play them, but you could build them, too. This line of thought brought the two worlds of music and mechanics together for me and after that, there was no turning back. I knew I had to figure out how to have a piece of this nirvana."

Making up his mind was the easy part. The hard part was telling his parents that he wanted to become a full-time guitar builder. "I remember my dad was reading the paper on the living room couch and mom was puttering in the kitchen," he says. "My announcement upset her and she said I could be a doctor or lawyer or something like that; that I was smart enough to do those things. She said to my dad, 'Dick, tell him. Say something.' And Dad folded the corner of his newspaper down and said, 'Ah, let the kid do what he wants.' And that was that. I had become a guitar maker."

After high school graduation Bob would go and hang out at the American Dream. He showed them the banjo neck he was working on and the guitars he had made, and Sam Radding and the other workers were impressed. Sam hinted that there might be a place for the teenager as an American Dreamer, but Bob had a road trip planned for part of the summer with his friend Mike Dwyer. He decided to go on the trip and talk to Sam when he got back.

"This trip was planned with Mike, who by now was engaged to marry my sister Georgi," Bob recalls. "My dad had just bought a new Datsun 510 sedan and he allowed us to use this new car to take this trip. We started in San Diego and drove east to New Mexico, and then up through the Rockies to Montana, and then into Canada, down into Washington, into Oregon, and down the coast of California. My guitar was finished when we left, but Mike's wasn't and I glued the bridge on and strung it up in a motel room in Santa Fe. I also brought along my banjo and we played music, sang and drove ten thousand miles on that trip. It took us a month and we had the time of our lives. I think I could go to the moon now and not feel as grown up or remote as I did on that first trip of mine. I remember we were driving along a country highway in Colorado, and looked over and saw train cars galore, and on the side of them it said "The Rock Island Line." So we pulled over to the side of the road and got out our instruments and sang the words of the old Leadbelly song. We sang, 'The Rock Island Line is a mighty fine road. The Rock Island Line is the road to ride,' for about two hours. I came back from that trip and talked to Sam Radding about work, and on September 15, 1973, just three months after graduating from high school, I began working at the American Dream."

"It was a hippie guitar shop." Tim Luranc

Living the American Dream

Sam Radding lives the American Dream. Luthiers helping luthiers. Dulcimers, banjos, and ukuleles. Bob Taylor meets future partners Kurt Listug and Steve Schemmer. Bob invents a bolt-on neck. Kurt, Bob, and Steve buy the American Dream.

Sam Radding and the American Dream

The American Dream was the perfect place for an aspiring guitar builder like Bob Taylor to hone his craft. The shop was owned by Sam Radding, a luthier who taught himself to build guitars as a teenager, much as Taylor had done. The Dream, as everyone called it at the time, consisted of three elements: a retail shop, run by Sam's brother Gene; a workshop that produced custom made acoustic and electric guitars; and a repair shop. Radding's workers included Kurt Listug, who ran the finishing department and would later become Bob's partner when they bought out Radding and started their own guitar company; Tim Luranc, who would become one of Taylor's first employees; and Greg Deering, the lanky banjo player Taylor met the previous year and who ran the repair shop. Along with building guitars, the shop sold hard to find guitar parts like plastic binding material, fret wire, and tuning machines. They would also resaw large boards of rosewood, mahogany, spruce, and other tonewoods into smaller pieces suitable for building guitars. This combination of services made the Dream the center of San Diego's growing community of luthiers as well as a popular place for musicians to hang out.

Brothers Sam and Gene Radding founded the American Dream in 1970. "I built the guitars, and Gene sold them," Sam recalls. "He came up with the name when we opened our first shop in San Diego. It had a tiny retail section in front, and most of the space in back was devot-

Sam Radding, proprietor of the American Dream, holding one of his guitars.

ed to instrument making." The venture was so successful that after a few months both the retail and instrument building parts needed more space. So Sam packed up his part of the business and relocated to a 1500 square foot building at 7936 Lester Avenue, Suite B in Lemon Grove, a small town east of San Diego.

When Sam set up his new shop in Lemon Grove, he had been building guitars for seven years. "I started building guitars in 1963, when I was in 11th grade," he remembers. "I had an old Stella acoustic guitar that was a pretty crappy instrument, but since I was getting into rock and roll at the time I wanted an electric guitar."

Over the course of a summer Radding had managed to save $125. He had his eye on a hollow-bodied Gibson ES-125 that was hanging on the wall at Apex Music, the same store Bob Taylor would haunt as a guitar obsessed teenager. One day he went into the store with a friend and tried to make a deal on the guitar, which was priced at $150. "I asked the salesman if he could come down a bit on the price," Radding says. "But he just stopped me in mid-sentence and said, 'No. There's just no way.' So I turned to my friend and said, "Well, I'm just going to have to build my own guitar." And the salesman stepped in between us and said, and I'll never forget this, 'You don't build guitars, you buy them in stores.' That really got me fired up and within a month and a half I was holding the first hollow bodied electric I built. A kid down the street saw it and asked if I could build one for him. I said, 'Sure, for a hundred bucks.' And with that I was in the instrument building business."

Article printed around 1973 about Sam Radding in a local newspaper called *The Independent*.

Sam Goes to the University

In 1965, Radding enrolled at San Diego State University, where he attended classes in biology and psychology, but he spent most of his time in the industrial arts department. "There was a huge Appalachian dulcimer craze going on during the mid-60s, so I figured out how they were made and I built a few in a workshop I had set up in my father's garage," he says. "I also started making acoustic guitars around this time. I got a copy of Irving Sloane's book *Classic Guitar Construction* and built a classical guitar. I decided that I had to make a steel-string acoustic so I built a Martin 00 sized guitar out of maple. When I strung it up I realized that I had something special."

Radding began to attract other schoolmates who were interested in building instruments. "Since I had already made a few instruments, I would help them out on their projects," he says.

> "I can look at something and tell you how it's built and suggest ways to build them a little better."

"I can look at something and tell you how it's built and suggest ways to build it a little better. Guitars are basically pretty simple so they were no problem for me to figure out. I could look at them and tell you how they were put together, and why they were built the way they were. Bob Taylor is one of the very few people I've met who seems to be hard-wired in the same way."

One budding luthier Radding helped out in the early days was Tony Graziano, who went on to become a well-respected builder of guitars and ukuleles. "I met Sam in 1969 when I was trying to make a dulcimer for a class project," he recalls. "Somebody mentioned there was a guy named Sam Radding in the industrial arts department who made instruments so I went and looked him up. He and his brother were constructing dulcimers in their garage and he showed me how they made them. He was happy to tell me what he knew and he didn't seem to mind

Sam Radding contemplates his future.

that I was building an instrument that competed with his. At the time it was weird to find out that people actually built dulcimers and guitars and that they weren't just made in a factory somewhere. It was great to be able to talk to a guy who actually built musical instruments. Sam was really generous with his time and he was a great source of information in a period when it was impossible to find out how instruments were made."

Another luthier who came into Radding's orbit in the 1960s was Greg Deering. "Sam was in a few of my classes in college," Deering remembers. "He and his brother Gene were building instruments in their parent's garage. The first time I went over there Sam was working on a guitar and I think his brother was making a clavichord. Somehow they were able to order parts wholesale and I had them get some banjo parts, fret wire, and plastic binding for me. I used that stuff to make my first banjo in 1969."

Deering was also there when Sam Radding moved the instrument building and repair facilities from the storefront in San Diego to the new location in Lemon Grove. "They moved in May of 1970," he says. "I remember that because I helped them move in the large band saw and some of the other big tools. We built a few benches out of plywood and two by fours and we were ready to go. I really wanted to be part of the American Dream, but Sam already had

"His first guitar had a few rough spots here and there – mostly minor cosmetic glitches – but that instrument was very good."

two partners, a guy named Lee Fulmer and Bob Morrisey, who was known as Captain Bob. While we were moving tools I overheard one of them say they needed a repairman. I quickly said I could do that. At first I had to take the repair work home and do it there, but after a couple of months they found a small corner of the shop for me to set up my bench." Radding remembers Deering as an excellent repairman, but he did have one failing. "He used way too much glue," Radding recalls. "There were always these puddles of glue on the floor around his bench."

The Dream began to attract people who wanted to learn to build guitars. "There were plenty of guys who wanted to dabble in guitar-making," Radding says. "They'd sort of fall for the supposed romance of the luthier's life, but they didn't realize how much work and dedication it takes to make a living with your hands." Over time Radding assembled a crew of workers and proceeded to shape them into luthiers. His crew built flattop steel strings, a few archtops, and the occasional solid body electric. Radding set up a system where each luthier was responsible for building an instrument from start to finish. "I looked at the American Dream as a co-op," he explains. "I owned all the equipment and I set the parameters for the guitars, but I didn't set the builders' hours. They were responsible for getting the job done."

The flattops were generally jumbos or dreadnoughts, but they sometimes made smaller guitars as well. The instruments had spruce tops and the back and sides could be made from Indian rosewood, Brazilian rosewood, or mahogany. They also used maple and walnut, which was quite unusual for the time.

A few months after the Dream opened its doors, Bob Taylor showed up with his first guitar. "Bob had been coming in, buying parts, and asking questions," Radding says. "His first guitar had a few rough spots here and there--mostly minor cosmetic glitches—but that instru-

Kurt Listug around the time he started working at the American Dream.

31

Old photo of the Master Toad banjo.

ment was very good. He was a highly capable builder from the start, even with no experience. He's one of very few people I've met who intuitively knows how to make a musical instrument. He just seemed to know how to make it sound good, and how it should be put together without being told. He knows that stuff better than I do."

Not long after Bob Taylor came in to show off his guitar, Tim Luranc purchased a new American Dream instrument. Unfortunately it was made by a builder who wasn't quite up to the job, and Luranc had to keep coming back for warranty work. But there was at least one consolation. "I liked hanging around the shop while it was getting fixed," Luranc recalls. "After a while I started working on some projects of my own and Sam let me use the tools. I had made surfboards and I had taken a few industrial arts classes, so I was familiar with how the tools worked. After he saw what I could do, he offered me a bench. I think that was early in 1973. That was how it was at the Dream. Sam never said you were hired, he asked if you wanted a bench. There was no contract and no paperwork, just a nod from Sam, and the statement, 'Here's your bench.'"

Luranc found that the Dream's laid-back approach to business suited him. "It was a hippie guitar shop," Luranc says. "Sam didn't run it based on standard legal practices. He didn't want to have employees as such, because of all the tax hassles of dealing with them, so he made everyone an independent contractor. There wasn't a time frame for completing a job. We could take vacations whenever we wanted. I once went to Hawaii for three months, and when I came back I still had my bench." The workers may have liked the easy-going hours, but Radding remembers being frustrated by the situation. "The guys sure liked the way the Dream was run back then," he says. "But looking back on it today, I have to say that way of doing business didn't make me any money."

Rather than pay his workers a salary, Radding took a percentage of the selling price of each instrument they made. Most of the orders came from the American Dream retail shop in San Diego, although occasionally a customer would track down the shop in Lemon Grove and stop by and place their order in person. There were a few customers who insisted that Radding himself build their guitars, but usually he would assign the order to the luthier he thought was most capable of building that particular instrument. It was common for customers to go through the stash of tonewoods and choose the set they wanted for their guitar.

Kurt Listug Gets a Job and Meets his Future Partner

A few months after Tim Luranc got his bench, Kurt Listug joined the crew at the Dream. He was attending college at the time, taking classes in German and philosophy, but he really wanted to work on guitars. "I tried to get a job at the American Dream for at least a year," he says. "I had some woodworking skills and I liked working with my hands, but I didn't know how to build a guitar when I started. Sam had an opening for someone to learn to do refinishing, which is what I started doing there. Greg Deering helped me out a lot. He taught me how to spray lacquer and also how to do a few minor repairs." A few months after he started at the Dream, Listug found a job in the refinishing department for a childhood friend named Steve Schemmer. "We grew up across the street from each other," Listug says. "He was a couple of years older, but since we both still lived with our parents, and were in our early 20s, we hung out together quite a bit. After I got him the job at the Dream, we sometimes drove to work together."

Listug was so excited about his new job spraying finish he barely noticed when a young luthier named Bob Taylor joined the crew at the Dream the same week he did. "I do remember he was so straight-laced," Listug says. "We didn't really talk to him when he first started at the Dream. He was a couple of years younger than we were. I was twenty and he was eighteen and just out of high school. One day, after he had been there a few weeks, we were all sitting on the couch and he came up to us and announced, "I'm Bob Taylor!" and that was how I met him."

It may have taken Kurt Listug a few weeks to notice Bob Taylor, but the other luthiers at the Dream saw he was something special immediately. "I sold Bob some of the parts to make his first guitar" Deering recalls. "This was the height of the hippie era and we had guys coming in all the time to buy wood and frets and stuff claiming they were going to build the best guitar ever. But they never seemed to finish what they started. They were always asking us to finish their half-completed projects for them. But Bob was one of the only guys to actually finish a guitar. In fact, he made three guitars while he was still in high school, which I thought was just amazing. When he started at the Dream he was working on a banjo as well. I helped him with the inlays. His banjo was a copy of a Gibson Mastertone, but rather than inlay that word in the fretboard, he inlaid a small pearl toad and called the banjo the Master Toad."

Tim Luranc also noticed Bob Taylor's abilities right away. "Bob's bench was next to mine," he recalls. "He came in out of high school and he just blew everybody with the speed and quality of his work. All he did was put his head down and go. I'd tell Sam I was going to cut out and go surfing for the rest of the day, or I'd head down to Mexico for a week, but Bob never did that. He just continued to work. You could just tell he was a better builder than everyone else. We weren't bad luthiers, but he just had a drive to excel that was unlike anything I'd ever seen." Greg Deering had similar thoughts. "Bob was notably different from everyone else there," he says. "He was the only person, apart from me and Sam, who wasn't a long-haired hippie."

On Bob Taylor's first day on the job he didn't waste any time. Even though he didn't have an assignment from Radding, he started work on a guitar. "It was a maple dreadnought with rosewood binding, a maple neck with a rosewood fretboard and bridge," Taylor recalls. "That first guitar was very exciting for me to build. It was actually my fourth guitar, but in my mind it was my first real guitar."

"I was 18 years old when I started my new career," Taylor says. "I got my bench from a builder named Dave Zucker, who was away on an extended leave. When he returned and I met him for the first time, he wasn't allowed to talk because of some New Age therapy he was involved in, so I knew him for about a month before he ever spoke a word. I never got the point of the silence and what he was supposed to achieve. It must have been a 60s thing. He was good at it, though, and he didn't say one word."

Sam Radding built this jumbo guitar around 1971. The moustache bridge was designed by a San Diego artist named David Randle. Taylor continued to use the bridge on their jumbo models for years.

A guitar-making bench at the Dream was crude but serviceable and consisted of a frame of two-by-fours nailed to the wall and a particleboard top for a work surface. You had to supply your own hand tools, but the shop had a table saw, band saw, planer, belt sander, drill press, and some routers and orbital sanders. There was also a crude spray booth that was an eight by sixteen-foot room with a hole at one end to vent the lacquer fumes.

Bob Taylor Learns the Ropes

Radding showed Taylor the various techniques to use to build an American Dream guitar, and the young builder attacked the job with enthusiasm. "I can recall almost everything about that first guitar," he says. "Sam's top bracing was different from the pattern I used on my instruments. Basically it was a variation of the classic Martin X-brace pattern, but it added two fan braces and two braces under the fretboard. I remember using a little Craftsman thumb plane and a chisel to shape and carve the braces into gentle sloping curves that died into the top toward the edges."

The neck joint was a unique T-shaped mortise and tenon that Radding dubbed the T-Block. "For some reason we all thought that it was easier or stronger than the standard dovetail joint that guitar makers used," Taylor says." But in fact it was a hard joint to make well and it was difficult to remove if you needed to reset the neck. It was also larger than the heel, which made it difficult to shape. I think the only advantage it had over a dovetail, and most likely the reason Sam thought of it, was that it could be made entirely with the table saw rather than complicated router fixtures." Radding had experimented with dovetail neck joints, but found them wanting. "I just think they take too much work," he says. "They're a nice joint for cabinets, but when you consider how much tension is on the neck, they're not really the best choice."

After the neck joint was completed, Taylor started on the fretboard, which was completed before it was glued to the neck. "I slotted it, cut it to taper, rounded the top surface, fretted it and then dressed the frets," he says. "Rounding the fretboard was fun. I'd double stick tape it to a long block of wood and set it down on the face of a 6" x 48" belt sander. Then I'd start rocking it back and forth, working it into a radius. It required a lot of skill and a good understanding of what a radial curved surface really is. The mistake most people would make was that they just rounded the edges and produced a flat fretboard with rolled off edges. I found that to make a radius you have to "think" 'radius'. Then your brain simply tells your hands and arms what to do. It's quite simple, really, when you're thinking properly."

He then glued the fretboard to the neck blank and trimmed the edge of the fretboard. After that, he shaped the neck with a Sureform and a spoke-shave. "Since this was only the fourth guitar I had made, I didn't really know much about how to shape a neck," he says. "I carved it so it was very thin and relatively flat. People seemed to like the feel of those skinny necks, and since they seemed to be stable, I continued to make them that way." In the early 1970s, builders such as Martin and Guild tended to make guitars with fairly large, rounded necks. Larger necks were more stable and less prone to warping or twisting than thinner necks, which was an important consideration for the guitar builder, but they were more difficult for guitarists to play. Bob Taylor continued to make guitars with slim necks when he started building under his own name. The slim necks were the first thing players noticed when they picked up a Taylor and his instruments quickly gained a reputation among musicians as one of the most playable instruments available.

Bob Taylor's first American Dream guitar progressed much more easily than the first three guitars he built in high school. He was more confident in his own abilities as a luthier, but he

"I can recall almost everything about that first guitar."

Sam Radding around 1973. >

also found that following Radding's blueprint took much of the ambiguity out of building guitars. Radding's plans meant that Taylor didn't have to puzzle over things like fret placement, scale length, or the proper neck angle, and could instead concentrate on just building the instrument and learning how the parts went together.

Everything was going well until he started the final process of spraying the finish. "I dropped the guitar in the spray booth and broke the top," he says. "It was late at night and I was getting it ready for a customer who had decided to purchase it. He wanted it to play at the Julian Banjo & Fiddle Contest, which began in about a week." Taylor was devastated by the accident and spent the next hour sitting at his bench and trying to figure out whet to do next. After pondering all of his options, he came to the realization there was only one thing to do. "I decided to rebuild the guitar immediately," he says. "I stayed up nearly all night making a new top. I removed the broken one, glued on the new top, and then rebound it. The next day I sanded it, started the finishing process and got myself caught up to within a day of being on schedule. I began to wonder if that particular pace could become the norm rather than the exception. It took me a month to build that first guitar, which was really far too long. I was only making a couple of hundred dollars on each guitar and I couldn't make a living if I was only building twelve guitars a year. At that time, my body and mind were the tools that I viewed as needing the most improvement, so I worked on my skills and attitude. I began to learn how to make guitars faster and better with my own bare hands. Later in my career I began to use tooling to speed up the construction process, but all of my ideas about building guitars more efficiently began with the one I dropped."

"What I think I did give him was the knowledge that you could make a living building instruments."

Radding was impressed with Taylor's woodworking abilities and with his work ethic. And although Taylor lacked experience when he started at the Dream, Radding feels he had little to do with the young luthier's development. "I don't believe I really taught Bob Taylor anything about building guitars," Radding now claims. "What I think I did give him was the knowledge that you could make a living building instruments. I also gave him a place where he could carry on conversations with other guitar makers about how to build instruments more efficiently, what types of tools to use, and stuff like that."

One of the good things about working at the Dream in those days was the steady stream of builders and aspiring builders who came through the doors looking for parts or advice. Radding was particularly willing to help out young builders and they would spend hours discussing various methods of carving necks, shaping braces, clamping bridges, and the dozens of other steps it took to build an acoustic guitar.

James Goodall, who now has a successful career building acoustic guitars in Hawaii, used to hang out at the Dream. "I never had a bench there," Goodall says. "But I think there was a real sense of mutual inspiration back then. We all learned together. I remember that Tim Luranc showed me how to bend the sides on my first guitar. He showed me where to put the pressure and how to keep the side from cracking. He was very helpful."

Radding remembers when James Goodall first came into the Dream. "He was making wooden Indian flutes that were nicely done," he recalls. "He was also a painter who did these wonderful seascapes. He traded a wonderful painting he did for some of the wood he used to build his first guitar. He became a very good builder." Although James Goodall was part of the San Diego's luthier's community he never worked for Radding or at Taylor. "A *Los Angeles Times* article claimed I was an ex-Taylor employee," Goodall says. "I really admire what Bob and Kurt have done over the years, but I never worked for them."

Sam Radding was a gregarious person and every few months he would hold a large potluck party and invite as many as two hundred people. These were held in the shop, but the party inevitably spilled out into the alley and the parking lot. Since all Sam's friends were musicians, there were always a number of bands that would play. "Those parties were a lot of fun," Listug recalls. "We'd go all out setting up for them. I remember we used to take a bunch of shipping pallets and stack them up to make a stage."

More than thirty years after the fact, musicians and builders still recall those huge potluck parties with affection. Another event that people remember about the early days was the American Dream Gun Day. "I'm relatively anti-gun but one day, and I don't really remember why I suggested it, but I decided that everybody should bring their guns to work," he recalls. "I was surprised to find out that I was the only person there without a gun, because these guys were such a bunch of hippies. I don't remember if Bob had one but I know Kurt did. I think he borrowed it from a friend of his. That day was very strange, but very funny. Customers would walk in to get their guitars worked on, and it would take a minute or two to realize that every workbench had a gun on it. Some of the guys set up a shooting range in back for pellet pistols and when I went back to check on what they were doing, they offered me the first shot. I had never fired a handgun before, but I paced off the distance aimed at the target and hit it dead center. I handed the gun back and decided to quit while I was ahead."

Bob Taylor's First Bolt-on Neck

Even with the parties Bob Taylor continued to build guitars at a fast rate and to experiment with ways to make the job go even faster. Sometime in late 1973, he came up with a different way of attaching necks that would later become one of his signature guitar building techniques. He was doing some repair work on a friend's Guild G-37 that required him to remove the neck. After examining the dovetail joint, he realized that it would take a lot of time to repair it. Drawing on the problem solving skills he learned in high school and working on his motorcycle, Taylor devised a way of bolting the neck back on. "I cut the dovetail off," he says. "Then I glued that block of wood into the body, drilled holes in it, filled it in, put some bolts in there, and I was done! I successfully 'repaired' it by converting it to a bolt-on neck, and the guitar played great. Fortunately, my friend didn't care that I'd changed the way it worked."

Bob Taylor built this walnut American Dream dreadnought in January 1974.

"That repair was one of the first things that really impressed me about Bob," Kurt says. "He just has this complete confidence in his abilities. I had done some guitar repairs but I would never have tackled something like that. He's not afraid to get himself into trouble on a guitar repair or a tool design, because he knows he can always figure out a way to make it work."

Interestingly, both Sam Radding and Greg Deering had experimented with bolt-on necks for acoustic guitars before Taylor. "In 1970 I built two small bodied travel guitars for a customer," Radding recalls. "The neck was held on with wing nuts so you could take it off for travel. I had forgotten I'd made those guitars until Bob told me about the repair job on that Guild."

Greg Deering was experimenting with bolt-on necks around the same time. "In the spring of 1970 I made a dreadnought with a slotted peghead," he says. "The back and sides were walnut and it had a bolt-on neck. I just didn't feel like doing a dovetail, so I theorized that bolts would work a bit more easily, and they did. I may have gotten the idea from building banjos, because they had bolt-on necks as well. Around that same time I built a plastic backed guitar for my senior project. That had a bolt-on neck as well. I built a few more of those, but after a while Ovation found out and sent me a cease and desist order."

Bob Taylor's attempt to make a repair job go a little faster was the first version of the neck attachment that would later become Bob Taylor's most significant structural innovation. Over the next few years he would continue to work on his designs for bolt-on necks, but for now he concentrated on completing his orders. "I spent the next year making these American Dream guitars," he says. "Along with learning to build instruments quickly, I was getting an education on meeting deadlines and keeping my customers satisfied. Often they would bring their guitars back a few days after picking it up for some tweaking. When that happened I got a chance to see what I did poorly and what I did well."

Taylor learned how to quickly assess a problem and because the customers were anxious to play their new guitars, how to quickly fix it. Every job at this time posed a new challenge. One time the two members of a local duo wanted to order a pair of matching guitars. After talking with them for a while, Taylor set out to make an identical set of maple jumbos. He cut the wood for the necks, backs, and sides from the same block of wood. "I did my best to make the guitars identical," he says. "But they turned out to be completely different. One of them was much better than the other. At the time I couldn't figure out why that was. After thinking about it for a while I came to realize that even though those guitars were made from the same pieces of wood by the same guy, they were in fact quite different. The guitars had different arches in the tops and backs, the tops had slightly different thicknesses, they each had different neck angles, and on and on. Just because I thought they were identical at first didn't mean they were. I think that was the time I seriously started thinking about making tools, jigs and fixtures, so I could build instruments with more control."

Contract between Kurt Listug and his father describing the terms for an emergency loan a few months after the Westland Music Company was founded.

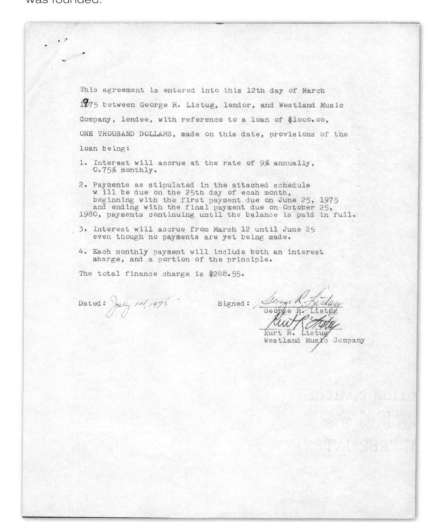

This agreement is entered into this 12th day of March 1975 between George R. Listug, lendor, and Westland Music Company, lendee, with reference to a loan of $1000.00, ONE THOUSAND DOLLARS, made on this date, provisions of the loan being:

1. Interest will accrue at the rate of 9% annually, 0.75% monthly.

2. Payments as stipulated in the attached schedule w ill be due on the 25th day of ecah month, beginning with the first payment due on June 25, 1975 and ending with the final payment due on October 25, 1980, payments continuing until the balance is paid in full.

3. Interest will accrue from March 12 until June 25 even though no payments are yet being made.

4. Each monthly payment will include both an interest aharge, and a portion of the principle.

The total finance charge is $288.55.

Dated: July 14, 1975   Signed: George R. Listug
                                      George R. Listug
                                      Kurt R. Listug
                                      Westland Music Company

By the middle of 1974 Sam Radding was getting tired of running the American Dream. Although he really enjoyed building guitars, he discovered he just didn't want to be the boss anymore. Radding used to have a pair of red socks and he noticed that whenever he wore them, the American Dream would make money. But eventually the socks lost their magic and the shop began to sink into debt. One day he announced he was going to close the American Dream, but after some of the workers urged him to reconsider he decided to sell it instead. Radding told the crew he was going to go backpacking for a week and when he returned he would consider any offers. Then he would present the plans to the crew, who would vote on who would be the new owner of The American Dream. Kurt Listug and Steve Schemmer decided to form a partnership to buy the business, as did Bob Taylor and his friend Jerry Pike.

When Sam Radding returned from his camping trip the two competing potential buyers laid out their offers. Listug and Schemmer surprised everyone by coming up with a well thought out business plan. "My father worked in the cost accounting department at an aerospace firm called Rohr," Listug explains. "He recommended that I go to the Small Business Administration, where I found out a group called SCORE, which stood for the Service Core of Retired Executives. They were able to set me up with a man named Herb Cooperman who helped me write my business plan. I was ambitious and thought I could take the idea of the American Dream and expand on it. We would continue to build guitars, but we would get more into retail, too."

Listug planned to borrow the money from his father, who quickly spotted the one thing missing in the plan. "The first thing my dad asked me was, 'Do you or Steve know how to make guitars?'" Listug recalls. "I had to tell him no, we didn't. He suggested that if we were going into the guitar building business, it might be a good idea to have a partner who actually knew how to build guitars. He asked me who the best builder at the Dream was and when I told him Bob Taylor was, he said he'd loan me the money if we could get Taylor to sign on as a partner."

A couple days after they gave their presentations, Kurt Listug and Steve Schemmer asked Bob Taylor if he wanted to be partners with them. "I still didn't know Kurt or Steve very well, but it sounded pretty good to me," Taylor recalls. "Kurt was interested in running a business and I was interested in building guitars. Kurt wanted to start with a $10,000 investment and he wanted to have both him and Steve to put in $3500 and me to put in $3000. He said the reason for this was that they didn't know me and with this arrangement they would have a larger say in the business than me, due to their higher percentage of ownership. It all made sense to me, so I agreed."

Bob Taylor went to his friend Jerry Pike and explained the situation. Taylor offered him half of his share of the new business, but after considering it for a couple of weeks, Pike decided to pass on the opportunity. Bob Taylor borrowed his $3000 share from his parents, who had recently moved to Spokane, Washington. Kurt Listug went to a lawyer and had the partnership agreement drawn up and on October 15, 1974 Listug, Taylor, and Schemmer bought the American Dream. They gave Sam Radding $3500 which covered the cost of the tools and paid off the out-

This agreement is entered into this this 26th day on June, 1975 between R. Pierre Taylor, lendor, and Westland Music Company, lendee, w ith reference to a loan of $500.00, FIVE HUNDRED DOLLARS, made on March 1, 1975, provisions of the loan being:

1. Interest will accrue at the rate of 7% annually, 0.583% monthly.

2. Payments as stipulated in the attached schedule will be due on the first day of each month, beginning with the first payment due on July 1, 1975 and ending with the final payment due on August 1, 1978, payments continuing until the balance is paid in full.

3. Interest will accrue from March 1 until July 1 even though no payments were yet made.

4. Each monthly payment will include both an interest charge, and a portion of the priciple.

The total finance charge is $68.60.

Dated: Signed: *R. Pierre Taylor*
                                            R. Pierre Taylor

                                            Robert Taylor
                                            Robert Taylor
                                            Westland Music

Contract between Bob Taylor and his grandfather describing the terms for his emergency loan.

"It all made sense to me, so I agreed."

Snapshot of one of the last guitars Sam Radding built before he turned the American Dream over to Taylor, Listug, and Schemmer.

standing debt. "I would never have done a thing as smart as getting the partnership agreement and having a lawyer handle the purchase," Taylor says. "But Kurt thinks that way. Everything was done legitimately with lawyers and contracts and all that kind of stuff. For a tiny $3500 business!"

The Birth of Taylor Guitars

But for all the care Listug took in drawing up the contracts, one important item slipped by him. It turned out the name American Dream wasn't included in the sale of the business. That name stayed with Sam Radding's brother Gene who still owned the retail music shop in San Diego. So the new partnership was formed under the name Westland Music Company. "We chose Westland because we thought it sounded so big, like a conglomerate," Listug remembers. "We were going to be selling guitar making parts and doing repairs. The guitar making was going to be just one part of the total picture." Since they couldn't call their guitars by the American Dream name, they needed to come up with something else to put on the peghead.

"We thought American Dream was the best guitar name ever," Taylor says. "We were really bummed that we couldn't use it. There was a lot of discussion about calling them 'Taylor' but both Kurt and Steve were worried and probably a little jealous about naming them after me. We thought of all kinds of names and even considered 'Listug' but decided that name would be more fitting for a line of drums. Besides that, everyone wants to say his name 'Lustig.' Final-

< The same guitar on Sam Radding's workbench.

An enthusiastic Kurt Listug stands on the roof of his Ford Falcon
and predicts great things for the Westland Music Company.

ly they decided Taylor was the best choice. "We all agreed that Taylor was a great name for an American built guitar and that it sounded as good as Martin," Listug says. "The only reason not to call it Taylor was that there were three of us involved in the company, but it sounded so good. Since Bob was the only real guitar maker among us, it made sense for us to use his name."

After deciding on the name, the three partners had to come up with a logo to use on the peghead. There was an old green thermometer hanging on the wall of the bathroom at the workshop that was made by a company that was also called Taylor. The new partners thought the thermometer logo had a nice typeface, so they used that as the inspiration for the Taylor peghead inlay.

Unfortunately, Taylor, Listug, and Schemmer had a minor falling out with Sam Radding during the period when the American Dream was changing into Westland Music. "Sam was going to continue working for us after the sale," Taylor says. "At the last minute his brother Gene decided that he was going to keep the phone number for his retail shop. Sam caved to the family pressure and ordered that the number be forwarded to Gene's store, The American Dream. The whole thing really annoyed us so we fired Sam and we didn't speak to each other for a while." The estrangement didn't last long however. And within a few months Radding was stopping by Westland Music to offer advice and help out his protégés however he could.

Radding has since gone on to do a number of different things besides build guitars. He has written a number of books on small-scale gold mining and is now regarded as one of the leading authorities in the field. In 1999 he got back into the guitar business when he started Go Guitars, a company that specializes in small-bodied travel guitars. "The design is based on those two guitars I made way back in 1970," he says. "You know, sometimes I kick myself for not keeping even a one per cent share of the business when I sold to Bob, Kurt, and Steve. If I did I would be sitting on a nice beach somewhere instead of making these travel guitars. But I don't begrudge them their success at all. They worked really hard to build that company, and they deserve all of their success."

Bob Taylor still remembers Sam Radding with fondness and respect. "I don't think he's received the recognition he deserves," he says. "The American Dream was an incubator for many of the innovations that revolutionized American guitar building in the 1980s and 1990s. He inspired a lot of great builders and he's one of the smartest craftsmen I've ever met. He recognized my potential when I was just a teenager and helped me become a better craftsman. He taught me how to build guitars and I can never thank him enough for that."

"We did the happy dance for a few minutes and basked in the glory for the next couple days. There is no feeling quite like selling a guitar that you made yourself." Bob Taylor

From Westland Music to Taylor Guitars

A soggy first day for the Westland Music Company. Greg Deering repairs guitars and builds banjos on the side. Building custom guitars. The 810 is born. The bolt-on neck evolves. Bob Taylor starts making tools. A candy man saves the day.

Original company logo for the
Westland Music Company.

Riding the Wave

Unplugged music was everywhere in the early 1970s, so it probably seemed like a great time to start an acoustic guitar company. In 1971 Led Zeppelin, now widely regarded as the prototypical heavy metal band, released their untitled fourth album. The record included soon to be classic rockers like "Rock and Roll" and "Stairway to Heaven" but the real surprises were the acoustic tracks. These included the mandolin driven "Battle of Evermore," a duet between Robert Plant and former Fairport Convention lead singer Sandy Denny, and "Going to California," a gentle acoustic performance that wouldn't have sounded out of place on a James Taylor record.

At the same time Rod Stewart was releasing a series of albums – *Gasoline Alley, Every Picture Tells a Story,* and *Never a Dull Moment* – that brilliantly fused folk, rock, blues, and country and featured the acoustic guitar playing of Martin Quittenton and Ron Wood. In 1972 Neil Young released *Harvest* featuring one of his most popular songs "Heart of Gold." The LP also included "The Needle and the Damage Done," a stark ballad with an infectious acoustic guitar intro that has become one of the standard licks in the unplugged guitarist's repertoire. That same year the Nitty Gritty Dirt Band released *Will the Circle Be Unbroken,* a celebration of country music's old-time legends that introduced Maybelle Carter, Earl Scruggs, Doc Watson, Norman Blake, Merle Travis, and Jimmy Martin to a new audience. That album sparked a revival of interest in bluegrass and early country music that continues to this day.

Tim Luranc (left) and Steve
Schemmer mop up the floor on Westland Music's first day of business.

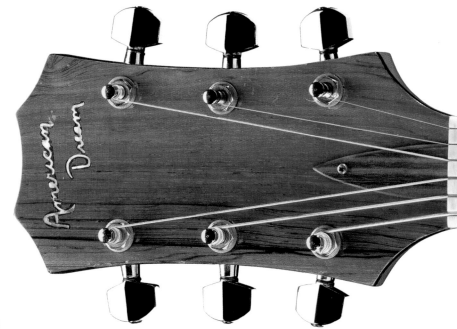

The singer-songwriter movement was also a major commercial force in the music industry at the time. The airwaves and record racks were full of countless performers who had followed Bob Dylan's lead and gave up traditionally grounded folk music in favor of a more introspective personal style of song writing. Solo performers like James Taylor, Arlo Guthrie, Janis Ian, Jim Croce, John Denver, Paul Simon, Harry Chapin, Don MacLean, and Cat Stevens routinely scored top ten hits with little more than a strummed acoustic guitar for accompaniment. And although musicians like Richard Thompson, John Prine, Loudon Wainwright III, David Bromberg, Leo Kottke, and John Fahey never scored top ten hits, they garnered rave reviews from critics and developed enthusiastic followings. And although the emphasis was on their singing, acoustic guitars were also integral to the sound of bands like the Eagles, America, Orleans, and Crosby, Stills, Nash & Young.

All of this unplugged music created a huge demand for acoustic guitars and the established companies like Martin, Guild and Gibson ramped up production to meet it. But even with the expanded production – Martin for example, made 5077 D-28s in 1974, as compared to 976 just a decade earlier—the companies couldn't supply enough guitars to the players who wanted them. Also, in an effort to simplify production, the big companies began cutting back on the numbers of different models they offered. In the early 1970s it was very difficult to buy a guitar from Martin, Guild, or Gibson that wasn't a rosewood or mahogany dreadnought.

This lack of choice inspired a host of individual builders and small production shops to step up and fill the demand for guitars with custom options like slimmer necks, larger or smaller bodies, different wood choices, and fancier ornamentation. When Sam Radding opened the American Dream in 1970, he was part of a luthier's revival that included John Gallagher in Tennessee, Stuart Mossman in Kansas, Jean Larrivée in Toronto (later he moved to British Columbia), Bruce Ross and Richard Hoover of the Santa Cruz Guitar Company in California, Michael Gurian in New Hampshire, and Thomas and Augustino LoPrinzi in New Jersey.

Bob Taylor, Kurt Listug, and Steve Schemmer probably had no idea they were part of a national movement when they went into work on October 15, 1974, their first day of business as the Westland Music Company. And even if they were inclined to ruminate on their place in the world of guitar makers, they quickly discovered they had more immediate problems to deal with. When they opened the door to the shop that day they discovered that a storm drain next to the building overflowed the night before and that the floor was covered in two to three inches of water. "Instead of working on guitars we spent the day cleaning," recalls Tim Luranc, who had stayed on from the American Dream. "I remember pushing all the soggy sawdust out the door with a push broom. We were really concerned about losing some of our wood, which was stacked on the floor. On the other hand, the shop was pretty dirty, so maybe the flood helped us get it cleaned out properly to get the business going. I remember that Bob, Kurt, and Steve weren't really that upset about the water, but they were concerned about the future."

One of the last American Dream guitars built. Notice the distinctive "three-scoop" shape that Taylor continued to use.

Early version of Taylor headstock with hand-cut pearl logo.

Bob Taylor working on dreadnought bodies circa 1975. Note the walnut back and sides of the guitar in the foreground and the three-piece maple back of the guitar Taylor is working on.

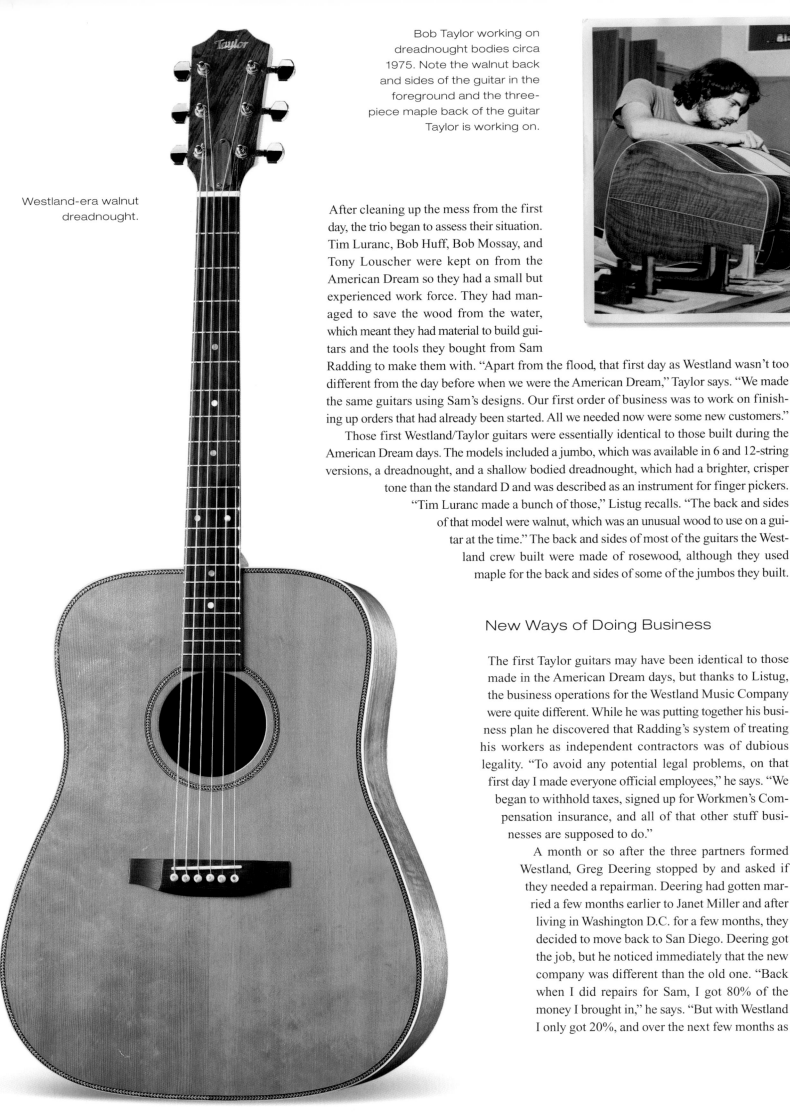

Westland-era walnut dreadnought.

After cleaning up the mess from the first day, the trio began to assess their situation. Tim Luranc, Bob Huff, Bob Mossay, and Tony Louscher were kept on from the American Dream so they had a small but experienced work force. They had managed to save the wood from the water, which meant they had material to build guitars and the tools they bought from Sam Radding to make them with. "Apart from the flood, that first day as Westland wasn't too different from the day before when we were the American Dream," Taylor says. "We made the same guitars using Sam's designs. Our first order of business was to work on finishing up orders that had already been started. All we needed now were some new customers."

Those first Westland/Taylor guitars were essentially identical to those built during the American Dream days. The models included a jumbo, which was available in 6 and 12-string versions, a dreadnought, and a shallow bodied dreadnought, which had a brighter, crisper tone than the standard D and was described as an instrument for finger pickers. "Tim Luranc made a bunch of those," Listug recalls. "The back and sides of that model were walnut, which was an unusual wood to use on a guitar at the time." The back and sides of most of the guitars the Westland crew built were made of rosewood, although they used maple for the back and sides of some of the jumbos they built.

New Ways of Doing Business

The first Taylor guitars may have been identical to those made in the American Dream days, but thanks to Listug, the business operations for the Westland Music Company were quite different. While he was putting together his business plan he discovered that Radding's system of treating his workers as independent contractors was of dubious legality. "To avoid any potential legal problems, on that first day I made everyone official employees," he says. "We began to withhold taxes, signed up for Workmen's Compensation insurance, and all of that other stuff businesses are supposed to do."

A month or so after the three partners formed Westland, Greg Deering stopped by and asked if they needed a repairman. Deering had gotten married a few months earlier to Janet Miller and after living in Washington D.C. for a few months, they decided to move back to San Diego. Deering got the job, but he noticed immediately that the new company was different than the old one. "Back when I did repairs for Sam, I got 80% of the money I brought in," he says. "But with Westland I only got 20%, and over the next few months as money got tighter, that was cut to 15%. They also discontinued the potluck jam sessions. Even though they were sometimes fun, they were a distraction from the guitar making."

The new company struggled in those first months. They found that as they finished up the outstanding orders, they were barely taking in enough new orders for guitars to really keep going. "We did a little repair work here and there to bring in some money," Taylor recalls. "And we sold some tuners, pickups, inlays and even some wood now and then, but hardly enough to prosper. It wasn't long before our $10,000 investment had dwindled to next to nothing."

The young luthiers were also learning some hard lessons about the business world. "We needed some ebony just after we started," Taylor remembers. "In those days, 'guitar wood' suppliers really didn't exist, so it was harder to buy wood for fretboards and such. Also, we were broke and didn't want to pay any more than absolutely necessary for wood. Bob Mossay and I went up to Los Angeles to a lumberyard that supposedly had some exotic wood with a blank check that Kurt had reluctantly given us. We found some small ebony logs and picked through all of them until we found what we thought was 'the one'. We paid $175 for it. That was just about all the money we had in our account, but we felt proud of our achievement, because we were going to get maybe 100 fingerboards out of this log, at a net cost of less than two bucks apiece. When we got the log back to the shop, we cut it open, and discovered to our dismay that it had been stained black on the outside to make it look like higher-quality ebony. The wood itself was actually light brown and streaked. It was a total waste. I don't think we got 12 usable fingerboards out of that log."

Kurt Listug building guitar bodies circa 1975.

Steve Schemmer spraying lacquer on
a rosewood jumbo circa 1975.

Things got so bad that by the end of the year the partners had to lay off their four-man work force, although they did keep Greg Deering on in the repair department. "I tried to be the manager at the beginning, to do all of the paper work," Listug says. " But after we got into debt we found that for any of us to make any money, the three partners all had to build guitars. We just didn't have the resources to hire people to work for us." Tim Luranc got a job painting houses and Robert Mossay opened his own music shop, which he called Moze Guitars. "After we laid him off, Moze became more successful than we were at the time," Taylor recalls.

Bob Becomes a Toolmaker

If he was ever going to make money at this, Bob Taylor realized that he would have to learn to make guitars more efficiently. But he also knew that he and his partners didn't have the money to buy new tools to do the job. Luckily, he was able to learn a few things from Greg Deering, who along with doing the repairs was making a few banjos on the side. "Greg was smart

"He showed me how to use a shaper to make patterns for necks and bridges and then cut them out accurately."

and had more experience with power tools than I did," Taylor says. "He showed me a few things that I started doing immediately. He showed me how to use a shaper to make patterns for necks and bridges and then cut them out accurately. We didn't have money for a shaper, but I found a mail order outfit that made spindles for shapers that they sold for something like $19. I made some plywood cabinets, found some surplus motors and made my own shapers."

Taylor used his new shapers to make both the patterns for the necks and bridges and the necks and bridges themselves. He discovered that not only did he save time, but the parts he made were of higher quality than the ones he previously cut out by hand on the band saw. "The bridges and necks were just more consistent," he says. "That was when I learned that higher quantity did not necessarily mean lower quality. That experience started me thinking of new ways to use jigs, fixtures, and machines to build guitars. After that, everywhere I went I noticed something that I could relate to building guitars, and my love for machinery grew. We used those shapers for several years in our production even though they were simple and cost us less than a couple hundred dollars."

Greg and Janet Deering sanding Stelling banjo necks on the porch of their house.

As helpful as it was for Bob Taylor to have Greg Deering around the shop to bounce ideas off, in March of 1975 Deering decided to leave Westland and build banjos full-time. "There was a customer named Geoff Stelling who used to come in and work with Greg on banjo necks," Taylor recalls. "He was an officer in the Navy and he played in a local bluegrass group. He had an idea for a new style of banjo tone ring so he'd come to our shop and Greg would make necks for the pots that Geoff would build." In March 1975, Deering and Stelling set up the Stelling Banjo Works in Geoff's garage. Stelling's new tone ring design proved to be popular with banjo players and they began to get more orders than they could build in their garage workshop.

Deering and Stelling approached the Westland/Taylor crew and asked if they wanted to share the shop space in Lemon Grove, which would help cut expenses for both companies. Mindful of their growing debts, Bob Taylor and Steve Schemmer thought the idea had merit, but Kurt Listug was adamantly opposed to the concept of splitting their shop in half. "I felt that sharing rent with Greg and Geoff would have just complicated our lives at the time," Listug says. "They were good guys, but I wasn't sure that I wanted to add another level of complexity." Bob Taylor was always more inclined to cooperate with people than Kurt. "I liked the idea of investors and partners, but Kurt never did," he says. "He was more willing to tough out our problems. It turns out that he was right, of course, and we're better off now for not having become entangled with other partners back then."

When their attempt to rent half of the Westland/Taylor shop failed, Deering and Stelling decided to form two different banjo companies. "Geoff's family convinced him that having a business partner was just not a good idea," Deering says. "So later that year I formed the Deering

Mahogany dreadnought from the Westland era.

Banjo Company and Geoff contracted with us to make the banjos for his company, the Stelling Banjo Works. I had quite a nice little business going there, and I hired Tim Luranc to work for me, along with the brothers Larry and Kim Breedlove, and John Gerlog. Those guys eventually wound up working for Bob Taylor. We built Geoff's banjos until the Thanksgiving of 1976, when we had a falling out. Geoff hired all of my employees away from me including Tim Luranc, John Gerlog, Larry Breedlove, and Kim Breedlove."

The Guitar Builders Envy the Banjo Makers

"Things were going really well over at Stelling," Taylor recalls. "We were amazed and envious. I mean they had cash just flowing into that joint. Geoff was a good promoter and made expensive banjos and sold them all. Sometimes Japanese collectors would come into his shop and all they could say was, "We want to buy a banjo!" and Geoff would sell them banjos at full custom retail prices and line his pockets. Things were booming over there."

After Greg Deering left Westland in 1975, Bob Taylor continued to work on refining the instrument construction ideas Deering had suggested to him. Now that Taylor was using shapers to make his necks and bridges, he began to alter Sam Radding's original designs. Taylor took the "three-scoop" peghead shape of the American Dream guitars and subtly changed its proportions. He also changed Radding's T-block neck joint. Taylor recalled the success he had with reattaching the neck of his friend's Guild G-37 with bolts, so he began to work on designing a new neck that attached with bolts rather than glue. His first attempt at a bolt-on neck consisted of a mortise and tenon that was held in place on the body by two bolts that went through the neck block. This design worked fairly well and he used it on the next 30 or so guitars he made.

But over the next year, he discovered a problem with the design. "It was hard to change the neck angle with that design," Taylor explains. "In those days when we sold a guitar, it was like we became the indentured servant to the person who bought it. We were making these guitars by hand and sometimes they just didn't go together that well. People would bring their guitars back for me to set up to their specs and Kurt and I would just work on it for hours until we found out what was wrong with it. We learned an incredible amount of information about how guitars worked doing that, but it was so nerve wracking, particularly when the customer would stay and watch us work. We were barely twenty years old and we had already taken their money, so what could we do? Because most of our customers were older than us it was like we were afraid they would beat us up or tell our moms if we couldn't get the guitar to play right."

Bob Taylor's original version of the bolt-on neck with a mortise and tenon joint.

Refining the Bolt-on Neck Joint

After taking off more than a few necks to correct the angle and make the guitar more playable, Taylor began to rethink his neck joint design. "After a while I just didn't see the need for the whole mortise and tenon joint," he says. "But I wasn't sure if I could make a neck joint without it." Around that time he read a new book called *The Acoustic Guitar* by the luthier David Russell Young, who advocated using an epoxied butt-joint to attach the neck. Taylor wasn't interested in the epoxy because he still wanted to make the neck easy to remove, but the idea of using a butt-joint intrigued him. "Sometime in 1976 I got rid of the mortise and tenon and switched to a butt-joint," he says. "I was attending some night school classes with James Goodall and it turned out he had a lathe, which we didn't have at our shop. He turned a number of different inserts that we could set into the heel of the neck. Jim experimented with a number of different thread patterns and eventually he came up with a design that worked. Since he was a budding luthier himself, he didn't want to get sidetracked into the metal working business, so we had them made in batches somewhere else. People often give me credit for inventing the bolt-on neck, but I didn't come up with it on my own. A lot of people like Sam Radding, David Russell Young, and James Goodall helped out either directly or indirectly. Like a lot of ideas that bubbled up back then in the San Diego guitar world, it was a group effort."

The new neck joint, combined with the slim necks they were already making meant that Taylor guitars were just about the most playable guitars around. But there were still other problems to be worked out. "We knew our guitars were crude in many ways," Listug says. "We knew we'd have to work harder on making them better. We'd get ripples in the back and the finishes didn't look too good, so we'd work hard on getting those kinks out." As they ironed out the wrinkles in their construction techniques, the three partners realized that they needed to standardize the instruments they made.

Invoice for a guitar purchased by Randy Northrup detailing some of the custom options Taylor offered in 1974.

QUAN.	DESCRIPTION	PRICE	AMOUNT
1	rose wood dreadnaught		450 00
2	ab top		50 00
3	ab rosette		10 00
4	ab back		20 00
5	ab around f.b on top		20 00
6	ab around head		25 00
7	D-45 inlay		20 00
8	fish on truss nut cover		5 00
9	handle bar bridge		10 00
10	binding on f.b		10 00
11	total		670 00
12	tax		40 20
13			710 20

No. 6474   office 286 4500   Date 4-23 19 74
Name Randy Northrup

1975 815 with dreadnought body. Bob Taylor hand-cut the pearl for the headstock logo.

Numbers, Numbers, Numbers

They started making various prototypes, and eventually decided that the Brazilian rosewood dreadnought with white body and fingerboard binding, zigzag pattern backstrip, diamond inlays, and spruce top would become the first standard model. They wanted to avoid the D or J prefixes that were the standard model names for companies like Gibson, Martin, and Guild. "We also rejected giving the guitar a name like The Prairie, or The Bluesman, or The Maple Leaf," Taylor says. "We thought they were kind of stupid. But we also wanted something to grow with and I had this idea for a numbering system that might make sense and allow room to add models in the future. We would start with a three-digit number such as '800'. "So we called that first dreadnought the 815, but I don't quite remember why I chose that particular number. But after thinking about it some more we refined that system."

In the new version the first digit would designate the wood used in the back and sides and the level of the cosmetic appointments. The middle number would designate whether it was a six or a twelve-string, with any number under 5 meaning six strings and any number 5 or above meaning twelve strings. The last number would be the body shape. Zero would denote a dreadnought while a 5 would denote a jumbo. "Under the new system the rosewood dreadnought we were making was an 810," Taylor explains. "Even though we put labels in the first few we built that called it an 815. There are a very few of those early 810s out there with that wrong 815 label, so if you ever see one, you now know the story of why that is. I believe the first or second 810 we made was designated as a 'second' for some cosmetic reason, and we got Geoff Stelling to buy that and another guitar at a discount. His purchase of those two guitars kept us alive for a few weeks."

Around the time they were working out the model numbering system, they started putting serial numbers in the guitars. The first number they used was #10109. The first digit indicated that the instrument was made in the first year of production. The next four numbers designated the sequential number of the guitar. So that first number would translate as the one-hundred-and-ninth guitar made in the first year of business. The new numbering system was an early indicator that the partners intended to succeed, and to succeed in a big way. Even though Taylor, Listug, and Schemmer were struggling to make ends meet that first year, and had yet to build forty instruments, they were ambitious enough to design a serial number system that would accommodate an annual production of 9999 instruments.

The new serial number system made sense, but it was designed from the beginning with one odd feature. "The first serial number we used in a guitar was #10109," Taylor says. "We did that for two reasons. The first reason was that we didn't want it to look like we hadn't made any guitars. If people looked at our serial number, they

Label from 1976, after Taylor had decided on the new format for serial numbers and model numbers.

would think we had made more guitars than we really had. And the second reason, which is sort of embarrassing now, is that we thought that someday we could come back and make the first hundred or so guitars and get rich off of them because they'd have low serial numbers and would be worth more." Westland/Taylor used that serial number sequence until 1977, when they realized that using the year they started production as the first digit didn't make much sense. That year they dropped the first digit, and went to a straightforward sequential numbering system.

Westland/Taylor now had a line of guitars to sell and a coherent serial number system. All they needed were some customers. Taylor and Listug realized that they had pretty much tapped out their local market for guitars and that if they wanted to grow, they would have to start selling over a wider geographic area. That meant selling wholesale through stores. Listug visited a few local music stores and discovered that they would have to sell their guitars to stores for considerably less than they were selling them directly to customers. "The three of us talked about it quite a bit," Taylor remembers. "Kurt and I thought that we needed to drop the parts business and close down the repair shop and just concentrate on building guitars and selling them to stores. Steve wasn't crazy about the idea of selling wholesale, but after discussing it quite a bit, he went along with me and Kurt." Taylor and Listug won that particular argument. At the beginning of 1976 they stopped retailing parts and wood, closed the repair shop and changed the name of their business from Westland Music Company to Taylor Guitars.

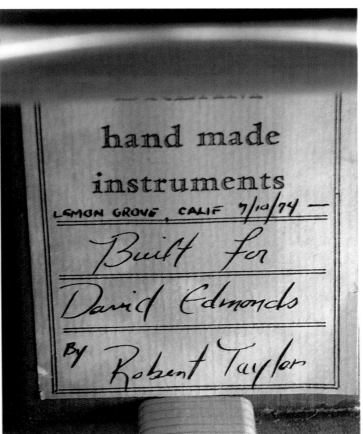

Label from 1974, before Taylor decided on a serial number and model number formats.

Going Wholesale

Now that the three partners had made the decision to start selling wholesale, they had to start rounding up dealers. They knew the local stores like Apex Music, the American Dream retail shop, and Moze's new music store, but they didn't know where else to try and sell their guitars. At that time they bought their cases from Geib, a respected case maker that had relocated from Chicago to Los Angeles. To save on shipping costs Kurt Listug used to drive there and pick up the cases in person. On one trip Listug brought along one of their new 810s and showed it to an executive there named John Levy and asked if he knew of any stores that might be interested in stocking Taylors. Levy was impressed with the slim neck and suggested that Listug use that as the main selling point. He also gave Listug the names of a number of stores in Los Angeles that he thought would want to see the new guitar.

A few weeks later Listug loaded up Bob Taylor's van with guitars and headed north to Los Angeles. He stopped at all the stores Levy recommended and managed to sell instruments to McCabe's Guitar Shop, Studio City Music, and Westwood Music. When he returned that evening to drop off the van at Taylor's house, the guitars were gone but Listug had something even better: a pocket full of checks. "We did the happy dance for a few minutes and basked in the glory for the next couple days," Taylor recalls. "I remember that night perfectly. There is no feeling quite like selling a guitar that you made yourself."

Along with money the stores that bought Taylor guitars offered lots of advice on how to improve the instruments. Fred Walecki, the owner of Westwood Music, was an early booster. He sold Taylors to David Crosby, Jonathan Edwards, and John David Souther. "Walecki made lots of comments and criticisms to us about our guitars and we worked on pleasing him with our work," Taylor recalls. "A dealer can have a very high level of influence on budding luthiers like we were at the time. His approval, and his business, kept us alive for a period. Anytime he'd withdraw his approval we felt we were in big trouble."

Westwood Music's repair shop was run by John Curruthers, who was also helpful. "I had some problems with my guitars at the time," Taylor says. "John helped me immensely by pointing out some techniques and skills he'd acquired from doing repair work. The guitars got a little better after I applied some of the things I learned from John. He was a little bigger than life to me at the time. I was still only twenty-one years old and he was way more experienced and knowledgeable about these things than I was at the time. I couldn't deny how impressed I was when I'd go into his shop and see road cases from every famous touring band on the music scene. This guy really had the clientele and I listened when he spoke."

McCabe'sGuitar Shop in Santa Monica was another early dealer. "When I first walked into McCabe's, the Mossman rep was on his way out with a large order for his guitars," Listug says.

Backroom of McCabe's Guitar Shop around the time they started carrying Taylor guitars.

"I remember that night perfectly. There is no feeling quite like selling a guitar that you made yourself."

"I remember Jack McKenzie, who was the store manager at the time, said they weren't ready to commit to our instruments, because they had just bought the Mossmans . But after playing my samples they went ahead and bought a few anyway. That really meant a lot to us at the time, and McCabe's has been one of our strongest dealers ever since."

As Bob Taylor increased production to supply the new accounts, he discovered that he wasn't able to get enough Brazilian rosewood to make the 810s, so they switched to Indian Rosewood. Brazilian rosewood, scientific name *Dalbergia Nigra*, is a dense tonewood that ranges in color from almost black to dark brown to light chocolate brown, with occasional streaks of red, orange, and even bright green. Guitars made from it tend to have a rich bass tone and clear, ringing trebles. It's always been expensive compared to other tonewoods, but even so, luthiers have been using Brazilian rosewood to make their instruments since the early 1800s. In 1965 the government of Brazil put an embargo on wood leaving the country in log form in an attempt to boost the local milling industry. The Martin guitar company, one of the largest users of Brazilian rosewood, wasn't happy with the quality of the milled timber coming from Brazil, so in 1969 they switched to Indian rosewood. Not long after they did so, other companies began to follow suit. Smaller companies continued to use Brazilian rosewood for a few more years, but eventually it got so scarce and so expensive that most builders stopped using it altogether, except for the occasional very pricey limited run.

Making Guitars Without Making Money

Even though they now had a number of stores stocking their guitars, the Taylor crew still wasn't making any money and they were having trouble paying their bills. But even though they were struggling financially, the guitars that Taylor, Listug, and Schemmer were building were earning an excellent reputation. In the autumn of 1976 Taylor was approached by Paul Rothchild, a record producer who was starting a new distribution company with his brother Ed. Although he wasn't well known to the general public Paul Rothchild was a legendary figure to music business insiders. He got his start as an A&R man and record producer at the jazz label Prestige in the early 1960s, but he was hired away by Elektra, which was the leading folk music label at the time. While he was there, he worked as a producer for many of the leading acoustic musicians of the day including, Judy Collins, Tom Paxton, Phil Ochs, 12-string wizard Fred Neil, Tim Buckley, and Tom Rush.

Rothchild also worked with electric groups like the Paul Butterfield Blues Band. Because he had recorded this last band and was familiar with their sound he was given the job of running the mixing board when the band backed Bob Dylan at his famous electric set at the 1965 Newport Folk Festival. Rothchild moved to Los Angeles in the late 1960s, where he signed the Doors to Elektra and produced their first LP. Rothchild knew everyone and he felt he would be able to get Taylor guitars into the hands of all sorts of famous musicians.

"Paul Rothchild and his brother, Ed, had a big dream," Taylor says. "They wanted to gather many of the smaller musical instrument manufacturers together under one roof and take those products to the retail stores. They had signed up companies like Larrivée Guitars, Augustino Guitars, Alembic Guitars, Oasis Guitars, Furman Sound Products, and Bartolini Pickups so it was a pretty powerful line-up for the time."

Rothchild explained that he had seen Taylor guitars and he was impressed with them. He felt they were under priced and that he would be able to net the young builders the same amount of money they were currently getting by selling direct to stores and still make money for himself. And since Rothchild would be handling all of the marketing, the Taylor crew would actually be saving some money. Bob Taylor and Steve Schemmer were interested, but Kurt Listug was skeptical and vetoed the idea. "After several days of discussion with Paul and Ed we finally told them 'no thank you' and went back to our bleak little existence," Taylor says. "When Kurt says 'no' he means it. He felt that we had to create our own future by our own effort so that when the business finally did succeed we wouldn't find ourselves sharing it with other people. He also had a sense that just because someone said they could solve our problems, that didn't mean they actually could."

> "After several days of discussion with Paul and Ed we finally told them 'no thank you' and went back to our bleak little existence."

After turning down the offer from Rothchild, business continued to get worse. Listug made a sales trip to San Francisco and failed to sign any new dealers. "We built guitars as best we could but production was difficult," Taylor says. "But no matter how bad production was, sales were usually worse. At any given time we would have several guitars in the shop that could be converted to cash if we could find someone to buy them. We managed to pay our bills late, very late, but still pay them. We didn't pay ourselves anything, but had a couple employees that we paid on time."

Listug managed to sell a guitar here and there and kept enough money coming in each week to keep going for another few days. Taylor was discouraged by the lack of sales and he spent all of his time working out the production problems in an effort to dispel his disappointment. "I was stressed out about the lack of money," he says. "But I was actually pretty happy during the day because I was actually building guitars and living my dream. Really the only reason that guitars needed to be sold, for my purposes, was so that I could keep making them. I was never disappointed or worried that I didn't have money to buy things for myself, I was just afraid that we'd go out of business and I'd have to get a job doing something that I hated."

Bob Taylor worked at coming up with methods to make guitars more efficiently. One of the procedures that took too much time was bending the sides. He was still using the round pipe

Kurt Listug leaning on sidebender. During this period his time was divided between building guitars and selling them.

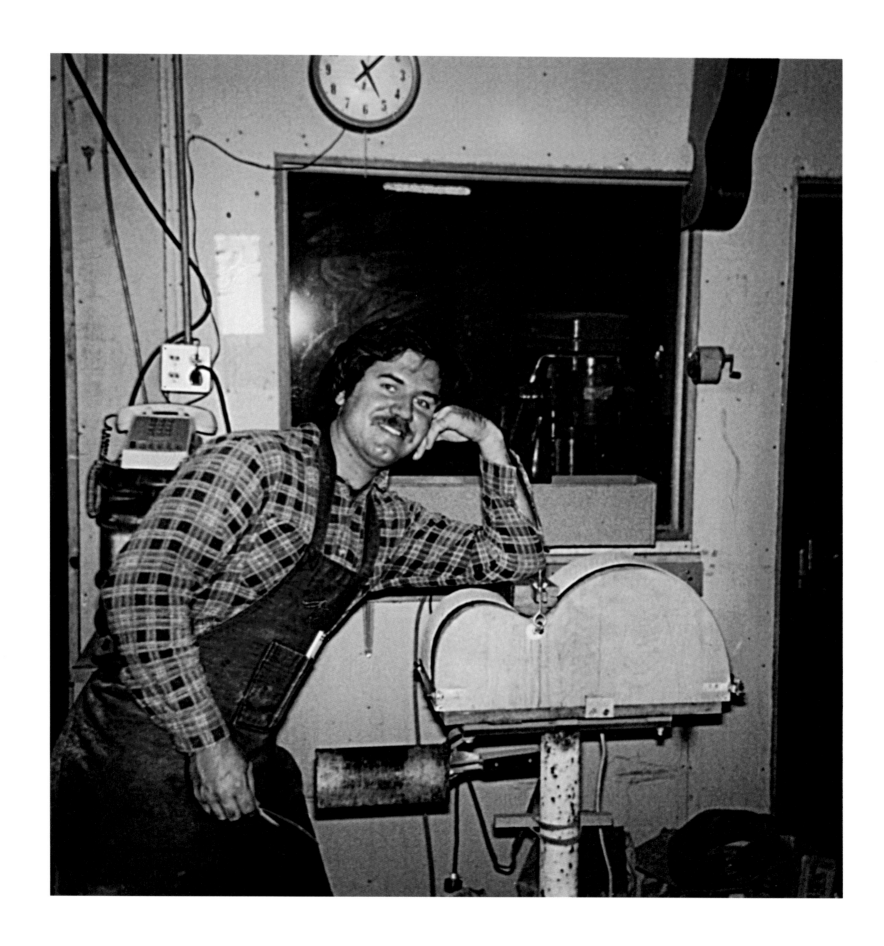

A tool called a fret buck that Matt Guzzetta and Bob Taylor designed to allow a worker to safely fret the section of fingerboard that extended over the body of the guitar. Note the Taylor logo cast into the metal.

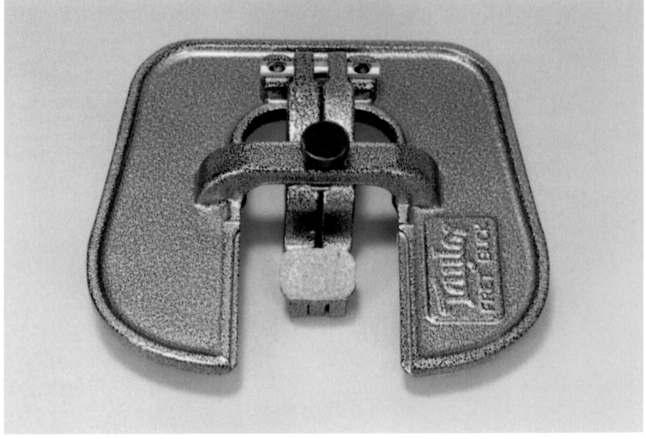

he built in high school to bend sides, but the results just weren't consistent enough for him. "I had seen pictures of factories where they had these heated molds shaped like half a guitar and they'd press the side to that and have a perfectly bent side," he says. "Our landlord ran a shop that made Formica counter tops in the back of our building and he had made his own machinery to form the tops around the no-drip edges. I discussed it with him and we decided that if I could get a half of a guitar made out of sheet metal I could then fill it with sand and put a water heater heating element inside with a thermostat. I found a sheet metal shop that formed and welded this mold out of stainless steel for me. Then, I got the heater and sand, filled it up, sealed it, set it on a bench and made a superstructure that had mating sections that screwed down. I put in a side and after a few adjustments I got it working and we were all pretty dang impressed."

Even that small success came with an unexpected aggravation. "One day a guy, who I'd never seen in my life, came in and said that I owed him $500," Taylor says. "I couldn't remember borrowing money or buying anything from him. He said I owed him for using his idea for the side-bending machine. He claimed it was making me a lot of money, which at that period was just a joke, and he demanded to get paid a royalty. Of course, I thought he was nuts and didn't pay him anything and I've still never figured that one out. Later on I discovered that he had a connection with the shop that bent the stainless steel for me, but that was the only clue I ever had about who he was."

By the end of the year they were so broke that they didn't have enough money to pay any bills, and they were talking seriously about closing down the company. One day, as they were getting ready to lock up and go home for the night, a customer wandered in and began to look at guitars. He looked at the guitars they had already made and was impressed enough to custom order a Brazilian rosewood 815 with abalone trim. "It turned out his name was Charles See and he was the grandson of Martha See of See's Candy," Taylor says. "Along with the jumbo he custom ordered a small guitar for an upcoming ski trip. He left us with a check for more than $1800, which was like a million dollars to us. That money allowed us to pay our rent and to keep going for a few more weeks."

"This was a huge step for us. It felt like we were at the threshold of a new era."

At the end of the year the Taylor team took stock of their situation. They had made 168 guitars in 1976, which was not a bad number considering all the difficulties they had gone through. They had a handful of dealers, but they realized that they were going to have to sign up many more if the new company was going to prosper. Kurt Listug had to stay in Lemon Grove to help build guitars, so he couldn't spend time looking for new accounts like he had earlier in the year. After some soul searching, Listug reconsidered his objection to getting involved with another company, and in late December the Taylor team called Paul Rothchild and set up another meeting to talk about a distribution deal. "This was a huge step for us," Taylor says. "It felt like we were at the threshold of a new era."

"Kurt, I just got my report from the field and it's goose eggs out there."

Taylor distributor Paul Rothchild

The Lean Years

A distribution deal with a music industry legend. Kurt Listug learns a hard lesson about the guitar business. The first paychecks. Bob Taylor goes to NAMM and becomes friends with some luthiers and builds even more tools. Good-bye to Rothchild.

Expanding the Line

Now that Taylor guitars were being sold through an exclusive distributor that would supposedly be getting them into new stores, the partners decided they should expand the line beyond the 800 series. They resurrected a birdseye maple model from the American Dream days, which they dubbed the 900 series. The new model had rosewood binding and a mix of abalone and pearl fretboard inlays. As with the 800 series the 900 series was available in both the dreadnought and jumbo shapes, with the latter size being the more popular of the two.

Paul Rothchild also suggested they build a less expensive model, so Taylor came up with the 700 series. This model had rosewood back and sides and a spruce top like the 800 series, but it had black rather than white binding and a simpler rosette. The Taylor workforce now consisted of four people, and they had a difficult time making enough guitars to sell to Rothchild Musical Instruments, or RMI as they came to call it.

Bob Taylor showing off a rosewood jumbo and a walnut dreadnought a few months before the deal with Rothchild.

Page from the original Rothchild catalog showing a 555 and a 710. Note the David Randle-designed moustache bridge on the jumbo guitar.

Detail from Rothchild catalog touting Taylor's compensated saddle. Taylor was one of the first acoustic guitar companies to offer a compensated saddle as a standard feature.

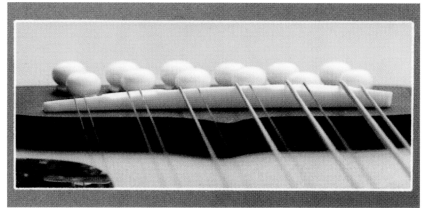

Rothchild had agreed to buy a set number of guitars each month as part of the distribution deal, so the first months were actually quite busy for the Taylor crew, who were working hard to fulfill the initial order. But RMI soon found they were unable to sell the guitars as quickly as Taylor could make them. That January, Taylor built only nine guitars, all of which were made to fulfill orders taken before they signed the deal with RMI. In February, they built twelve guitars, ten of which went to RMI. In March, they sent out eleven guitars and in April only five instruments were shipped.

It was Kurt Listug's job to call RMI and ask how many Taylor guitars they sold in the past week, and all too often he was given bad news. "It got to where I hated making those calls," Listug says. "Paul Rothchild would say, 'Kurt, I just got my report from the field and it's goose eggs out there.' That was his way of telling me there were no orders. I think that RMI had too many acoustic guitar lines, what with us, Larrivée and LoPrinzi."

Rather than hire experienced woodworkers, who would cost more than the company could afford, Bob Taylor recruited workers from the local high schools. "I'd call the wood shop and metal shop teachers at the local high schools and have them send me their best seniors," he recalls. "We hired some pretty talented kids that way. It was also the only way I could figure to get employees who were younger than I was. I knew I was a good craftsman but I was still learning how to be a leader. The thought of telling some guy who was twenty-five or thirty years old what to do, when I was just turning twenty-two myself just made me nervous."

Bob Taylor eventually got over his nervousness and began hiring older workers. "I had this one guy who looked like a mountain man," Taylor recalls. "He had managed a water bed factory before working for me and he was an okay woodworker. One Saturday, I came in and found him bending sides to get ahead for the next week. But on the floor next to the side bender was a pile of fifteen broken sets of rosewood sides! He couldn't figure out why he kept breaking them so he just plowed ahead and kept breaking them over and over. I thought I was going to die, or maybe kill him. We couldn't even pay the bill for that rosewood, and there it was in a

A bearded Bob Taylor working on a guitar.

useless pile on the floor. It was just another one of those excruciatingly painful incidents that seemed to be the norm back then." But even with setbacks like that they were able to increase their output to 21 guitars in May, 38 in June, and 31 in July.

That same year Bob Taylor became engaged to Cindy Rich, and they planned to get married on June 25th. The impending marriage and the responsibilities it would bring made Taylor more aware that he and his partners, Kurt Listug and Steve Schemmer, were working hard for basically no pay. "It was one thing to be broke and single," he says. "But it was quite another story as I thought of getting married. I was still living with my sister at the time and I spent many nights sleeping in my van in front of the shop. Every time I needed gas I had to scrounge money from my family or tell Kurt that I needed a draw, which always was embarrassing to me. It was a strange situation to find myself in. Here I was this owner of a company that was actually selling something but I had to borrow ten bucks to buy gasoline to get to work."

Bob Taylor, Listug, and Schemmer sat down and tried to sort out their money situation. They saw that they were paying their vendors for wood, tuners, shell, pre-cut inlays, pre-cut abalone rosette arcs, strings, insurance and electricity; they were paying their new employees to build the guitars; and they were paying RMI a commission on the guitars they sold. But they weren't paying themselves.

The partners realized that they would have to budget money for their salaries, so Schemmer and Listug took a hard look at the books, and found out the most they could afford to pay themselves at the time was $15 a week. It wasn't much, but it was a start. "Believe it or not, I was satisfied with that," Bob Taylor says. "At the time it was almost a matter of principle to me, that we get paid for our hard work, even if it was a token payment. Besides, that fifteen bucks would buy me some gas and, most importantly, I could count on it." After a few $15 weeks, the trio instituted a policy of giving themselves a $5 raise every week until they were each making $85 a week.

The weekly salary wasn't much, but it was steady. When combined with Cindy's salary as a schoolteacher, it allowed the young couple to buy a house of their own, which they moved into the day after their wedding. Bob and Cindy's new home was tiny—the bathroom was so small that Bob couldn't stand upright in it—but it would later play an important part in the history of the Taylor company.

The First NAMM Show

That same June, just before Bob and Cindy got married, RMI asked one of the three partners to represent Taylor guitars at the National Association of Music Merchants Summer Market in Atlanta. The NAMM Show, as most people called it, was a trade show where musical instrument makers of all sorts met with their retail dealers. Up until now Kurt Listug had been the public face of Taylor, thanks to his road trips, but the trio thought that retailers might be more interested in meeting the man whose name was on the headstock, so even though his wedding was coming up, Bob Taylor went to Atlanta. Also, it would give Bob a chance to meet other guitar builders and perhaps pick up a few secrets.

"That first NAMM show was a big deal to us," Taylor remembers. "We gathered all our employees around and talked about it. I knew I'd be meeting with other guitar makers, and all the guys in the shop wanted me to ask them all kinds of guitar building questions. My workers wanted to know things like, 'How do other makers prepare the sides after the kerfing is on in order to glue on the top and back?' And, 'Do they extend their back braces all the way out and then route binding slots and let the binding touch the end of the brace?' And, 'What do you do if the wood shrinks?' There was a long list of answers I was supposed to bring back."

When Bob Taylor arrived in Atlanta, he was impressed with the way his guitars looked in the RMI booth, but his eye was also drawn to the instruments of his booth mate Jean Larrivée. "I couldn't believe how nicely his instruments were made," Taylor recalls. "Jean's guitars made me feel like I had a long way to go in order to call myself a guitar maker."

Jean Larrivée was a Canadian luthier who had apprenticed with the German classical guitar maker Edgar Mönch. Larrivée had started his own guitar company in Toronto in 1969, where he built highly regarded steel string and classical guitars. He had more experience as a luthi-

Interior of the Lemon Grove shop. Note the tools that Bob Taylor painted green.

er and as a businessman than Bob Taylor, and he was happy to share his knowledge with the younger man.

"We became instant friends," Taylor says. "I can't say that any one person taught me how to make guitars, but I can say that there are certain people who taught me a few key points. One good idea here and there is enough to change my life, and Jean had some very good ideas."

Bob Taylor had been struggling with a way to make necks that were consistent from batch to batch. At the time, Taylor guitars were fretted before they were attached to the body. Sometimes, after the frets were installed, a neck would bow, twist, or warp. This meant that a worker would have to pull the frets, sand the fretboard flat and then refret it. Taylor had tried fretting the necks after they were attached to the body, but for some reason the fret ends wouldn't stay down.

"Jean taught me the secret of how to fret a guitar neck while it was attached to the body," Taylor says. "The key to the whole process was the fret wire. It had to be soft." Hard fret wire required more pounding to seat firmly, which made it difficult to install fretboards that were already attached to the relatively delicate guitar body, which could get damaged by the shocks caused by the hammer blows. But softer wire went into the fret slots more easily and the process of pounding the wire into the fretboard actually made it more durable, a process that was known as work hardening. Not only did Jean Larrivée solve Bob Taylor's fret problem, he gave him the address of the firm in Holland that sold the fret wire.

"I think Jean Larrivée is one of the best guitar makers alive."

"I think Jean Larrivée is one of the best guitar makers alive," Taylor says. "All he does is make guitars and, like me, he never quits thinking about the subject. He could probably think a guitar into existence, and if he figures that trick out, I'm going to copy his technique."

After Bob Taylor returned to California from the NAMM Show, he began to work on streamlining his production line, using some of the ideas he picked up in Atlanta. But even though he was able to increase the numbers of guitars his crew built every month, RMI just wasn't selling as many guitars as they promised they would. Rothchild used the slow sales as an excuse to get Taylor to lower their prices, which they reluctantly did. "We shipped 36 guitars in the first four months of 1977 which was no better than our 1976 shipments," Bob Taylor says. "Except now we were getting less money per guitar. That didn't seem fair."

Bob Taylor was getting his crew to build more guitars to meet their RMI commitments, but the bad news just kept on coming. One example of the rotten luck that kept dogging the company was the time Bob Taylor built a drill jig to pre-drill the tuner hole screws on the back of the peghead. He designed it to work with a particular set of Schaller tuners that had two screw tabs. After drilling a batch of 12-string guitar headstocks he found that the Schaller tuning machines he had just ordered had only one screw tab. There was no way of filling the extra hole without making it look bad, which meant that unless he could find the right style of tuning machine, he would have to make new necks for that batch of guitars. He called the Schaller distributor, but they didn't have any of the two tabs gears left in stock. In a state of desperation he called his new friend Jean Larrivée and asked if had any of the proper gears in stock.

"I was in a world of hurt and was pretty stressed," Taylor remembers. "Jean must have heard that in my voice because he said that he was just finishing a batch of twelve strings and he'd check the tuners for them. He called me back and said that the tuners he had were what I needed and that he'd send them down that day. I said, 'What about your guitars? Don't you need them for those?' He answered by saying, 'Don't worry about that, eh? The important thing is to get you guys going.' I'll never forget that. Ever." Around this same time Larrivée sent Taylor a particularly nice piece of German spruce. Bob Taylor later used it to make an 810 for himself, which he has continued to use as his main guitar ever since.

1977 finally ended, leaving the three partners discouraged by the slow pace of their progress but not yet ready to give up. Bob Taylor continued to work on ways to build guitars more quickly and efficiently. He now had a workforce of eleven people. The crew worked ten-hour days, four days a week, while the three owners worked six or seven days a week, depending on what needed to be done. The stated goal was to make a dozen guitars a week, but somehow they were never able to achieve it.

The Taylor crew made guitars in batches of ten or twelve, and then try to produce a batch a week. This method seemed to them to be the most efficient way of building guitars, but the Taylor workers found it was fraught with difficulties. If something happened to one guitar along the way, say a worker accidentally dinged the top, or a jig was set up incorrectly, or there was a problem with the finish, that entire batch was held up while the problem was dealt with. Because of the length of time it took for the glue to dry and the finish to cure, it could be quite a while until a batch was ready to ship. This meant that there were some periods where no money was coming into the company for weeks at a time.

Helpful Friends

Bob Taylor attempted to come up with a way to overcome this problem, but he had no success coming up with an answer on his own. He was still puzzling over possible solutions when he attended his second NAMM show in June, 1978. Rothchild put Taylor in a hotel room with Augie LoPrinzi, another luthier who sold guitars through RMI.

Augustino LoPrinzi, who everybody called Augie, was a barber who was inspired to build his first guitar in 1958 when a customer mentioned that he just bought his son a guitar for $145. When LoPrinzi remarked, "For that money, I'll make one myself," and the customer said he couldn't, LoPrinzi took it as challenge. He set up a workshop in the backroom of his barbershop and within a few weeks he had built his first guitar.

Over the next few years LoPrinzi made classical and flamenco guitars, flattop steel-strings, archtops, mandolins, and even a few lutes in the back room of his barbershop. In 1972, he and his brother, Thomas, started the LoPrinzi Guitar Company in New Jersey. His guitars quickly gained an excellent reputation and in 1973 his company was purchased by the Maark Corporation, which was a subsidiary of the huge AMF conglomerate. LoPrinzi saw his operation grow from a small shop where he hand built guitars to a factory that produced eighty guitars a month. He found he didn't like working for a large corporation so in 1978 he left Maark and set up a small guitar workshop in Florida. Because Maark owned the rights to the LoPrinzi name, he built guitars under the name of Augustino.

As with Jean Larrivée the year before, Taylor and LoPrinzi became instant friends. After the NAMM show was over LoPrinzi invited Taylor to visit his shop. While they were there, LoPrinzi took Taylor to visit friends at the nearby Martin guitar factory, which led to an embarrassing incident. "When we switched from Brazilian to Indian rosewood in 1976, we bought a large stock of Indian from Martin," Taylor says. "I think it cost around $1200. We were doing so badly at the time that we couldn't afford to pay the money back, which made me feel awful. Augie was good friends with some of the Martin workers and he introduced me around. When

we came to the guy who was in charge of the wood division he said, 'Taylor Guitars? Hey, when are you going to pay us that money you owe us for the wood we sent you years ago?' I was so embarrassed I thought I'd die right there. After a year of trying to collect they sent us notice that they'd written it off, but the guy in charge of the wood still remembered. We weren't able to pay off the bill until after we split up with Rothchild."

But the trip to visit LoPrinzi wasn't all embarrassment. "He had some very interesting jigs in his shop," Taylor recalls. "Of course, when I got back to San Diego, I made my own versions of them. But more importantly, Augie told me how to solve my production problem. While I was there he mentioned that he made his guitars 'one at a time.' In other words, every day he'd set up jigs and make the parts he needed for that guitar that day. I argued with him saying that it was more efficient to set up the jigs once and make all the parts for a batch at that time. I explained to him how we made our guitars ten at a time to take advantage of the set up times. Then he asked me a question that forever changed the way I made guitars. He said, 'Bob, which would you rather have, one done guitar or ten half-done guitars?' It only took a second for me to get the idea, and I immediately saw this idea was the way to help solve many of the problems that were plaguing us, from the erratic cash flow to the training of new craftsmen."

Augie LoPrinzi remembers that Bob Taylor was very young, but he knew his stuff. "He was real interested in the way I had set up my jigs and fixtures," LoPrinzi says. "In some ways, I liked finding new ways to make a part like a guitar bridge rather than making the bridge itself. Bob seemed to have a bit of that way of thinking in him as well. I also thought he was starting more guitars than he could really finish with his crew at the time. That's when I asked about whether he wanted one completed guitar or ten half-completed ones. Boy, did he take my offhand comment and run with it."

Bob Taylor returned home, eager to put the new concept into practice. He realized that if he were to literally follow LoPrinzi's advice and made guitars one at a time, that the best he could hope for was to make four guitars a week. (Remember, Taylor employees worked a four-day workweek.) After considering the abilities of his crew, he decided that they could produce three guitars a day. He divided the crew into departments and began to create schedules for them to follow.

Bob Taylor now knew, for example, that the neck department would have to make three necks a day. On the first day of making a neck they would cut out the neck blank, shape it, and cut out the basic headstock shape. Then they would install the truss rod and the brass inserts for the neck bolts and glue on the headstock veneer. Then they would plane and slot three fingerboards, cut them to shape, glue on the binding, install the inlays, and round the top surface. On the second day the neck blank was run through the shaper and put through some drilling processes for tuner holes. The peghead was shaped, bound, and inlaid. Finally the fretboard was glued on. Also on the second day, the neck department would start a new batch of three necks. On day three, the first batch of necks got their final shaping and sanding, after which they were taped for finish, and sent on to the finish department. At the same time the second batch of three necks was getting drilled for tuning machines and being bound, while a new batch of three necks was getting started.

While the necks were being made, there were people making three tops, people bending three sets of sides, and so forth. It took a while for the crew to catch on to the new system. "It was very difficult for the guys doing the work to be able to resist the desire to put just three fretboards through the slotting process," Taylor recalls. "I think it's programmed into the DNA

< Kurt poses for the cover of a novelty issue of
Rolling Stone at the 1978 NAMM Show

of every person who ever worked in a factory to want to go ahead and make dozens of whatever it was they were making at the time, since they were doing it anyway. We tried doing it that way by, for example, slotting 70 fretboards at a time, but we found it didn't work.

"But I kept repeating Augie's question. 'Would I rather have, one done guitar or ten half done guitars?' The way I saw it was that if we spent any time doing jobs that weren't directly related to those three guitars we were trying to finish, then that time was being wasted. We had limited money to see us through until the guitars were sold and so I wanted to convert our work and effort into money in the shortest time-span possible. That way I could have enough money to do the process again and, hopefully, do it better the next time."

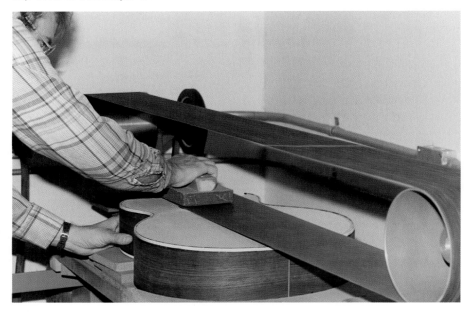

Bob Taylor tries out the stroke sander he built out of salvaged parts on the top of a rosewood jumbo.

The workers eventually saw the wisdom of the new building system when they began to complete three guitars every day instead of a batch of ten or twelve every few weeks. The steady production created a snowball effect that helped every aspect of the company. The new system meant that the instruments were being sold daily instead of every few weeks, which meant money began to flow into the company in a more predictable fashion, which in turn made planning for the future much easier.

Bob Starts Building Tools in a Big Way

Bob Taylor and Greg Deering spent much of their off hours thinking of new ways of using tools to make the parts for their instruments. Deering would sketch out plans for a jig to glue up banjo resonators while Taylor would think about tools like large buffers and stroke sanders that he couldn't afford. Together, Deering and Taylor would visit local salvage yards and scavenge motors and other parts to make their own tools. At first they did it out of necessity, but they quickly learned that there were real advantages to custom making tools to do specific jobs.

Taylor wanted a stroke sander, a type of belt sander used to sand large, flat surfaces like doors or tabletops. In the late 1970s a stroke sander sold for around $2500, much more than he could afford. Also, since they were designed for sanding doors, the machine would have been too big to fit in Taylor's increasingly cramped workshop. So he managed to find the various parts he needed at various salvage yards and surplus stores and for about $500 he built his own stroke sander that was just the right size for sanding the tops and backs of guitars after the binding had been glued on.

Taylor and Deering also began taking evening classes in a metal shop at a local school. The teacher was named Steve Shoemaker, who discovered that there were all kinds of tools available as government surplus. He could get them for free, if he came up with a way to pay the freight. After thinking about the problem for a while he decided to install a couple of soda machines in his classroom, and in a few weeks he was able to pay the shipping costs with the profits generated by his thirsty students.

When Bob Taylor heard that story, he knew he'd found someoné as resourceful as he was, and that he would enjoy studying with Shoemaker. "Steve's shop was great," Taylor recalls.

Neil Young plays his new 855 in concert. >

The 810 Bob Taylor built for himself using the spruce that Jean Larrivée gave him. Bob Taylor still owns and plays this guitar.

"There were several metal lathes and he had forging and foundry equipment, several vertical and horizontal mills, a huge radial arm drill press and even some hydraulic three dimensional copy mills. There was also every kind of welding machine and a pantograph flame-cutting torch that could follow patterns that we cut from plywood. Greg and I were delighted to have all this at our disposal. James Goodall also used to show up and make tools to build the flutes and recorders he made along with his guitars."

Taylor made excellent use of his time at the school, and he built buffers, gluing presses, and special clamping fixtures for end blocks and braces. After moving his new tools to the Taylor factory he painted them all green. "I chose green because it looked gray to me," he says. "I didn't know it was green until my wife, Cindy, saw them after I painted the tools. I chose the paint from a paint chip card that only listed the order numbers and not the names of the colors. I guess that company never thought that color-blind people would be ordering paint from them."

While Bob Taylor was figuring out new ways to make guitars, his partners concentrated on running the business end of things. Steve Schemmer would spend part of his day finishing guitars and the rest working in the office. Kurt Listug would build guitar bodies and then work on the books, and try and figure out ways to make the company profitable. He was also learning that his initial misgivings about getting involved with RMI were well founded.

The other instrument companies RMI represented were also having difficulties. Alembic Guitars co-founder, Rick Turner, says that RMI refused to release financial statements to his bank, which made it impossible to get loans to let him expand his company. "We had guitars on backorder, but we couldn't prove it to the bank," Turner says. "I think that Paul Rothchild had a great eye for quality, but he didn't really have any interest in running the business. We usually dealt with Paul's brother Ed, who sold electronic calculators for Texas Instruments before he started selling instruments. I don't think he really knew what he was doing."

Turner was impressed with Taylor guitars from the moment he saw them. "Taylors were the first acoustic guitar I recall seeing with slim, electric guitar style necks," he says. " At the time acoustic guitar necks tended to be really clubby and the action was almost always set too high. An electric guitar player could switch from his Strat to a Taylor without having to make a huge mental or physical adjustment. And their 12-strings were excellent, as well."

Other luthiers weren't the only ones to notice the unique features of Taylor guitars. Neil Young bought an 855 12-string at a music store in Florida, making him the most famous musician to play a Taylor up to that point. Although he was vacationing at the time, Young called his guitar technician Larry Cragg and asked him to buy a second one immediately. Young played the 855 on his *Rust Never Sleeps* tour and it featured prominently in the movie he made of some of the concerts. Although Young never officially endorsed Taylor guitars, he choice of the 855 gave the struggling company some much needed public exposure.

Although it was exciting for the luthiers to see their guitar in the hands of a rock legend like Young, it didn't really translate into sales. Paul Rothchild would tell Kurt Listug that part of the problem was that guitarists were unfamiliar with the Taylor name. He suggested that they come up with some less expensive models, so Taylor came up with the 500 and 600 series. The 500 series had an unstained mahogany back and sides, which gave the guitar a very light, almost salmon-pink color, a spruce top, a two-ring rosette, black binding and a rosewood fretboard and bridge. The 600 series was a slightly fancier version of the same guitar with white binding, a three-ring rosette, and an ebony fretboard and bridge. The back and sides were also stained a darker, more chocolate colored brown. The new models boosted sales slightly, but because it cost almost as much to make them as the fancier 800 and 900 series, the extra sales didn't help Taylor's financial situation.

"Any guitar, no matter how simple it is in construction, is almost as hard to make as any other," Taylor says. "The 500 and 600 series still had to go through nearly every process that the 810 went through. We probably saved an hour of labor and $25 in materials when we made a 510 back then. By then I had made some tooling to save time and we worked hard and fast, and I applied my attitude that quantity was every bit as important as quality. Still we sold those guitars out our door to RMI for $150. I still don't know how we did it, but we did. We just put our heads down and plowed through. Kurt required RMI to place a large order for these new affordable guitars and he also required them to pre-pay 50% of the invoice for the first 100 guitars or so. This gave us an infusion of cash and helped us survive again. At $150 per guitar, multiplied by 100 guitars, divided by 2, we got an "infusion of cash" of $7500. You can tell how broke we were when $7500 made that big of a difference. But it did."

The money from the sale of the 500 and 600 series only help alleviate the money problem for a brief period. The company continued to lurch from financial crisis to financial crisis, never really catching up on their bills. "Things were looking bleak and I thought that maybe I could take a loan on my house," Taylor recalls. "I mentioned the idea to Kurt and Steve and they agreed that it sounded good to them. I figured I could borrow about $7000, which would give us a big shot in the arm. Only I wasn't interested in loaning the money to the company, I was interested in investing the money. And I wanted some percentage of their shares for my trouble. Steve was against that proposition but Kurt thought it was fair and so we all agreed that if I put in $7000, they would each sign over 3% of their shares. We started with them each owning 35% and me owning 30%. With this transaction I now owned 36% of the company and they each owned 32%."

Saying Good-bye to Rothchild

Just like the money from the sale of the 500s to Rothchild, the cash infusion from Bob Taylor's home loan only helped for a little while. "Days came and went and we did our thing in the factory, hiring, training, negotiating, and of course, facing bad news," Taylor says. "By the end of 1978 we were beginning to talk about what life would be like without RMI. We were getting tired of fighting with them just to get them to take another guitar that we only received $150 for anyway.

"And I was getting exhausted physically and mentally and the fight in me was waning. We were just so broke, but at least we got our $85 a week, and I was happy about that, even though often times we couldn't cash the check. I would relate everything to my situation. I remember watching a re-run of *Hawaii 5-0* and Danno was complaining about how his cop job sucked and he'd better move on to something else because the pressure was just too high. I yelled right out loud right to the TV that he was a wimp because at least he got paid and could cash his check."

Bob Taylor began to think about quitting the guitar business. "I realized that in order to go out of business I'd have to pay all my debts first," Taylor says. "And if I could actually do that, then what would be the point in going out of business? Then I also thought of all the people I'd run across over the next few years and they'd say, 'Hey, Bob, how ya doing? You still making guitars?' And I'd have to say, 'No, I quit that.' And then they'd say, 'Wow, really? I thought you were doing so well in that.' And I'd have to say, 'Yeah, well, not really, I just couldn't make it.' Oh, the thought of facing all those little conversations just drove me back to my workbench."

To make things worse, even apparent good news turned out to be bad news in disguise. American Airlines sent Taylor a check for around $500, which they immediate deposited. Later it

The Taylor crew standing in front of the
Lemon Grove shop circa 1986.

turned out that check was sent in error and that it was a duplicate payment for a guitar Taylor had shipped COD. American Airlines didn't recognize their mistake, but when the luthiers had the money a couple of years later, they paid off the debt.

December rolled around, and by the end of the year it was apparent that implementing LoPrinzi's idea was bearing fruit. By the end of 1978 Taylor produced 449 guitars. There were eleven people working in the small Lemon Grove factory, which was full of Bob Taylor's custom-built green tools. But while the total number of guitars was impressive, they were still making very little money on them.

Taylor, Listug, and Schemmer began to realize that perhaps their biggest problem was the deal they had with Rothchild. True, RMI had placed Taylor guitars in lots of new stores, but then they did very little to help those stores sell the guitars. Rather than try to market the existing models, Paul Rothchild insisted that Taylor come up with cheaper guitars.

At the end of 1978, the three partners flew to San Francisco to attend a meeting with the few companies that had had elected to stay with RMI. By now, Larrivée and Augustino had both severed their relationship with RMI and Alembic was in the process of leaving. The meeting with Paul and Ed Rothchild and their remaining clients was tense, but after all these years, Bob Taylor remembers very little of what was said that day. "The only thing I remember about that meeting, and you'll probably think me heartless for this, was the incredible hamburger I had when we went out for lunch," Bob Taylor recalls. "It was at a gourmet hamburger place

"I took one look at their display at that NAMM show and knew it was time for us to go."

in downtown San Francisco and they had ingredients listed on the wall of your booth. You made up your own hamburger off that list. I had a half-pound burger with mushrooms, avocado, Swiss cheese, and grilled onions on a big San Francisco sourdough roll. I look back with delight on that meal from time to time, but I almost never think about that meeting."

In January 1979, Bob Taylor went to the Winter NAMM show in Anaheim, and he was very disappointed with RMI's booth. "I took one look at their display at that NAMM show and knew it was time for us to go," Taylor says. "They had our guitars in a dark corner of the exhibit hall where they couldn't really be seen. They had trouble selling our stuff, and after looking at the booth I knew why. But we couldn't do anything to help ourselves because of the exclusive arrangement we had with them. I called Kurt on the phone and said that I was ready to leave RMI. He came up to the show right away to see things for himself and agreed that things didn't look good."

The two partners returned to Lemon Gove and began to figure out what it would take to get out of their contract with RMI. They realized that they were obligated to make a certain number of guitars over the next few weeks, so they set about making them. On January 27, 1979, Taylor shipped their last batch of guitars to RMI and Kurt Listug called Paul Rothchild to tell him they wanted to end the distribution deal. "When I called him he was working as the music director on the set of Bette Midler's movie *The Rose*," Listug recalls. "He wasn't happy with our decision, but the fact he was working on a movie was a good sign that his heart wasn't really in the guitar business."

The relationship between Taylor and RMI ultimately proved to be a failure. The concept behind RMI was interesting, but their mix of high-end acoustic and electric guitars and expensive pro-audio gear ultimately proved to be too difficult to sell to enough stores to be profitable. Paul Rothchild had a good eye for quality, but he preferred to spend his time working on movie sets and in recording studios instead of in an office selling guitars over the phone. And Ed Rothchild, who was an able calculator salesman for Texas Instruments, never really adapted to the quirkier musical instrument market.

But the experience wasn't a total loss for Taylor. Because of RMI, Bob Taylor met Jean Larrivée and Augustino LoPrinzi, both of whom proved to be valuable friends. Kurt Listug learned that making good guitars wasn't a guarantee that they would sell. In a market that included venerable names like Martin, Gibson, and Guild as well as more recent builders like Larrivée, LoPrinzi, Mossman, Gurian, and the Santa Cruz Guitar Company it was more important than ever to set your product apart from the rest.

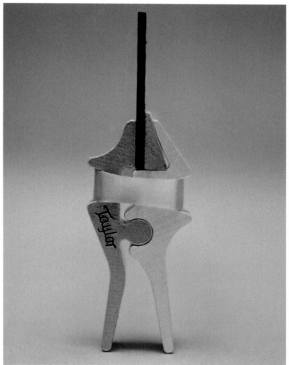

These Guzzetta-designed aluminum clamps were designed to hold the kerfed linings in place while the glue dried. Before the kerfing clamps were designed, Taylor workers used wooden clothes-pins to do the job.

"I was making the bodies, Steve was doing the finishing, and Bob was making the necks, doing the final assembly and then stringing the guitars up." Kurt Listug

Learning How to Grow a Company

And then there were three. Fireworks. Kurt Listug hits the road to sell guitars. A brief sojourn in Mexico. Koa. Steve Schemmer leaves. Old friends return. Westland Music Company becomes Taylor-Listug, Inc. Sea monsters and possums.

Downsizing

Now that Taylor, Listug, and Schemmer were free of Rothchild, they began to brainstorm on ways of improving business. One of the first things they did was to drop the mahogany 600 series from the line. The eleven-man crew had built 449 guitars in 1978, and the three owners felt they should be able to sell at least that many on their own without Rothchild's help. Kurt Listug had spoken by phone to all of the dealers that had signed on during the RMI era and he felt that he would be able to retain them now that Taylor was on its own. There was one minor hitch in the beginning, though. They had just sent RMI a final batch of guitars to fulfill their contract and RMI promptly began to sell those instruments to their dealers at heavily discounted prices.

Taylor felt the immediate effect of that last shipment and they only shipped 12 guitars in February. March was much better, with shipments of 56 guitars and in April they shipped 38 guitars. True, they were making more money on each guitar now that they weren't selling through a distributor, but it still wasn't enough to pay themselves and their workers. So, for the second time in their brief history, Bob Taylor and Kurt Listug made the hard decision to lay off the entire workforce.

"During this time I went back to the 'I'm getting rid of everything that stands in the way of profits' type of thinking," Bob Taylor recalls. "And when Kurt agreed, I laid off our employees. Every one of them. They were just kids so they weren't too upset. And so once again it was just Kurt, Steve, and me. We figured if we couldn't make guitars at a level to support our measly lifestyle, then we weren't going to be able to hire some kids to do it for us."

After laying off all of their employees, they began to look for other ways to economize. They were renting two 1,500 square foot units, and after deciding that was too much space for just the three of them, they gave one of the units up. "Our feeling was that we were spending money, and not making a dime," Listug says. "So we stopped spending money. We had a meeting and looked over our bills and decided what could go. One thing that went was our business insurance. Bob said that he had made most of our tools, and if the building burned down he figured he would just make some more." And since the sales weren't increasing they decided to cut back production as well.

"When we had almost a dozen guys here, we were trying to make sixteen guitars a week," Taylor says. "We decided that it made more sense to try for eight guitars a week. There were only three of us now, but we thought that if we really focused our energies, we could pull it

"I was making the bodies, Steve was doing the finishing and Bob was making the necks, doing the final assembly and then stringing the guitars up. We had the system set up so that the completed guitars were ready to go out on Friday."

off. We had a number of guitars in various states of completion around the shop. They had become like a bank account, however unintended it was. This meant that I didn't have to buy wood for a long time, and the month's worth of tuners I had in stock was now two months worth, and so on. We began to experience some income without the back breaking outflow of cash to negate it."

Even though they had cut production in half, that meant that they still had to build eight guitars a week with only three people. Because Bob Taylor had designed a number of methods to make the parts for guitars more efficiently, it was surprisingly easy for three committed individuals to do the work that was previously done by eleven workers. "I was making the bodies," Kurt Listug recalls. "Steve was doing the finishing and Bob was making the necks, doing the final assembly and then stringing the guitars up. We had the system set up so that the completed guitars were ready to go out on Friday."

The new set up required everyone to work very efficiently, and when Steve Schemmer began to fall behind in his work, Taylor and Listug began to get more and more annoyed with him. "Steve was a good worker, but he just had different priorities than Bob and I did," Listug says. " He want-

No, it's not a young ZZ Top. It's Kurt, Bob, and Steve at the NAMM show in Chicago.

ed to keep the same sort of working hours we did back in the American Dream days, which meant he didn't always get his work done in a timely fashion. There were lots of times in the early years when Bob stayed up all night Thursday doing the final assembly on the guitars that Steve had just buffed out so we could ship them on Friday. Sometimes Steve seemed to be more interested in working on his sailboat than in building guitars."

Even with the heavy workload, Bob Taylor continued to refine the guitars. In 1979 he started to scallop the top braces on the 810. Until then the rosewood dreadnought had straight braces, which were stronger, but tended to give the guitar a brighter tone that some players described as tinny. Scalloping the braces made the top lighter and more flexible, which in turn increased the bass response. Over the next few months Taylor would switch to scalloped braces on all of the higher end models.

Even though there were only three people building guitars at Taylor, by the end of 1979 the trio managed to complete and sell a very respectable 399 instruments by the end of the year. In fact, they found that they were making more guitars than they could easily sell. They had to skip the 1979 NAMM Show because they felt they couldn't afford to attend. In 1980 they realized that they had to sign up more dealers, so they felt that they couldn't afford to miss the 1980 Summer NAMM Show, which was being held in Chicago.

Since they didn't have any cash to pay for the hotel rooms, Listug applied for a credit card that would only be used for show expenses. "We would use that for food and hotel rooms," Listug says. "When we got back home, we'd put the card in a drawer and forget about it. Then we'd spend the next 12 months paying off that bill."

Johnny Lane from Arnold and Morgan music. At the time they stocked more Taylors than any other music store in the country.

Bob Taylor spent a lot of time and effort designing an attractive booth to display the guitars. He had a carpet made with the Taylor logo on it and built a small soundproof listening room so prospective buyers could hear the acoustic instruments over the wail of the people trying out electric guitars and the ceaseless thunder of the drummers. "Kurt, Steve, my wife Cindy, and I hopped into my brown '78 Volvo, in Lemon Grove," Bob remembers. "We had a U-Haul trailer hooked to the back and just enough money to buy gas to get us to the NAMM Show. We didn't stop until we got there, 52 hours later."

When the weary crew finally made it to Chicago, they discovered that their 10-by-20-foot booth space had two concrete pillars in the middle of it. "They were each four feet in diameter, and right beside each other," Taylor recalls. "Complaining to the authorities did no good, so we cut the new carpet to smithereens, set up our booth, and tried to make the best of it. I even got my 'soundproof room' rearranged and set up. Unfortunately I had neglected to build a roof for it, so it really wasn't very good at keeping out the noise. And to make things worse, when we showed up on the first day of the show, we discovered that someone had pushed the door of the booth in, breaking it right off the hinges and leaving it in a heap of splinters."

The Taylor booth was across the aisle from Dean Guitars, an electric guitar company who was famous at the time for their ads featuring scantily clad women. The Dean Girls, as they were known, were at the booth and were attracting a steady stream of staring men. "I remember Dean's booth looked amazing with nice leather couches and his blue and gold macaw," Taylor says. "People would pass by our little booth, say something like, 'Cool! Taylor! They make a killer 12-string!,' and then go look at the Dean Girls and the parrot. Our best dealer at the time was Arnold and Morgan Music in Texas, and they came by and bought all nine of the guitars in our display, at a discount. Larry Morgan was one of the first dealers to really support us. Another dealer, Ed Taublieb, ordered two guitars. That was it. There were no other orders."

After the show was over the dejected crew began to pack up, and Bob Taylor unwittingly ran afoul of one of Chicago's infamous unions. "We wanted to get the guitars shipped off to Arnold and Morgan as quickly as possible so we could get paid as quickly as possible," Taylor recalls. "But I had to go and mouth off to a Chicago union steward. He wanted me to hire one of his union guys to remove that last screw, and even if I had the money to pay him, I didn't want to do it.

"Mysteriously, the guitars we were shipping by truck got air-freighted all over the country before getting to Arnold and Morgan. The trucking company sent us large collection bills for this tour de farce, and we ended up having to go to court. To this day, I just imagine the union steward purposely messing up the bills of lading we left on our crates, causing them to take this huge detour, and delaying both their arrival at the music store and our eventual receipt of payment."

The drive back home to California was long and hot. There was a heat wave and the air conditioning in Bob Taylor's car was broken. In Missouri, Taylor and Listug bought some fireworks in an attempt to cheer themselves up. They set most of them off in the desert, saving one bottle rocket to shoot off to celebrate their return to California. "We arrived back at my little shack in Lemon Grove, where we launched that last bottle rocket," Taylor recalls. "It promptly set fire to the dry bushes across the street. We stomped it out as our last act of that NAMM Show trip."

Listug remembers making numerous calls to the trucking company to get a refund on the large air freight-bill. After being constantly rebuffed, he eventually took them to small-claims court. "I brought the lid from the packing crate into court to show the judge that the label said 'ship via truck,'" Listug says. "When the trucking guy saw that he didn't offer much of a defense. We got our money, but it made me angry that we had to go through that. In those early years we were always struggling to be taken seriously by other businesses. It seemed that just because we were young, they thought they didn't have to take us seriously."

Bob Taylor would relieve the stress in those days by playing in a band he started with his brother-in-law, Mike Dwyer. They started playing in church on Sundays and were so well received that they were soon playing fifteen to twenty times a month at other local churches. The chance to actually play guitar helped to ease the frustration that was caused by making and then trying to sell them. And as he had done on the disastrous NAMM Show trip, Bob Taylor found a more explosive way to amuse himself.

"I discovered these big firecrackers that came from Mexico," he explains. "I loved these explosives. Some friends and I used to blow up things in a field across from my house. One day I remembered I had an old guitar that I think I got from Greg Deering. I think it was an old Vega guitar or something like that, and I had planned to fix it up. But after thinking about it for a second I decided to blow it up instead. I had one more of these little poppers and we went into the front yard, lit the thing and dropped it right into the soundhole. Where there once was a guitar, there was now no guitar."

Bob Taylor enjoyed the spectacle so much he began searching for another candidate for destruction. Unfortunately for future guitar historians, he turned his attention to the trio of guitars he built in high school before he started working at the American Dream. "Only one of those three guitars has survived," he says. "The other two suffered death at my own hand, the hand of their master. I didn't think they were all that great at the time and I was working on making a reputation. I never thought that I'd ever be famous and could use them as museum pieces. I just wanted to destroy the evidence of any bad work I'd done. The first one simply went into the fireplace one evening and we all watched in awe as the lacquer lit afire and danced up the face and around the sides. After a while the pearl inlays began to fall out of the charred fretboard, having survived the heat better than the wood, and soon there was nothing left but a lone truss rod in a pile of grayish ash."

> "I was way, way too stupid at the time to realize what a wonderful thing they had given me, so this guitar was soon on my hit list."

Taylor decided that the next guitar should have a more spectacular demise. "This one was actually the first guitar I built, and the second one I destroyed," he says. "I had sold it to a friend of my brother-in-law and he and my sister got it back for me several years later and presented it as a gift. I was way, way too stupid at the time to realize what a wonderful thing they had given me, so this guitar was soon on my hit list. I'd always thought that it would be exciting to lay scratch with my motorcycle on a guitar." Taylor planted the rear wheel of his motorcy-

cle on the top of the guitar, revved the engine, and popped the clutch. "That guitar shot out about fifteen feet to the rear," he says. "Then we jumped on the remains like the boys in *Lord of the Flies* and walked away satisfied. Now I don't regret my past too much and I sure had fun at the time, but I'd sure like to have that guitar right now."

< Some of the tools Taylor bought with their $30,000 loan.

Luckily Bob Taylor balanced his destructive urges with more creative ones. In 1980 he built his first guitar out of koa. Koa is a hardwood from Hawaii that was used quite a bit on instruments built during the Hawaiian music craze of the 1920s. While the vast majority of instruments made of koa then were ukuleles, companies like Martin and Weissenborn made a fair number of guitars out of koa as well. When the Hawaiian music fad died out in the early 1930s, luthiers switched back to using mostly rosewood, mahogany, and maple, and koa was forgotten on the mainland.

In the 1970s guitar makers began to take a second look at koa. The wood is beautiful, with a color that varies from a light honey color to a rich, golden brown. Its grain pattern ranges from a very straight pattern similar to mahogany to a flamboyant tiger stripe that rivals the fanciest maple. Builders James Goodall, Richard Hoover at the Santa Cruz Guitar Company and Michael Gurian were among the first luthiers in the 1970s to work with koa.

Bob Taylor built his first koa guitar out of very plain wood he found at a local lumberyard. His experiments eventually led to him adding a series of koa guitars to the line in 1983. In a break from their numeric naming system they dubbed the new dreadnought koa model the K-10. They also made a version with a koa top instead of spruce that they called the K-20. The koa series of guitars would go in and out of production over the years depending on the availability of the wood, but the style was always popular with customers.

Kurt Hits the Road

In an effort to share the workload, the trio had split the dealer base up into three equal shares with each partner being responsible for selling guitars to their assigned stores. Bob Taylor and Steve Schemmer discovered that they didn't really have the knack for selling guitars like Kurt Listug did. That same year Kurt bought himself a green Volvo and started going on short road trips showing guitars to stores. Over the next few years his short trips would grow in length until he was spending weeks at a time on the road and racking up tens of thousands of miles on his odometer.

By the end of 1980 the trio's production had dropped to only 100 guitars. As they had proved the year before, they were capable of making far more than that, but since they weren't selling as many as they wanted, they had to cut back on production to save money. Even though they were making more guitars than they could sell, Bob Taylor was always thinking of ways to build them even more quickly and efficiently. One of the biggest obstacles he wanted to overcome was the problem of manufacturing the essential components like bridges, braces, and linings in a consistent and timely manner.

At the time, they had to make different parts on the same few machines. This meant, for example, that they would have to set up a shaper to make bridges, then reconfigure it to make necks, and then reconfigure it yet again to do some other operation. It sometimes seemed that the trio was spending more time disassembling and reassembling power tools than they were building guitars.

So they applied for and got a $30,000 bank loan. "This was our first real, live bank loan to buy equipment," Taylor says. "We thought it was important to establish a relationship with a banker and move one notch closer to being a real business. Of the $30,000 we borrowed, we used about two-thirds for equipment. To save money, I actually made most of the machinery myself. We bought some new shapers, a resaw, a dust collector, and a table saw, while I built the stroke sander, a buffer, and various clamping fixtures. We created a few dedicated machines to make parts on more or less a daily basis, so we could just walk over and do it, instead of making a big, hairy mess. The way we'd been making parts was so tedious. So, this was our first foray into adding a little more 'horsepower' to our woodworking."

Taylor Goes to Mexico

Not long after getting the loan, a man named Nobel Field stopped by the Taylor shop with a luthier from the Mexican town of Paracho, a small town in Michoacan that produced most of the guitars made in Mexico. Field explained that the Mexican man was named Francisco Andrade and he was working for the Mexican government on a project intended to help improve production and living conditions for the people in Paracho. The two men were impressed with the small Taylor operation, and were particularly excited to learn that Bob Taylor had built most of his own tools. Field asked if Andrade could work in the shop for a week or two to see if Taylor's tools and methods might be applied to improving the working conditions in Paracho.

Paracho is a little town in the mountains of Mexico about 1800 miles south of San Diego. It currently has a population of around 15,000 people, although in the early 1980s it was quite a bit smaller. Nearly the entire population is involved in building stringed instruments in one way or the other. (There are a number of towns in Michoacan devoted to specific crafts such as Tzintzuntzan, which is famous for pottery, Santa Clara, which is home to numerous coppersmiths, and Taxco, which is devoted to making items out of silver.) Most of the instruments made in Paracho are very inexpensive and are designed to be sold to tourists as decorations, but quite a few local luthiers produce very high quality guitars, along with uniquely Mexican instruments like the *guitarron*, the *bajo sexto*, and the *vihuela*. In the early 1980s most of the luthiers built their instruments using nothing but a very sharp knife called a *cuchillo*, which they would use to carve the neck, cut the kerfed linings, shape the top, and cut the bridge.

Bob Taylor remembers that Francisco Andrade showed up for work in overalls and offered his labor in exchange for studying Bob's building techniques. "Francisco's history came out over a period of time," Taylor recalls. "Through our broken Spanish and his broken English we found out that he had owned and operated some furniture factories in Mexico. He was so successful he was eventually asked to change careers and work with Fidepal, which was the part of Mexico's social security system designed to help improve working conditions. The gentleman who brought him to us was Nobel Field, a former buyer for Montgomery Ward who had moved to Mexico to open his own furniture factory."

After working at Taylor for a week, Francisco offered to hire the three partners as consultants for Fidepal. He would take them to Paracho to show the local craftsmen some of the guitar building techniques Bob Taylor had come up with. "I knew and understood high production methods since I'd visited many factories by then," Taylor says. "But our own methods were based on cheap, homemade tools and lots of handwork which was exactly what this town of Paracho needed. In May 1981, we were invited to travel with Francisco to Paracho for an eight-day excursion, and so we literally locked the doors of the shop and took an all expense paid tour of this area of Mexico."

Taylor, Listug, and Schemmer toured the town and visited the homes where the luthiers did their work. "One house we visited was a simple stone structure with a wooden roof and a dirt floor," Taylor remembers. "Mama was cooking food over an open fire pit in the middle of the fifteen foot square room, and about six or seven children were either being attended to or attending to another. Papa was over on his workbench finishing guitars with what was described as a gasoline finish. It was a lacquer base of some sort, or maybe varnish and the solvent was gasoline. The smell of the gasoline permeated the entire dwelling as there were four or five open containers and about six guitars hanging from the ceiling to dry. The finish was applied with a brush or a rag under the light of an electric bulb hanging from two bare wires with the aid of masking tape."

Bob Taylor attended meetings with the luthiers, and over the course of the next few months explained his methods and techniques for producing guitars more efficiently. Unfortunately, the funding for the modernization of Paracho eventually dried up, and the town's luthiers were unable to buy the tools to put any of Taylor's ideas to work on their own guitars. In recent

The Taylor crew with Francisco Andrade.

years things have gotten better. Today, luthiers still use their *cuchillos* to make most of the parts of their guitars. But there are now a number of shops that are set with a few power tools, and these shops will rent time on their tools to other luthiers who might want to take advantage of a table saw or a power sander.

The Paracho adventure took quite a bit of time from guitar building, but the extra money the Taylor partners made from the consulting fees helped take up the slack. To help boost sales they re-introduced the 600 series, but this time as a guitar with maple back and sides. Taylor decided the maple on the new version of the 600 should remain unstained, making it one of the very few blond flattop maple guitars on the market. The new model, which had a smooth, mellow tone, helped boost the bottom line a bit, but overall sales were still sluggish. It's not that guitarists were shunning Taylor guitars specifically; the problem was that musicians at the time weren't buying acoustic guitars at all.

Punk rockers began to smooth their rough edges, and call themselves new wave musicians.

When Taylor Guitars opened for business in 1974, acoustic guitars were an important part of the general music scene. But in 1976 things began to change. Disco was becoming the most popular music in America when people decided that they wanted to shake their booties instead of listen to earnest singer/songwriters emote about their failed relationships. (On October 15, 1976, the Taylor Guitar company's second birthday, the number one song in America was "Disco Duck," which should have been an obvious sign that things were changing.)

Punk rockers began to smooth their rough edges, and call themselves new wave musicians. By the early 1980s bands like Blondie, the B-52s, and the Talking Heads began to appear regularly on the charts. Country music was overrun by smooth, middle of the road singers like Eddie Rabbit, Kenny Rogers, and Olivia Newton-John, and mainstream pop was full of even smoother performers like, Lionel Ritchie, Christopher Cross and Air Supply. Rock music was going through one of its periodic quiet spells, but even so bands like Styx, Supertramp, and REO Speedwagon kept the sound of electric guitars on the radio. None of these best selling early 1980s bands had anything in common, except the fact that none of them had any use for acoustic guitars.

The dire situation wasn't helped when MTV went on the air in 1981. The new cable channel introduced new musicians like Duran Duran, the Eurythmics, Gary Numan, and Thomas Dolby who created their distinctive sounds using synthesizers and samplers. In this new, electronic world, acoustic guitars were seen as almost unbearably old-fashioned. Sales at the larger acoustic guitar companies like Martin, Gibson and Guild plummeted and a few smaller companies like Gurian simply went out of business. In 1974, the year Taylor began, Martin made 6184 guitars in the popular D-35 style. In 1982, one year after MTV went on the air, they made 599.

Bob Taylor responded to the slowdown in sales by working even harder to refine his building techniques, which would help them make each guitar more profitably. Meanwhile, Kurt Listug began going out on the road on longer and longer selling trips. Each trip brought in enough orders to keep the business struggling along at its current pace, but there never seemed to be enough money to expand the company to the next stage. "We had no maneuvering room," Taylor recalls. "The worst part about economic failure is spiraling all the way down and not having any options. So, Kurt and I sort of tag-teamed it; we called Arnold & Morgan Music in Texas and offered to sell them 100 or so guitars at a huge discount. I actually told them that I would cook them Thanksgiving dinner, because it was about that time of year. Part of the deal included me going to their store on a Saturday for a meet-and-greet workshop. I spent the whole day there."

Listug remembers that the unsold guitars were just piled up everywhere around their small workshop in Lemon Grove. "We couldn't sell them, we had bills piling up, and we couldn't pay ourselves," he says. "It was bleak. The Arnold & Morgan deal wasn't great for us financially—I think we gave them an extra 25% discount—but it did net us around $13,000. Bob had an excellent understanding of the financial hole we were in. He rightly said that if we just pay off our bills with the money, we're going to have to do this again in a few months. We needed to come up with some more dealers to increase our cash flow. We talked about the situation and decided that I should hit the road one last time and not come back until we had enough new dealers to help us grow our business to the next level." So in October of 1982, Kurt Listug got into his green Volvo and traveled across the country trying to open new dealers. He didn't come back to San Diego until just before Christmas.

Bob Taylor and Steve Schemmer stayed behind to make guitars along with Don Miller, who was hired to cover for Listug. "I remember staying up until midnight making guitars," Taylor says. "Kurt would call in every day with progress reports. He would go into a new town, open the yellow pages to find the local music stores and head over and take orders based on the guitars he had in his trunk."

Buying Out Steve

While Listug was on the road, the problems and disagreements he and Bob Taylor were having with Steve Schemmer came to a head. "I would talk on the phone to Steve and he would always be complaining about how bad he thought things were going," Listug recalls. "But then I'd talk to Bob and he'd be really enthusiastic. He'd say, 'This is working. We're beginning to turn this around. But I can't get Steve to come in to do his work.' It was the same old problem. Steve just wasn't getting his work done and Bob was still staying up until two or three in the morning on Wednesday and Thursday getting the guitars ready to ship on Friday."

Listug's long road trip had its rough moments, such as the time his car broke down in Madison, Wisconsin on his 30th birthday. Then there was the un-festive way he spent the Thanksgiving holiday. "I was in the Detroit area for the holiday," he recalls. "Since all the stores in town were closed, I drove across the Canadian border to Windsor, Ontario to visit some stores there. When I got back that evening I stopped at the Denny's restaurant next door to my hotel for dinner, but they had already sold out of turkey. That was a sad day."

But it wasn't all bad. By the end of the trip he had taken lots of orders and he had realized that it wasn't that hard to sell guitars after all. "I was on my way home and stopped in Nashville on a Sunday because the weather was so bad," he says. "I sat in my room and watched the San Diego Chargers beat the San Francisco 49ers. I had been on the road for two months, but I was feeling really good. I had a pocket full of checks, I was on my way home, and my football team had won. And most importantly, being away from the shop for so long helped me realize that it was time for me and Bob to do something about Steve.

Learning How to Grow a Company

"I ended the trip by selling the last of my samples to Alan Levin at Washington Music Center, and I drove home. When I got back, Bob and I went to a lawyer and figured out how we were going to buy out Steve." Fortunately, the original partnership agreement had a buy/sell provision, which, ironically, was there because Listug thought he and Schemmer might have to buy out the then unknown Bob Taylor at some time.

Taylor Guitars had grossed about $100,000 the previous year, so using that as the value of the business, Taylor and Listug each borrowed $15,000 from their families and bought out Schemmer's share. After the final accounting, it turned out that Bob Taylor actually had a few more shares than Listug because Taylor got some extra shares when he mortgaged his house to pay off some outstanding bills. Taylor decided to give Listug enough shares to make them equal partners, and in March 1983, the Westland Music Company had two equal partners instead of three. In November the Westland Music Company officially ceased to exist when the partners transferred all of their assets into their new corporation, Taylor-Listug, Inc.

"Bob and I had been unhappy with Steve for quite a while," Listug says. "I remember driving up to Los Angeles with Bob in 1976 and we just spent the entire trip complaining about him. It was hard to make the decision to buy Steve out because we had been friends since we were boys, but once I made it, I knew it was the right thing to do. Once Steve was gone, the bottleneck in production opened up and we were able to almost double our production in the next year."

The first order of business was to find a replacement for Steve Schemmer. Bob Taylor had kept in touch with Tim Luranc, who was spraying finishes for the banjo maker Geoff Stelling. They offered him a part-time position, which quickly turned into a full time job. "They offered me $400 a week, which was more than I'd ever earned in my life," Luranc recalls. "Obviously, it was also more than Geoff Stelling was paying me, so I jumped at the chance. But I told Bob that I wanted to train other people how to spray finish, because I didn't get back into the guitar business just to spray lacquer. After a while he hired a couple of guys to help out with the finish and I moved on to final assembly, attaching necks and gluing bridges and that sort of thing. Bob also let me build my own guitars in the evening, which was a nice perk."

Around that same time Taylor hired Larry Breedlove, a luthier who was also working at Stelling's shop. Breedlove was an old friend of James Goodall, and he had been taking classes in advanced furniture design at San Diego State University. Breedlove was a skilled craftsman, with some innovative design ideas that would play an important part in the success of Taylor guitars.

The return of Tim Luranc, who was one of the luthiers that stayed on when Taylor, Listug and Schemmer bought the American Dream in 1974, injected some of the easy-going feelings that were the hallmark of the early days. Things continued to go wrong, but now the incidents were more comic than tragic.

Luranc recalls the time that a possum wandered into the shop after a work crew tore down the abandoned house it was living in. "When Bob saw the possum, he tried to chase it back out the door," Luranc says. "But the possum got spooked and ran deeper into the shop. Finally, Bob grabs a stick and starts poking at the thing, and actually gets it to head for the door, but at the last minute, it takes a turn into the small bathroom we had and lodges itself behind the toilet. By now, Bob is really annoyed, and he starts prodding the thing with this stick, but the more he pokes, the madder the possum gets, and they get into this long standoff, with Bob yelling and poking and the possum hissing and snarling from behind the toilet. Bob was determined, though, and he finally got the thing out the door. Of course, possums don't exactly run, they sort of waddle. I still laugh at the image of this possum waddling as fast as it can down the street, with Bob in pursuit, poking it."

< Tim Luranc in the spray booth that Taylor traded for a new 815.

The American Dream feelings got even stronger when Bob Taylor's old friend and former West-land Music repairman, Greg Deering, opened his new banjo company in the building next to Taylor's tiny factory. "From the very first we used to have keys to each other's shops," Deering recalls. "I had a welder Bob would borrow and I would use his big band saw and stuff like that."

Not long after Deering moved in to his new shop, the city poured a new concrete drive-way. It rained quite a bit that winter and before long that driveway was under ten inches of water. In true Dream fashion, everybody dealt with the situation with good humor. "There was a cab-inet shop nearby and they cut out a plywood sea monster and stuck it in the water," Deering recalls. "We set up a fishing pier by our shop and one of my employees brought a canoe that we used it to paddle back and forth from my shop to Bob's."

The combination of buying out Steve Schemmer and the close proximity of old friends seemed to inspire the small Taylor crew. Bob Taylor began to work on designing a completely new gui-tar with a smaller body; Larry Breedlove started work on a custom guitar that would spark a mini-revolution in guitar design; and the dealers that Listug signed up during his marathon road trips began to reorder instruments. At the end of 1983 there were five people at Taylor who built 493 guitars. The overall acoustic guitar business was still bad, but for the first time Tay-lor and Listug could sense that the situation was going to improve.

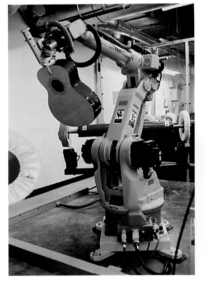

Robotic arm that was purchased in 2000 and programmed to buff guitar bodies. The Taylor crew nick-named it Buffy.

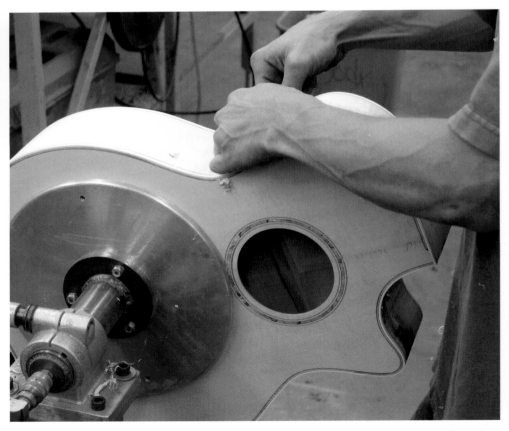

A clamp designed by Matt Guzzetta that held the guitar in place using the suction of vacuum. This method of clamping allowed the worker more access to the guitar body and reduced the chance of scratching or otherwise damaging the body.

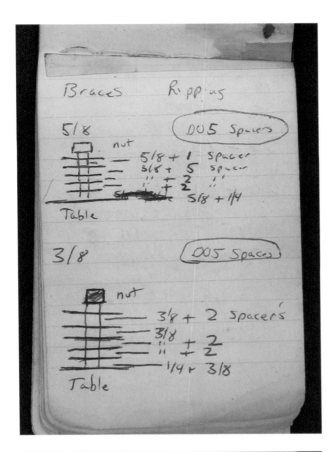

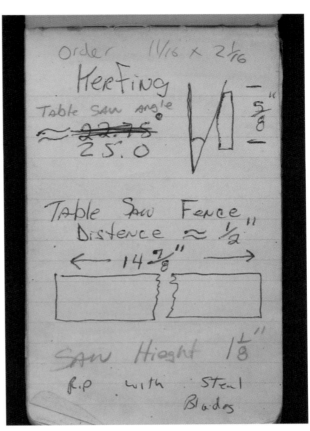

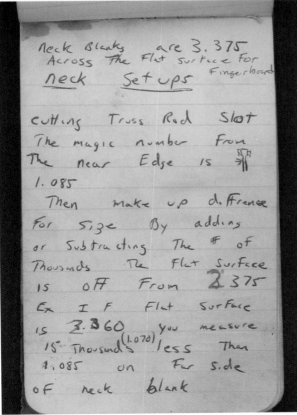

Some more pages
of Bob Taylor's
notebook.

The Art of Taylor

When Bob Taylor first started working at the American Dream in 1973, all of the decorative inlays were cut by hand out of pearl or abalone shell. Today, Taylor and his crew still cut the inlays from pearl and abalone but they also use a wide of variety of materials including hardwoods such as bloodwood and koa, synthetic material like Color Core, as well as shells such as agoya. And instead of using a jeweler's saw to cut the individual pieces, they use high-tech tools like lasers and CNC mills. The new tools and materials have inspired Taylor's inlay artists to create designs that would have been impossible to do even a few years ago.

2003 John Denver Commemorative Model (JDCM)

The inlay on this koa grand concert guitar was laser-cut from koa, maple, walnut, and yellow heart. The soundhole rosette is made of flamed maple.

2002 Doyle Dykes "Desert Rose" Signature Model (DDSM-LTD)

The headstock inlay on this grand auditorium is made from abalone and pearl and the desert scene is made from stained maple, green Formica Color Core, and a sliver of pearl for the moon.

2003 Cowboy Sunburst (CS-LTD)

This sunburst maple dreadnaught with checker-board binding was created to emulate the inexpensive guitars that were sold through catalogs in the 1930s and 1940s.

**2003 Hot Rod Guitar
(HR-LTD)**
The inlays and soundhole rosette on this
guitar were inspired by the flames painted
on the sides of old hot rods.

2003 Jars of Clay Signature Model (JCSM)

The simple pearl inlay on the headstock of this guitar is a replica of the band's logo. The inlay on the back is a reference to the biblical verse – "But we have this treasure in jars of clay to show that this all-surpassing power is from God and not from us"– that inspired the band's name.

2 cor 4:7

2003 Pelican Guitar (PG-LTD)

The pelican inlays on this guitar were designed by Pete Davies, Jr., and were laser cut out of koa, satin wood, walnut, and myrtle wood.

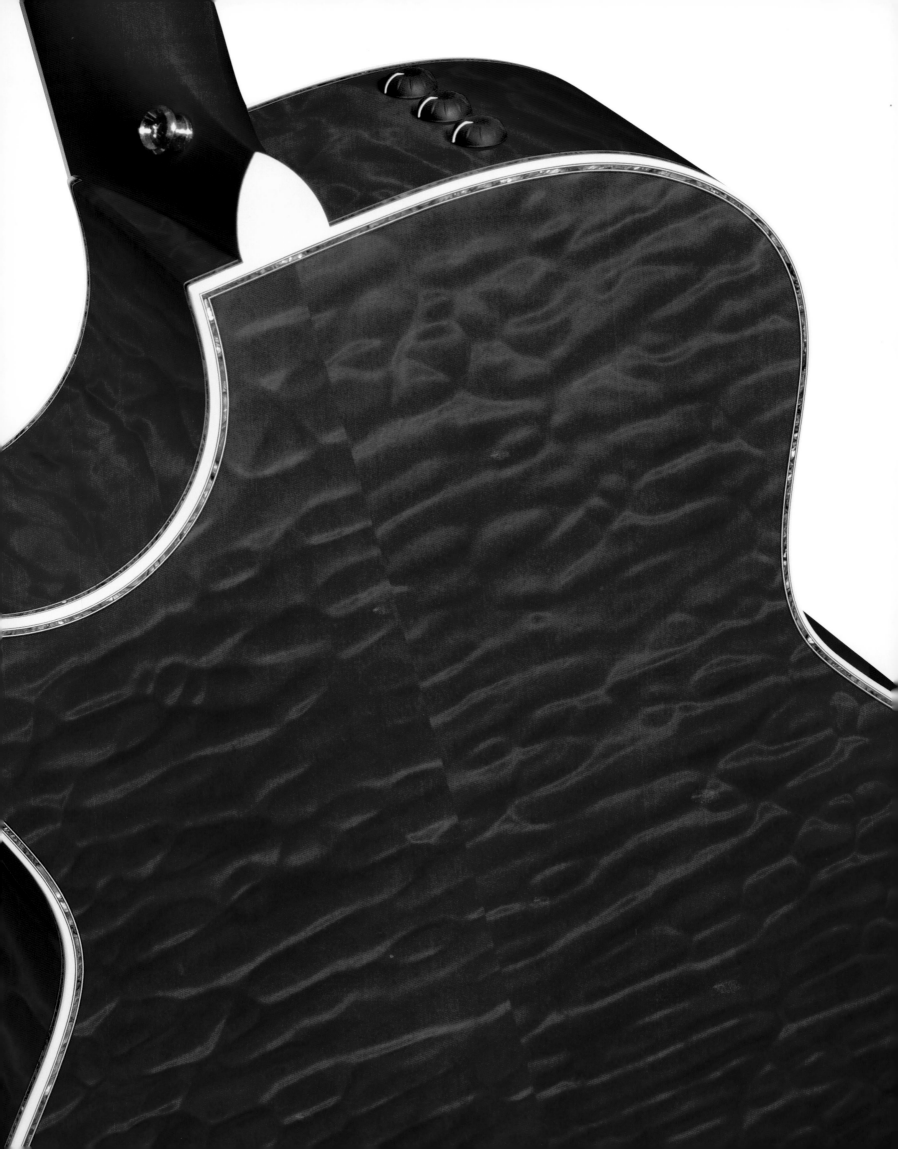

**2003 Presentation Series
Limited Edition "Ruby Red"
(PS-LTD)**
The tree-of-life inlays and body bordering on this
limited edition guitar are cut from abalone shell.

2003 Running Horses (RH-LTD)

Pete Davies, Jr. also designed the running horses inlay on this instrument. They were laser-cut from pieces of maple and koa.

**2003 Russ Freeman
Signature Model
(RFSM)**
The beret-sporting jazz cats on this
guitar were inspired by drawings from
the covers of Russ Freeman's albums
Sahara and Brave New World.

**2003 Windham Hill
Commemorative Model
(WHCM)**
The headstock inlay on this guitar is cut from
figured maple while the fretboard logo is cut
from pearl.

2003 NS72ce-LTD
The leaf-pattern soundhole rosette on the nylon string model was etched using a laser.

2003 NS62ce
As with the NS72ce-LTD, the soundhole rosette on this maple sides and back NS62ce was cut with a laser. The body was bound in rosewood.

1973 Rosewood Dreadnought hand-built by Bob Taylor.

The fretboard inlays on this guitar were based on the "Hearts and Flowers" inlay from a Gibson Granada banjo.

1978 810

This guitar sports the diamond shaped pearl inlays that Taylor used in the early days of the company. This is Bob Taylor's personal guitar.

"Bob wakes up in the morning and wants to make the guitars better. Kurt wakes up and wants to make the company better." Chris Proctor

Success at Last

A new body size. The blue guitar and the purple guitar. Chris Proctor and Harvey Reid. The Dan Crary Signature Model. Kurt Listug wears out one Volvo on his road trips. Time to move to a bigger building. Solving a difficult case.

A New Body Style

In January 1984, Taylor and Listug headed up to Anaheim, California to exhibit their guitars at the Winter NAMM Show. Unlike previous NAMM Shows, where they appeared with an assortment of dreadnoughts and jumbos that were not that different from the instruments of other guitar makers, this time they had two very different guitars to show off. The first was a small body grand concert-sized guitar. Taylor gave the new body size a 2 designation and brought two versions, a 512 and an 812, to the NAMM Show. Later that year they added the maple 612, the rosewood 712, the spruce top and koa back and sides K12, the koa top, back and sides K22, and the fancy fiddleback maple 912 to the line. They also offered a pointed Florentine cutaway as a custom option. The other special guitar was a maple dreadnought that Larry Breedlove had stained bright blue as a custom order for a music shop in Santa Monica.

Chris Proctor giving a workshop at Guitar Showcase around 1985.

The first grand concert model, which was built for fingerstyle guitarist Chris Proctor.

Bob Taylor had been thinking about making a smaller bodied guitar for at least a year, but he hadn't made much progress in coming up with a workable design. He wanted to add a new model to the line and stores, particularly those that specialized in acoustic instruments, wanted a guitar that would appeal to the new breed of fingerpickers that were starting to appear on the scene. These young players had grown up listening to the great blues players like Gary Davis and Mississippi John Hurt as well as country players like Doc Watson and Merle Travis, but they wanted to create their own music using the instrumental techniques of their heroes.

In the 1960s players like John Fahey and in the 1970s Leo Kottke produced a series of records that rearranged folk, blues, classical music, jazz, and whatever else seemed to be lying around into surprising new forms. These records inspired countless numbers of budding players, and by the early 1980s there were avid fingerstyle guitarists all across America and throughout Europe. Some were playing the gentle New Age styles pioneered by William Ackerman and Alex de Grassi; others were playing complex ragtime and gritty blues, while players like Michael Hedges were creating entirely new sounds using open tunings and radical techniques such as slapping the strings. As these musicians stretched the boundaries of music, they began to realize that the guitars they were currently playing weren't always up to the job.

One of these players was Chris Proctor, an up and coming fingerstyle guitarist from Utah. Proctor had taken first prize in 1982 at the National Fingerpicking Championship in Winfield, Kansas, and in 1983 he released his first album, a collection of instrumentals called *Runoff*. "I was a guitarist on a quest for an instrument I couldn't find in the marketplace," Proctor recalls. "So, I went to several NAMM Shows just to talk to manufacturers, trying to find a company small enough to do what I wanted, but big enough to make it happen." At the 1983 Summer NAMM Show in Chicago, Proctor met Bob Taylor. The show wasn't a very good place to discuss the subtleties of acoustic guitar tone and playability, so a few weeks later Proctor went to Lemon Grove to talk at greater length about what he was looking for.

Proctor had previously owned guitars made by Martin, Mossman, Gurian, Franklin, and Charlie Hoffman, and while each instrument had elements that he liked, none of them wrapped everything up into one package. The last two instruments on the list were made of koa, a wood that Proctor felt sounded particularly nice. "I knew I wanted a small body, a wider neck, perfect action, a compensated saddle, and a lower-than-normal nut," Proctor says. "Bob had already worked out the low action and the good intonation on his guitars. Now I wanted to see if he could get the sound I wanted. Most of the guitars that were available then were jumbos or dreadnoughts, all with narrower fretboards. Those guitars play well if you use a flatpick, but they just didn't work for the spidery fingerings that fingerpickers use. And most of those larger bodied guitars are just too boomy on the low end. We like guitars with the well-balanced bass and treble that a smaller guitar like the grand concert has."

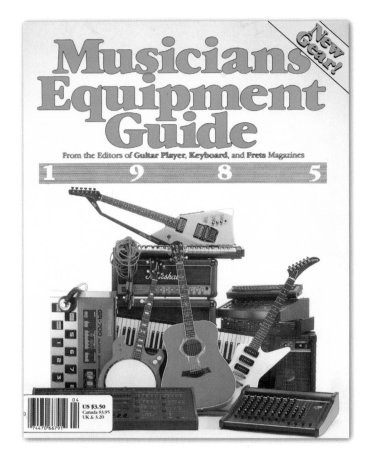

Cover of the Musician's Equipment Guide from 1985 showing Larry Breedlove's blue guitar and Greg Deering's red Crossfire electric banjo.

Bob Taylor appreciated Proctor's insights into what guitarists wanted. "By the time Chris came around I felt that my ability to build guitars had grown beyond my ability to play guitar," Taylor says. "To get to the next step as a luthier I needed to build guitars that really good players responded to. Chris was the perfect guy to bounce ideas off." Taylor made a couple of prototypes that Proctor played and critiqued before they built his custom guitar for him; a koa back and sides, spruce top K-12C with a sharp, Florentine cutaway and a 1 7/8 inches wide fretboard. Bob Taylor considers this to be the first official grand concert guitar.

The Blue Guitar and the Purple Guitar

The other special guitar that Taylor introduced at the 1984 NAMM Show was a maple dreadnought that Larry Breedlove stained with a translucent blue finish. The guitar was a special order for McCabe's Guitar Shop in Santa Monica, California, who wanted a guitar that had a striking visual appearance but wasn't covered in abalone trim, a look that was becoming something of a cliché.

Larry Breedlove had been taking graduate level courses in furniture design, including a class on advanced finishing techniques. "I had taken some workshops in surface decoration," Breedlove recalls. "Around the time the McCabe's custom order came in, I had taken a class on staining wood with watercolors. I did a couple of test samples on some maple scraps—the

Larry Breedlove at the Lemon Grove shop.

technique is most effective on blond wood like spruce and maple—and I showed them to Bob. He thought my samples looked good and he told me, 'Go for it!'"

The 1984 Winter NAMM Show was dominated by revolutionary synthesizers like Yamaha's digital DX-7, and the buzz about the new Musical Instrument Digital Interface (MIDI), that was announced the previous year. But even though the music industry was focused on digital instruments, Breedlove's blue guitar managed to create a major stir, perhaps the only acoustic guitar to do so that year. It wound up being pictured in all of the music trade magazines and was featured in consumer music publication like *Frets* and *Guitar Player*. But it almost didn't make it to the show. "I don't remember exactly what happened," Tim Luranc recalls. "But somehow we broke the top on it. We scrambled to fix it as quickly as possible and in the process developed the repair technique for replacing a top, which we still use."

Kurt Listug remembers thinking that Luranc's technique was very clever. "Tim took a laminate trimmer, which is basically a small, hand-held router, and he carefully cut the wooden top out while leaving the binding in place. Then he fitted a new top in place. It was a tricky operation, but it saved us from having to rebind the guitar, which would have meant refinishing the whole guitar."

Before long Taylor began to get requests for other colored guitars, including a very special one from Glenn Wetterlund who worked at Podium Music, a Taylor dealer in Minneapolis. At the time another Minneapolis music store was doing quite a bit of business with Prince, who had just had a massive hit with his movie Purple Rain and the accompanying LP of the same name. Prince was working on his next project and wanted to rent a jumbo 12-string guitar. The dealer Prince was working with didn't have a guitar he liked so they contacted Wetterlund and asked if they had something suitable they could rent. Wetterlund sent over a Taylor 555, which Prince wound up using in the sessions that produced the LP *Around the World in a Day*.

Wetterlund, who was anxious to get more business from Prince, suggested to Kurt Listug that Taylor make a purple jumbo 12-string on spec on the off chance that the star might buy it. "Kurt liked the idea a lot, so we basically cooked something up over the phone," Wetterlund recalls. "Taylor made a purple-stained guitar in a fairly short time. We sent it to Prince, who loved it. He subsequently used it on a couple of videos. I know that his guitarist, Wendy Melvoin, played it on 'Raspberry Beret'. I still think that was something of a watershed for Taylor."

The video for "Raspberry Beret" came out in early 1985 and immediately went into heavy rotation on MTV, which meant that the purple guitar was seen by millions of television viewers. Unfortunately, Prince refused to perform with instruments that had the maker's name on them, so his custom 12-string had no Taylor inlay on the headstock. But even that lack of advertising turned out to be a minor advantage as curious guitarists wrote to guitar magazines asking who made the mystery guitar.

"You know, Kurt and I sometimes get a bit indignant when people point to the Prince guitar as being the 'turning point' for us," Taylor says, "It's as if all of those years we struggled didn't really count and that we might not have made it without Prince's intervention." While Prince's use of the Taylor 12-string may have had only a small impact on

The purple jumbo that was made for Prince. Note the exaggerated soundhole flames that were hand painted by Larry Breedlove.

the company's fortunes, it did signal a change in the types of musicians who were playing acoustic guitars. "Until Prince came along, I think too many guitarists saw acoustic guitars as a folkie thing," Listug says. "Maybe it was some sort of reaction to the music of 1960s and early 1970s, but people just weren't buying acoustic guitars by the early 1980s. With the colored finishes, we made an acoustic that a hip electric guitarist wouldn't be embarrassed to play. The Artist Series just didn't have the same old, plain acoustic guitar look."

Taylor began to get so many custom orders for the colored finish guitars that in 1985 they were added to the line as the Artist Series and given an A prefix. The A-10's came in blue, a salmon colored red, a dark charcoal gray, and a natural finish version with an abalone rosette instead of Breedlove's hand-painted, multi colored flames. The Artist Series guitars also had a Breedlove-designed inlay pattern and new bridge shape that echoed the curves of the inlays. Breedlove applied the translucent colors over the maple and spruce guitars and painted on the multicolored flame rosettes by hand. "I had only planned to make the first blue one, but the style really seemed to catch on," Breedlove recalls. "It was a cool idea but it was a lot of bother to do. If I had known they were going to be so popular at first, I would have made the sound-hole design easier to do. As nice as they looked, I wasn't sorry when we stopped making them in 1989." Along with Prince, other famous musicians who bought Artists series guitars included Jeff Cook of Alabama, who had a green one, Dan Crary, who had a natural finish A-55 12-string, and Michael Hedges, who bought a blue A-10 on impulse but quickly traded it back in for a black one.

"I had only planned to make the first blue one, but the style really seemed to catch on."

The First Clinicians

Around that same time another excellent fingerpicker entered the Taylor orbit. His name was Harvey Reid, and like Chris Proctor, he had taken first prize in the National Fingerpicking Championship in Winfield, Kansas. "Harvey demonstrated our guitars when we first exhibited them at the Winter NAMM Show in Anaheim in 1984," Listug says. "Then, we built our 'sound booth' for the summer show in Chicago and Harvey and Chris came and were doing stuff together. We figured that you couldn't hear our guitars in that setting, anyway, so we might as well have someone demo our guitars through an amp. We had a little 10-by-10 booth and Harvey would play and we'd try to get people to stop and pay attention to our guitars."

< Three A-10s and a black A-15 jumbo are
photographed for the catalog.

Reid remembers playing Prince's purple 12-string at one of the NAMM Shows and drawing quite a crowd. "I noticed people stopped to listen to what I was doing when I played that guitar," he says. "They didn't do that when I played a plain brown guitar at previous NAMM Shows. So right after that I custom ordered a ruby red maple jumbo 12-string. Bob Taylor personally did the tree of life inlay in the fretboard and Jean Larrivée's wife Wendy did the inlay on the headstock. Larry Breedlove told me that he lost the formula for that particular shade of red and that he hasn't been able to duplicate it since."

Reid was attracted to Taylor guitars because of their playable necks and excellent intonation. "I liked Bob Taylor's philosophy that a guitar that plays well and plays in tune may be more valuable than one that just sounds good," Reid says. "I found I could play things on a Taylor that I couldn't play on other instruments. Larry Breedlove was hand-carving those necks, and I think he made some of the best necks I ever played."

Harvey Reid was among the first people outside of the Taylor work crew to witness first hand the major advantage of Bob Taylor's bolt-on neck design. After a couple of years of hard road use, Reid's custom 810c with a 1 7/8ths-inch wide fretboard needed a neck reset. On a guitar with a dovetail neck joint a neck reset is a major operation that requires steaming the joint to loosen the glue, a process that can damage the finish if it's not done carefully. After the neck is reset, it needs to be clamped in place for at least 24 hours, during which time, the neck can slip slightly, negating the entire operation. Taylor's new neck joint turned what was a major repair job that was done only if it was drastically needed into a minor tweak.

"I remember visiting the Taylor shop in Lemon Grove," Reid says. "Bob looked at my guitar and thought the neck angle could be a bit better. It was after hours so he ordered a pizza and he had the neck out and back in at the proper angle before the pizza arrived. I think the whole process took about 22 minutes. I knew then that this was the wave of the future and that before long more builders would come around to his way of thinking. Now everyone makes a well playing, well intonated guitar and I think we have Bob Taylor to thank for that."

Business started to pick up, but they weren't making enough money to launch a full-scale advertising campaign. Fortunately, Chris Proctor came up with an idea that would help get the word out about Taylor guitars for much less than the cost of a series of magazine ads. "Chris came to me with the idea of doing in-store workshops, which we would partially finance," Listug explains. "Chris was on the road a lot, and he was looking for something to do on the off days between gigs. He suggested that he could give a two or three hour clinic on fingerstyle guitar at a local Taylor dealer a day or two before his concert. I thought it was a good idea for everybody. Chris got paid for the workshop and was able to promote his gig; we got to have Chris, who is very articulate along with being an excellent guitarist out there demonstrating our guitars; and the store got a roomful of potential customers. That was the start of what has become our Taylor Clinicians program."

Proctor became something of an evangelist for the grand concert. "I had talked with Kurt and Bob before they made the smaller guitar," Proctor recalls. "I remember saying that this would be a viable guitar, and not just for me. I said there was no guitar out there for fingerstyle players; no guitar for people who play sitting down; no guitar for classical players who want a steel-string; no guitar for a woman who doesn't want to wrestle with a dreadnought or a jumbo. I became a spokesperson for Taylors in general and the grand concert model in particular."

Proctor and Reid soon began giving workshops and clinics at various Taylor dealers across the country. Reid, who lived in New Hampshire, covered the eastern part of the country and Proctor, who lived in Utah, covered the west. Over the years Taylor would add clinicians in a variety of styles, including bluegrass pickers like Beppe Gambetta, rockers like Laurence Juber, and folkies like Artie Traum.

Harvey Reid demonstrates an 810 at the 1985 Winter NAMM Show.

Bob Taylor was excited that players of Reid and Proctor's caliber were interested in playing the guitars he built. "I remember the Summer NAMM Show in Chicago, when Harvey was demo-ing our guitars," Taylor says. "He and Chris were there and we all went out to dinner one night. We're all walking down Lake Shore Drive, on the waterfront, and Chris and Harvey are cracking me up. The night before they had been out jamming, and here we were talking about guitar models, and I thought, 'Boy, I really like these guys. These are some of the first really good guitar players I've met, and I feel like I'm finally getting to players, instead of it being just me and Kurt and the dealers. These guys can actually play an acoustic guitar.'"

The Staff Begins to Grow

Sales started to increase, which meant that Taylor would have to expand their workforce. Bob Taylor had learned that hiring semi-trained woodworkers from the local high schools may not have cost as much as finding skilled craftsmen, but the young workers required too much super-

Bob Zink at his work bench around the time he joined Taylor.

vision to be really cost-effective. He had excellent luck with Tim Luranc and Larry Breedlove, both of whom had extensive experience as luthiers, so he began looking for potential workers with similar qualifications.

One of the people Taylor hired in 1984 was a local banjo maker named Bob Zink, who was co-owner of a combination folk music school/music store called the New Expression. Zink had once sold a banjo that Bob Taylor made, and the store was stocking Taylor guitars, so he was a familiar face. "Then, one day, I was out in El Cajon visiting the Deering shop," Zink recalls. "Bob Taylor was there, and he said, 'Let's go to lunch.' He told me all about his guitar shop in Lemon Grove, and I sort of off-the-cuff mentioned that I'd grown tired of being the New Expression's banjo maker, publicist, PR person, bookkeeper, and custodian all rolled into one, and of never having time for a vacation. I said if he ever had an opening to give me a call. He called me two weeks later saying he needed help sanding necks."

Zink spent the next few months sanding necks at Taylor from 4:30 in the morning until noon, and then heading over to the New Expression to work from one in the afternoon until seven in the evening. This schedule soon exhausted him and he decided to start working for Taylor

Tim Luranc and Steve Baldwin at the Lemon Grove shop not long after Baldwin joined the crew.

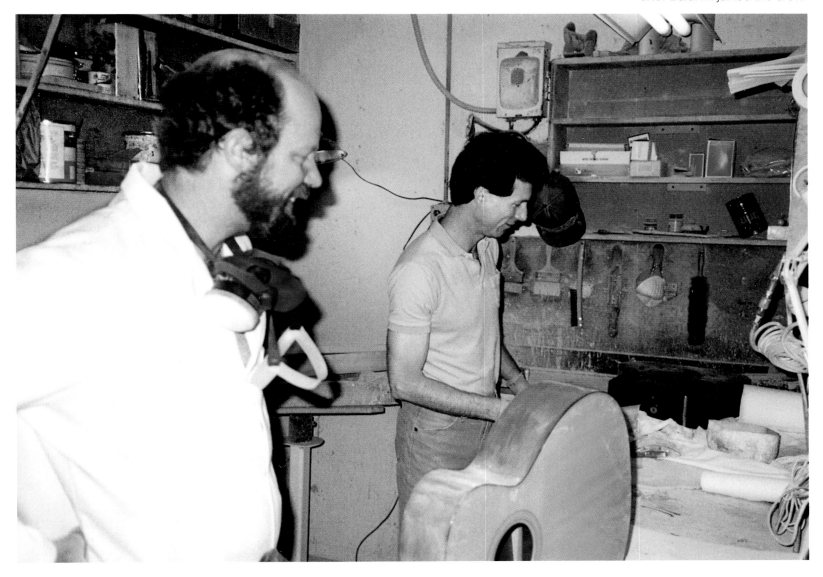

full-time. "Taylor seemed to have some potential," Zink says. "There were only a handful of us in those days. I was the 'body department', Steve Baldwin was the 'finish department' Tim Luranc was the 'string-up department', and Larry Breedlove was the 'neck department'."

The small crew was turning out high quality work, but the small Lemon Grove building was beginning to become a liability. "We had to fight swarms of termites," Zink recalls. "That's not a good thing for a place that makes solid-wood guitars. And the whole shop was about as big as the broom closet of our current plant, with no wall or ceiling insulation. The front of the building was a south-facing wall, which was great in the winter, because we'd have the benefits of natural sunlight. Summer was a different story. The sun started hitting us real early in the morning, and when we anticipated a real scorcher of a day, we would put a thermometer on the wall just to watch it rise. We had days when it topped out at 105 degrees. And that was indoors. Normally, we used water to moisten pieces of maple during the sanding process, but on those hot days, we didn't need a wet rag; we'd just lean over and drip perspiration onto the wood."

Taylor and Listug also knew that they had outgrown their tiny 1500 square foot facility. The guitar making tools had so completely filled the small shop that Listug had to rent a small 600 square foot office to conduct his part of the business. "There just wasn't any room in the workshop for storage," Taylor recalls. "I had to use the bathroom in Kurt's office to stack and dry the spruce blocks that we'd buy to make tops out of," he recalls. "I had to arrange all the machines so that you could open a door to feed wood in and out of them. If it was raining, we couldn't do some operations, because too much of the wood would be hanging out of the building while we worked on it. The 'spray booth' was a room with a hole in the wall and a 20-inch fan hung on a nail to exhaust the fumes. One time it fell, sparked, and the whole room burst into flames, all in about 10 seconds. Luckily, we had a sprinkler system that put it out, or we would have lost the business." Even with all of these problems the crew, which was now up to eleven, built 681 guitars in 1985.

Dan Crary

At the 1986 Winter NAMM Show Taylor and Listug introduced the Dan Crary Signature Model (DCSM), which was the first guitar added to the standard line that was designed for the playing style of a specific musician. Dan Crary was one of the leading lights in the progressive bluegrass movement, a group of musicians that included pickers like banjo players Bela Fleck and Tony Trishcka, mandolin players David Grisman and Sam Bush, fiddler Mark O'Connor, and guitarist Tony Rice.

Crary grew up in Kansas in the 1950s, where he started playing guitar in church. In he early 1960s he fell under the influence of the legendary guitar player Doc Watson, and devoted the next few years to emulating Watson's intricate flatpicking. In 1968 Crary co-founded a band called the Bluegrass Alliance and made two records with them. Crary's blazing single note picking with the Alliance helped liberate the guitar from its role as just the timekeeper in a bluegrass setting. Crary left the band to pursue dual careers as a solo guitarist and as an academic. (Crary later earned his Ph.D. in communications.)

Page from the 1986 catalog showing Dan Crary with his new Signature Model.

Taylor Guitars

Dan Crary
SIGNATURE
"My Taylor is Astonishing, Loud and Sweet"

◆ Special bracing
◆ Designed for acoustic lead work
◆ Vintage look
◆ Soft cutaway
◆ Loud, projecting tone

The Dan Crary Signature Model guitar was designed by Bob Taylor and Dan Crary from the "ground up" to meet the needs of flat-pickers, bluegrass players, and other acoustic soloists.
"In the past, you had to choose either a powerful bass or treble in an acoustic guitar," Dan says. "But my Taylor delivers consistent loudness across the tonal range, a loudness which is beautiful and penetrating, but not harsh."

We believe it is a new advance in the development of the steel-string guitar.
The bracing of this guitar has been completely redesigned and the top is thinner. The outcome of the new design is a louder, more responsive treble, and a more musical bass. Now the high mid-range overtones that should be part of the bass can be heard.
We devoted maximum attention to the appearance of Dan's guitar, combining modern features with the beauty of traditional design.

The golden top and white binding, along with the gold tuners and engraved snowflake position markers, help achieve an exquisite vintage feeling.
The soft cutaway allows easy playing in the high registers and the neck has the feel and playability that has made Taylor guitars famous.
Best of all, it sounds great!

Listug and Taylor first met Crary in the 1970s. "He was the most famous guitarist we had met up until that time," Listug says. "We were really nervous to be around him, but somehow we got up the courage to ask him if we could build a guitar for him. He was polite, but he said no, he was happy with his Mossman. But he did say he liked our 12-strings and he might like to get one someday." In the early 1980s Crary followed through on his statement and bought a custom maple A55 12-string, which he describes as possibly "the most incredible guitar I own."

Once again Bob Taylor offered to build a six-string for Crary, and this time he said yes. "I told Bob that I thought Taylors were great guitars, but that he tended to emphasize scalloped-braced six-strings, which were not the kind of guitars I played," Crary explains. "A scalloped-braced guitar is weighted toward the bass side, because when you scallop braces, you sacrifice some treble overtones. Now, over the years, Taylor guitars have gotten to the point where that trade-off is much less than it was, and certainly much less than the current industry standard. Still, if you take your average scalloped-braced guitar, and go to about F# on the first string, you'll notice the volume dropping off dramatically. And, if the volume's dropping off on the first string, so are treble overtones throughout the whole thing."

Bob Taylor took Crary's words to heart and he began to work on creating a guitar that would win Crary over from the Mossman Great Plains he had been playing for years. "A scalloped-braced guitar has a beautiful, rich sound when you're sitting with it in your lap," Crary says. "But microphones don't hear it the same way; the average dynamic microphone will turn that bass-heavy tone into distortion. A microphone likes a balanced tone, so you can get a lot of gain without distorting the EQ."

Taylor started with an 810 model and modified the scalloped braces to a taller, blade shaped brace. This increased the treble response and slightly attenuated the bass response, giving the guitar the more balanced sound Crary was seeking. The addition of a rounded cutaway so Crary could reach the high notes completed that package. Dan Crary was so pleased he allowed Taylor to put the guitar into production, making the first signature model in the line. "Now, I guarantee you that the Dan Crary Signature Model is a guitar that sound technicians -both studio people and stage people -absolutely love, " Crary says with pride. "They listen to it and say, 'Hey, this is great. I don't have to do this or that, because it sounds good even EQ'd flat.' We tried to create a guitar that was better for 'pros' to play."

That same year Taylor switched the back and sides of the 900 series from maple to Indian rosewood. More and more musicians were requesting a fancy rosewood guitar, so the move made economic sense. One of the first players to get a rosewood 900 was Chris Proctor, who supplied his own wood. "I had a few sets of Brazilian rosewood that I bought when I was working at the music store in Utah," he says. "I brought it to Bob who used it to make what I believe was one of the first rosewood 900 series guitars. It was a grand concert of course, and it had the floral inlays that Bob designed for his wife Cindy. It sounds beautiful, but I got scared traveling with it so I eventually retired it."

While Bob Taylor added new guitars like the DCSM to the line and tweaked existing models like the 900 series, Kurt Listug concentrated on selling the guitars to dealers. "I spent lots of time in the early 1980s on the road," Listug says. "By 1983 I had completely worn out my green Volvo. Since I was traveling so much, Bob and I decided that the company should buy my next car, so I got a two-year-old burgundy Volvo. I continued racking up the miles until the spring of 1985,

Dan Crary Signature Model from around 1992.

when I found that being on the road was just taking up too much time to be cost effective. I had opened a lot dealers by this time and I felt that I could continue to maintain those relationships by phone."

Business was picking up, but the lack of money continued to be a problem. "We still paid ourselves each week," Listug says, "but we couldn't always cash the checks. Sometimes I'd have four or five uncashed paychecks in my wallet. In 1986 I just got tired of it and decided I would really have to figure out how to increase the sales of guitars to dealers over the phone."

Listug used to maintain the list of pending orders on a large white board on a wall in the shop. If a store ordered a particular guitar it went on the board in black ink. If the Taylor crew was making a guitar for stock, hoping they could sell it when it was finished, it went on the board in red. Listug was pre-selling a fair number of guitars, but most of the entries on the board were in red.

Bob Taylor remembers when Listug began to turn things around. "One day, Kurt just seemed to turn on his 'sell the guitars' switch," he says. "It was as if one day he just thought, 'I wonder how many of these things I could sell, anyway?'"

"Every couple of hours, Kurt would walk into the shop, take his thumb and erase a red entry, and replace it with black, then disappear back into his room."

"It just had to be done," Kurt explains. "I had to figure out how to do it somehow, even though it was so hard, because we were all doing so many things. I had only a couple of hours a day to talk to our dealers. Somehow, though, I managed to get on the phone, push through, and get stuff sold. Before long our guitars were back-ordered, which meant that dealers who used to call and order instruments only when they had sold one, now had to start scheduling their next few orders over the coming months. This helped Bob and the other builders because they knew what they would be making in the immediate future."

After struggling for more than a dozen years, Bob Taylor and Kurt Listug finally discovered the balance of labor that would make their company successful. Chris Proctor described the dynamic between Taylor and Listug by saying; "Bob wakes up in the morning and wants to make the guitars better. Kurt wakes up and wants to make the company better."

While that is a good description of how the two men work together, it glosses over the fact Taylor is an astute businessman himself. His drive to make guitars as quickly and as efficiently as possible is partly mechanical perfectionism, but he also knows that wasted wood and lost time are unprofitable. Listug, for his part, spent years making guitar bodies, sanding necks, and finishing the instruments. He probably has more hands-on guitar making experience than any other executive in the guitar industry and because of that, he understands why investing in expensive but time-saving machinery is actually a smarter business move in the long run than hiring a few more workers.

Bob Taylor looks back on that moment when Listug started seriously selling guitars as the moment when the business finally turned the corner. "Every couple of hours, Kurt would walk into the shop, take his thumb and erase a red entry, and replace it with black, then disappear back into his room," Taylor recalls. "Everyone in the shop was like, 'Dude!' Slowly, the whole board transitioned from all 'red-ink' guitars to all 'black-ink' guitars. Our lives were never the same after that. Although there were a couple of really tough times to come, we were getting paid, our employees were getting paid, and we were doing well. We never went back to those bad old days."

Time to Move

Taylor and Listug soon found that success brought its own set of problems. The Lemon Grove shop had always been cramped, but now that they were producing 22 guitars a week, it was just getting too difficult to work there. "We had 13 people working there and that little building was just filled to bursting with wood, tools, cases, and people," Taylor says. "But we didn't move until we really needed to. We'd wanted to move as early as 1981-82, and we actually looked at a few locations, but then we thought about the list of bills we couldn't pay and quickly got back to reality."

Kurt checking out the worksite where the new Santee factory was being built.

Kurt at the new Santee
plant in a familiar pose.

In late 1986 they finally made the decision to move and they broke ground on a new building in the nearby town of Santee. The new factory was 4700 square feet, more than twice as large as the old shop with its office annex. Before they made the move though, there were still a few minor details to work out with the guitars. In February 1987, Bob Taylor decided to make all of the bridges and fretboards on the guitars out of ebony, rather than using the less expensive rosewood on the lower-end models and ebony on the higher end models. Rosewood is more resinous wood than ebony and it had a tendency to clog the saw blades when cutting frets. Bob Taylor felt that the slightly higher materials cost was more than offset by not having to stop and clean the fret saws every time they cut a rosewood fretboard.

Finally, in May 1987, they moved into their new building. "We left Lemon Grove with 13 people on the payroll, and we were able to make the transition without a loss in production," Bob Taylor says. "We did this by building all new benches and equipment for the Finish, Final Assembly, and Shipping departments in the new building. Then over the course of one weekend we moved those departments along with the offices. For the next two weeks we operated from two buildings, making the bodies and necks in the old Lemon Grove digs, and bringing them over at the end of each day to continue production. During that two week period, we got ourselves organized and did a weekend move for the rest of the shop." The last guitar made in Lemon Grove was a 510c, serial number 5300. The Taylor crew built it in the old building, but transported it to Santee to string it up.

"We left Lemon Grove with 13 people, just busting with success," Listug says. "It was the most success we'd ever had. After 12 years in that building, 10 years of which were nothing but bad news, it was pretty exciting when that last year turned out to be much better. The difference was so great, that when we finally moved in the Santee building, it was like our lives began again."

Once they moved into the building, Kurt Listug got a bit over-eager and pressed Bob to increase production too rapidly. They hired more workers and quickly increased production from four guitars a day, to six and then eight guitars a day. Listug was an excellent salesman, and even though there were a lot of back-ordered guitars, there weren't enough orders to justify doubling production. Listug and Taylor cut back to building six guitars a day and even though they decreased production, they managed not to lay-off any of the employees as they had in the past. Most of 1987 was spent getting used to the new facility, but at the end of the year the workforce of 18 still managed to build a record 1202 guitars.

Terry Myers (left) backstage with Bonnie Raitt.

Kurt Listug congratulates T.J. Baden on making Guitar Showcase Taylor's largest dealer in 1984.

As 1988 began Bob Taylor hired Terry Myers, who began to work in the final assembly department. Myers had an eye for detail and a perfectionist streak and was soon responsible for the final inspection of guitars, a job that Bob Taylor had previously reserved for himself. Bob Taylor had begun to step back and let his workers take even more responsibility. Myers also proved to have a knack for streamlining various jobs around the new factory, and his new techniques cut the time it took to do certain tasks in half.

Myers soon found out that now that he had more authority, Bob Taylor expected him to be ruthless in eliminating inefficiency. "I started a whole new sanding method for straightening fingerboards when I arrived that gave us results we hadn't gotten previously," Myers remembers. "But it was labor-intensive and hard to train people to do it. At one point, we started using a fretboard sanding machine that was just an overgrown vertical belt sander with a motor at the bottom. As Bob later said, we were trying to straighten an already radiused, planed fingerboard from the shaper, rather than just round it and plane it all at one time with the sander. After many attempts to use the thing, it just wouldn't work right, and one day Bob just pitched it in the Dumpster. I didn't know Bob well enough yet to say, 'You must be nuts,' which is what I was thinking. But that forced us to find a better way to sand fretboards."

The business was growing so quickly that Kurt Listug also felt he needed to hand over some of his duties as well. "I thought I'd continue to sell guitars indefinitely, because I liked doing it and I liked the dealer relationships," Kurt remembers. "I thought, 'How can I ever delegate that?' But suddenly, it became really clear that this business couldn't grow unless I began to devote my time solely to management and marketing. I knew I couldn't sell more guitars without neglecting my other duties. So one day, Bob asked me, 'Who could we hire?'"

Listug remembered a young salesman named T.J. Baden who worked at a store in Northern California called Guitar Showcase. When Baden started at the store, they were a strong, but not spectacular dealer for Taylor. Baden fell in love with Taylor guitars and in the next few years he turned Guitar Showcase into one of Taylor's most successful dealers. Listug called Baden to feel him out about the possibility of moving south and joining the Taylor team. It turned out Baden was about to get married and was thinking seriously about his future. Baden felt that working for Kurt and Bob was a great opportunity. So he and his new bride moved down to San Diego and he became the company's first official sales representative.

Baden used the expertise he gained in his years at Guitar Showcase to help him educate dealers about Taylor guitars and to help them sell the instruments to customers. When Baden started at Taylor, many of their dealers sold more solid-body electrics that flattop steel-strings and the sales staffs at the stores were not that familiar with acoustic guitars. Thanks to Baden's efforts, the better informed store employees began to sell more Taylor guitars and by the end of 1988 the company sold 1,849 guitars and racked up over a million dollars in sales for the first time. Over the years Baden's duties began to include more than just selling guitars. He got more involved with artist relations and has become the driving force behind many of the successful signature models Taylor has produced.

The musical culture was undergoing one of its periodic shifts. In 1980 acoustic guitars were seen as hopelessly old-fashioned. Now, in 1989 they were once again cool. After a period of flirting with mainstream pop, country music was in the throes of a traditionalist revival. Singers like Randy Travis, Lyle Lovett, and Dwight Yoakum were scoring hits and posing on their album covers clutching acoustic guitars. Rootsy rockers like Tom Petty, John Mellencamp, and Bruce Springsteen included acoustic tracks on their records. Even heavy metal bands began to include acoustic sets at their concerts. On November 26 1989, the acoustic guitar revival became official when MTV aired the first episode of *Unplugged*, a show where popular musicians performed acoustic versions of their hit songs.

An 812c rests in the elegant new Taylor case.

The Best Case Scenario

Taylor had survived the worst period in history for the acoustic guitar, and now that things were about to get really crazy, they found that were having trouble shipping guitars for a reason they had no control over. Taylor was having trouble getting enough cases for the guitars they were building. "Often we would have over 100 guitars in stock waiting for cases to arrive," Taylor recalls. "That is a lot of guitars, representing a lot of needed income at a time when the production was only about 30 guitars per week. The cases would arrive and the quality would be sub-par, but we'd use them anyway because we had to ship guitars or go broke."

Bob Taylor approached the problem in typical fashion. "I set a goal of making our own cases when our production rose to 10 guitars a day," he says. "It did, and so we did. We started the case factory because being dependent upon suppliers was hampering our growth, our cash flow, and the quality of our presentation."

Cases had always been a problem for Taylor. The shape of their dreadnoughts and grand concerts were subtly different from Martins, Gibsons, and Guilds, and practically all of the cases manufactured in the US were designed to fit one of those three brands. In August 1989, Bob

Taylor's first Fadal.

"I came back and told Kurt, 'That's our future, find the money.' That was in November, and by the time we went on Christmas vacation our first machine was on order and financing was approved."

Taylor began making cases that fit his guitars perfectly. The shell was a five-ply poplar laminate and the covering was a dark brown tolex with a maroon velvet interior. Now that they could make their own cases, the shipping bottleneck opened, and the dealers began to get their guitars in a timelier fashion.

As the year and the decade drew to a close, Bob Taylor discovered a tool that would completely change the way he built guitars. It was called a computer numeric controlled milling machine (CNC) and it was built by a company called Fadal. "The Fadal came to our attention when Tom Anderson, of Tom Anderson Guitarworks, wanted to see our factory," Bob recalls. "I'd met Tom at a trade show, and he said he'd 'heard about the great Taylor Guitars.' He came down with a couple of his guys, and I showed them around our factory. When we came to our fret cutting gang saw, Andersen says, 'That's a pretty neat machine.' I asked him how he cut frets, and he says he said he used a computerized mill. Now, I'd heard about CNC equipment a little bit, and I said, 'Folks, the show's over. We're going to your place!' Within three days, I was up at Andersen's shop looking at his Fadal, which he'd learned about through his friendship and working relationship with Dave Schecter of Schecter Guitar Research. Dave had sold that company to a Japanese firm, and had gone to work for Fadal. One day, Dave called Tom to tell him about Fadal's machines. Tom took one look at the machine and knew he could use it to make guitars; he was the first person to use a CNC milling machine to make his electric guitars. I'm often credited with introducing that technology to acoustic guitar making, but Tom Andersen was the real CNC pioneer in the guitar world.

"I came back and told Kurt, 'That's our future, find the money.' That was in November, and by the time we went on Christmas vacation our first machine was on order and financing was approved. It was delivered over vacation, and we started using it in January. We started 1990 with a brand new machine that we had to learn how to use."

"One of the things that sold me on the idea of working with Bob and trying this 12-string was that Bob is the first person I'd run into who can talk as long as I can about guitars." Leo Kottke

New Ways of Building Guitars

The Fadal. The Leo Kottke Signature Model. The acoustic guitar business rebounds. The 410 breaks the $1000 barrier. Kurt Listug redefines the guitar advertisement. Time to move to a bigger building, again. UV finish. The Acoustic Bass.

Brave New World of Guitar Building

When Bob Taylor and Kurt Listug took delivery of their first Fadal, they had no idea they were about to change the way acoustic guitars were made in America. In 1990 people built guitars in pretty much the same way they did a century earlier. The rough shaping of components like bridges and necks may have been done on power tools, but the final shaping and finishing was still done using hand tools like draw knives and spoke-shaves. Tops, backs and sides were sanded by hand, braces were carved by hand, and fretboard inlays were cut by hand. A luthier magically transported from 1890 to the 1990 shop floor of Martin, Gibson, or Taylor would have easily recognized that the various power tools like saws, drills, and lathes were just electric versions of the familiar tools he used everyday. But the Fadal would have been completely alien to him.

The Fadal was a computer controlled vertical milling machine that was capable of carving complex parts with an extremely high degree of precision. Unlike a standard power tool such as a drill press or a shaper, which required a human operator, a Fadal did its work essentially unattended. (Fadal was the brand name for what is generically known as a computer numeric control (CNC) machine.) Basically a worker would place a piece of wood in the machine, make sure it had the proper cutting heads installed, and call up a particular program on the computer. Then the Fadal would proceed to cut perfect bridges, accurately slotted fretboards, or whatever other parts the machine was programmed to make.

At least that's how a Fadal worked in theory. Bob Taylor quickly discovered the truth behind the old computer programmer's axiom: a computer does what you tell it to do, not what you want it to do. The Fadal was capable of doing any number of wonderful things; he just had to learn to program it to do those wonderful things. The Fadal was controlled by a program called Mastercam, which consisted of two parts. The first was a 3-D graphics application known as a computer aided design or CAD program. The second was an application that translated the CAD graphic into a series of instructions for the Fadal to execute. This program was known as a computer assisted manufacture, or CAM program.

Bob Taylor began to devote most of his evenings to teaching himself how to program his new machine. "After everyone went home, I would sit down and write and draw something, and then run the program on the Fadal to see if the part came out the way I imagined it would," he says. "As I did this, I'd play Nanci Griffith's *Storms* CD, over and over and over, like a thousand times. Every time I hear that CD, it takes me back to the time when I was learning CAD

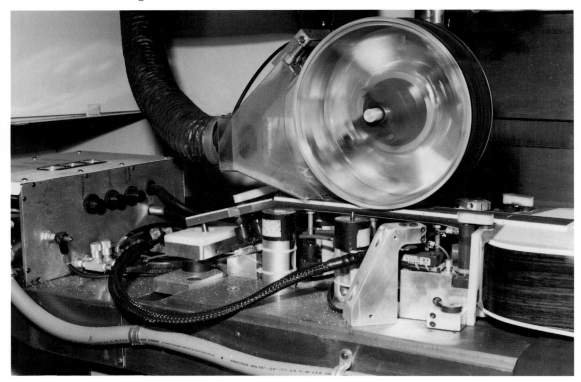

The new Fadal sanding a neck on an 810.

work on Mastercam. When I got my first version of the program it didn't even have an instruction manual, you just turned on the program and figured it out."

Matt Guzzetta Joins the Crew

The Fadal was still an exotic machine at the time and before long local luthiers and machinists began to stop by the Taylor shop to see how it worked. One of the first visitors was Matt Guzzetta, who used to work for Don Vesco Products, a company that manufactured motorcycle gas tanks in a shop a couple of doors down from the old American Dream workshop in Lemon Grove. (Don Vesco was a motorcycle racer who held the motorcycle speed record in the 1960s and early 1970s.) In 1984 Guzzetta designed a motorcycle that was so aerodynamically efficient he was able to cross America from California to Florida on a single tank of gas. In the late 1980s he dropped out of the motorcycle business to devote his time to building a new long bow he had invented. Bob Taylor and Matt Guzzetta became friends in the early Dream days, back when Taylor divided his time between motorcycles, scuba diving, and guitar making.

Matt Guzzetta hard at work rewiring the Fadal to sand necks.

Guzzetta remembers the parties that Sam Radding used to hold on the weekends and how things changed when Taylor, Listug, and Schemmer bought the American Dream. "We'd have maybe four local bands going at these parties," Guzzetta says. "If you ask me, Bob and Kurt ruined everything when they bought the business and the parties stopped. After that, it was all downhill as far as I was concerned."

In 1976 Guzzetta decided to move his shop. Bob Taylor mentioned in passing that he was looking for a spray booth. Guzzetta didn't need his old spray booth, and since Taylor didn't have enough money to buy it, they worked out a trade. Even though Guzzetta didn't play gui-

Matt Guzzetta standing in front of the Fadal.

tar, he accepted an 815 rosewood jumbo in exchange for his booth. Because the guitar was never really played it is still in almost perfect condition, making it the cleanest early Taylor in existence. "A few years ago, I brought that guitar into the Taylor shop to have the guys work on it," Guzzetta says. "Bob intercepted it. 'Nobody's going to work on this guitar,' he said. 'It's one of the rarest Taylors out there, and should stay just the way it is.'" Bob Taylor thinks that Guzzetta took him too literally. "To this day, it has the original strings on it," he says.

Matt Guzzetta initially stopped by the Taylor factory to see the Fadal and to make a few small parts for his longbow project. Bob Taylor realized that Matt Guzzetta had a profound knowledge of machining and would be a valuable addition to the growing workforce, but Guzzetta wasn't really interested in working at Taylor. So Bob Taylor came up with a plan to ease Guzzetta into a job. He'd hire the machinist to work on a small project every now and then. "I worked a couple of hours a day at first," Guzzetta says. "Then four hours, and so on." After a couple of years Guzzetta found himself working full time. Guzzetta eventually became the senior tool and machine designer and proved to be invaluable as Taylor began to increase production.

The first guitar component Bob Taylor was able to produce on the Fadal was a new bridge. The shape was based on the design Larry Breedlove created for the multi-colored Artist Series guitars. Most of the workers, including Bob Taylor felt the Artists Series guitars sounded fuller and had more sustain than the standard line. At first they attributed the sound difference to the maple necks on the Artist Series, but after some experimentation they discovered the slightly larger Breedlove design made guitars with mahogany necks sound better as well. So Taylor started using the new CNC carved bridges on the entire line.

At the same time they used the Fadal's arrival as the excuse to discontinue the hand carved moustache bridge on the jumbo guitars. The fancy bridge was always popular with customers, but the Taylor crew hated carving them. They took too long to make and it was impossible to make each one exactly the same shape, which made replacing them under warranty a nightmare.

Leo Kottke

That same year, Taylor introduced the 12-string Leo Kottke Signature Model (LKSM). As with the Dan Crary Signature Model, Bob Taylor designed the LKSM by working closely with the artist. Leo Kottke first entered the guitar world in 1969 when he released *6 and 12 String Guitar*, a brilliant album of acoustic guitar instrumentals. Over the next decade he toured extensively and released albums such as *Mudlark*, *Ice Water*, and *Guitar Music* that stretched the boundaries of acoustic guitar. By the early 1980s the combination of his relentless touring schedule and extremely dynamic right hand picking technique damaged Kottke's arm and wrist. He spent the next few years completely revising his picking technique. Unfortunately, the neck on his Gibson B-45 12-string proved to be too uncomfortable, so he had to give up playing 12-string altogether.

Then in the late 1980s he was performing in Clearwater, Florida, where a friend named Ken Spooner who owned a music store brought a new Taylor 555 mahogany jumbo 12-string by Kottke's hotel room. He discovered that the slender, well-shaped neck didn't exacerbate his

Page from the Taylor catalog announcing the introduction of the Leo Kottke Signature Model.

sore hands, so he bought the guitar. "I did what I frequently do with a 12-string," Kottke recalls. "I took out my pocket knife and started carving on the braces. I didn't do much of that, because I had learned by then that most of that impulse is pathology on my part."

Bob Taylor was excited to discover that it was his guitar that got Kottke playing 12-string again. He was also intrigued to hear that Kottke had modified the braces as well. The luthier got in touch with the musician and proposed that they work together on designing the ultimate 12-string. They started with the mahogany jumbo shape, and went from there. "The bulk of the experimentation had to do with the bracing," Kottke recalls. "I essentially wanted less wood than is common on a 12-string, and I also wanted it built to be tuned down, instead of up to pitch. I don't think a 12-string makes sense tuned to pitch. If you want that, I think you should play a mandolin. I think the real virtue of the 12-string is that it can just explode out of the bottom. So, that's what we aimed for."

Over the next couple of years Bob Taylor would make a guitar, send it to Kottke, who, after trying it for a few months, would offer his comments. Taylor made guitars with tops of Engelmann spruce or Sitka spruce and the back and sides made of Honduran mahogany or African mahogany. "Bob did what he said he'd do," Kottke says. "He built me a guitar I wanted. You know, one of the things that sold me on the idea of working with Bob and trying this 12-string was that Bob is the first person I'd run into who can talk as long as I can about guitars."

The final version of the Leo Kottke Signature Model had Central American mahogany back and sides, a Sitka spruce top, and an ebony fretboard with no fret markers except for the words "Leo Kottke" inlaid at the 17th fret. The binding was rosewood, which gave the guitar an austere but elegant look. Rather than use a sharp Florentine or a rounded Venetian cutaway, the LKSM had a flat cutaway similar to the one used on the French built Selmer guitars. The LKSM was designed to be strung up with heavy strings and tuned down to C-sharp.

Taylor's two new signature models, the Dan Crary and the Leo Kottke, were not designed to be sold to the mainstream acoustic guitarist. Instead, they were built to appeal to tiny, but influential, niches in the guitar world. But Taylor's next guitar was aimed directly at the heart of the acoustic guitar market. By the early 1990s practically every guitar in America that sold for under $1000 was made overseas.

Japanese guitar makers like Yamaha, Yairi, and Takamine and European builders like Levin, which were sold under the Goya name, and EKO had started producing inexpensive guitars of surprisingly high quality in the early 1960s. These instruments were imported in huge numbers during the 1960s and they usually played and sounded better, and cost less than the guitars made by the American companies that made cheap instruments such as Harmony, Kay, and Regal. By the mid 1970s all of the American firms that made lower end instruments had gone out of business.

Over the next couple of decades, as the value of international currencies began to rise in relation to the dollar, the prices of the Japanese and European instruments began

The guitar that got Leo Kottke playing the 12-string again.

to go up. By the end of the 1980s most distributors had stopped exporting European guitars to the US while the prices of the higher end Japanese guitars were about the same as the lower end Taylors, Martins, and Guilds. Kurt Listug and Bob Taylor saw this situation as an opportunity to expand their line in a new direction. Up until now Taylor had been competing with venerable but high-end guitar companies like Martin, Guild, and Gibson as well as with smaller companies like Gallagher and Mossman. Now Listug and Taylor realized that they could successfully compete against the Japanese builders on the lower-end of the price scale as well. Bob Taylor and his crew set about designing a new model that would take advantage of the new CNC technology, and at the Winter NAMM Show in 1991 they showed the fruit of their labors to the world.

410 model and hard shell case

❖ Solid wood construction

❖ Satin finish

❖ Custom case included

The 410 makes it easier to own a high quality acoustic guitar. Many companies bring in inexpensive imports when adding a lower priced guitar to their lines. But, the 410 is made right here in the Taylor factory, with the same high quality you'd expect from Taylor.

The 410 body is made of rich mahogany with a spruce top. The hand-rubbed satin finish enhances its natural beauty.

The sound is loud and well balanced from top to bottom, typical of all Taylor guitars. The neck is sleek and easy to play.

Advanced technology, new design features, streamlined production and eliminating costly options have made it possible for Taylor to make such a great guitar for such a great price.

And the 410 comes with a custom-shaped hard shell case, which Taylor makes in their own case factory.

Now you can own an American made solid wood guitar for the same price you'd pay for an import brand made of wood laminates.

Play a 410 today. It's the best value in American made acoustics. And it's a Taylor.

Page from the 1992 catalog announcing the introduction of the 410.

"Bob Taylor talked for quite a while about how he programmed his Fadal and how he was using it to make more precise parts."

The 410

When Taylor introduced the 410 with its $998 list price in 1991, there wasn't an American built, all-solid wood steel string guitar that had a list price of less than $1000. Martin's least expensive model, the D-16, had a list price of $1330, Guild's D-25 listed for $1100, and Taylor's own 510 listed for $1156. Taylor got the 410's price down by using CNC milled parts and ruthlessly stripping every non-essential cosmetic feature off the instrument.

The first version of the 410 had mahogany back and sides, and a spruce top. The fretboard and bridge were made of ebony, which was rare on inexpensive guitars. (Most lower end guitars had rosewood fretboards and bridges, which cost less, but didn't wear as well as ebony.) The bridge was an unusual pinless design, where the strings fed in through the back of the bridge, rather than through holes drilled into the top. The pinless bridge design required fewer steps to install than the traditional pin bridge, which saved on labor costs, and the lack of pins saved a few dollars in parts costs.

The 410 was finished in a non-gloss satin finish. Using a satin finish meant that Taylor could cut out the entire final polishing stage, which was a huge time saver. They even managed to save a bit of money by cutting the headstock logo inlay out of plastic instead of pearl. The 400 Series also got a unique serial number sequence. The new number began with the numeral 4 and was followed by a four digit number. The first 410 was serial number 4-0001.

As expected the 410 was an immediate success. One of the persistent problems from the early days was that the Taylor crew was always making more guitars than they could sell. Now they found that they had to add a second shift to meet the demand for the new model. By the end of the year the 400 series was expanded to include the grand concert 412 and the acoustic-electric 410e. They also made a short run of 400s out of rosewood, which they called the 410SE, for Special Edition. (This model was later renamed the 420.) The final 400 made in 1991 was serial number 4-1132, which meant that the new series made up a significant portion of the 4,800 guitars that Taylor made that year.

The large guitar builders immediately recognized that CNC technology was the wave of the future, but the smaller companies and independent luthiers were still skeptical. Many builders sniffed that Taylors were now being made by robots and that the CNC machines weren't capable of making a guitar with a "soul." Bob Taylor began to change people's minds with the lecture he gave on how he used the new technology at the convention of the Association of Stringed Instrument Artisans (ASIA) at Lafayette College in Easton, Pennsylvania. The ASIA convention is held every two years and features workshops and lectures on building techniques, an instrument exhibit, and the chance for hundreds of luthiers to schmooze with one another.

Among the attendees that year was Richard Johnston, the co-owner of Gryphon Stringed Instruments, which started carrying Taylor guitars in the mid 1980s. Johnston was an expert on American guitars and a former luthier himself. He attended Bob Taylor's lecture, which he remembers as being in a hall packed with people. "Bob Taylor talked for quite a while about how he programmed his Fadal and how he was using it to make more precise parts," Johnston says. "I had made about forty guitars with my partner Frank Ford in the late 1960s and early 1970s and I remember how long it took to do things like make bridges and carve necks. The work was also repetitive and took a fair degree of skill to well. Once you decided on a basic design, there really was no reason not to cut them out on something like a CNC machine.

"I remember when Bob was taking questions at the end of his lecture and a machinist stood up and said that if Bob switched to another cutting head he would be able to carve a neck in less than half the time. Bob's answer was that he wasn't after speed, but precision. He said that carving necks at a higher speed tended to leave tool marks that had to be sanded out and that the cutting head was more likely to catch on a small imperfection in the wood and tear out a chunk and ruin the neck. Bob also mentioned that the Fadal was so precise that there was very little waste wood left over."

Johnston visited the Taylor factory a few weeks later and was surprised to find that it took so long to carve the necks on the CNC machines that they were loaded up with wood blanks at the end of the day. Then, while the factory was deserted, the machines spent most of the night carving the necks for the next day's production. Before long other luthiers began to make the trek to Santee to see how the CNC machines worked. Even though many of these builders were his direct competitors, Bob Taylor happily told them everything he had learned. "I always remembered how helpful and open Sam Radding had been when I was starting out," Taylor says. "And Jean Larrivée and Augie LoPrinzi were really helpful to me as well. Since then I've felt that I should be as free with my knowledge as those builders were with theirs."

Time to Move Yet Again

The success of the 400 series, combined with a general revival of the acoustic guitar in popular music meant that Taylor was making so many guitars that they were quickly outgrowing their building in Santee. Bob Taylor and Kurt Listug began scouting for a location for their new factory, and Bob Taylor began designing the facility with his computer drafting program. He spent countless hours working out how the guitars in progress would most efficiently flow from one department to the next. He decided what the floor plan was going to be, where every machine was going to go, and where each builder's workstation was going to be. "I designed the entire building," Taylor says. "Every electrical drop, every air compressor outlet, even the size of every office and the width of the doors."

Bob Taylor, Kurt Listug and their employees spent the first months of 1992 preparing to move into the new factory. He and Listug had settled on a location in the nearby town of El Cajon. Because they outgrew the Santee location so quickly, Listug and Taylor decided they would build a facility they could grow into. At 1500 square feet, the first shop in Lemon Grove was almost too small to be called a factory. The second Taylor factory in Santee was 4700 square feet, which later expanded by another 2500 square feet. The addition of the separate 2500 square foot case factory gave Taylor 9700 square feet of factory space by the end of 1991. The new building in El Cajon was going be more than two and a half times larger than that and measured in at 25,000 square feet.

Because of the massive effort required to get the new facility ready, Bob Taylor put all of his other projects on hold and spent most of his time overseeing the construction of the new facility. But even though he was putting in long hours day and night, he still found time for

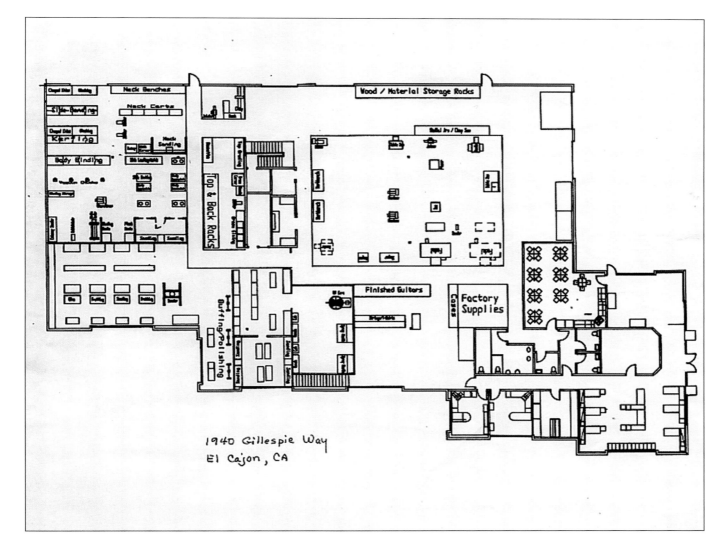

The blueprints Bob Taylor drew for the new building on 1940 Gillespie Way in El Cajon.

his family. Bob Taylor's daughter Minét recalls him taking her and her sister Natalie to the El Cajon factory while it was being built. "It was a big empty building, but to me it looked like a roller rink," she says. "I skated there for hours. Natalie and I even brought our bikes occasionally. We'd take turns pushing each other on the flat-bed dollies, and sometimes dad would even lift us high into the air on the forklifts."

Bob Taylor and Kurt Listug had picked exactly the right moment to expand production, as the acoustic guitar was about to undergo an amazing revival of popularity. Singer/songwriters had come back into fashion and new performers like Mary Chapin Carpenter, the Indigo Girls, and Nanci Griffith were selling records by the truckload. Older performers like James Taylor were also getting airplay again. There were major music festivals across the country devoted to formerly niche styles like blues and bluegrass. Players like Michael Hedges, Leo Kottke, and Pierre Bensusan were redefining what was possible to play on an acoustic guitar. There was even a new magazine devoted to the instrument, which of course was called *Acoustic Guitar*.

But the event that really marked the acoustic guitar's return was Eric Clapton's appearance on the *MTV Unplugged* television show on March 11, 1992. *Unplugged* had been on the air since 1990 and had featured an eclectic mix of players including Paul McCartney, Elton John,

Kurt Listug and Bob Taylor posing for a photo that was used in the 1993 catalog.

REM, Ratt, Vixen, Sinead O'Connor, and Crosby, Stills and Nash. Most of the shows had a loose, improvised feel, with plenty of flubbed notes and lots of laughter. But Eric Clapton approached his appearance with surprising seriousness. Although he was regarded as one of England's premier guitarists in the 1960s and 1970s, his 1980s output received increasingly lukewarm reviews. When his record company released the four-CD retrospective *Cross-roads* in 1988, they were essentially admitting they felt his best work was behind him. In 1990, Clapton's life took a tragic turn when his young son Conor was killed when he fell out of a window. Clapton, with Will Jennings, had written a moving song about the incident called "Tears in Heaven," which had appeared on the soundtrack for the movie *Rush*.

When Clapton appeared on *Unplugged* he played a combination of classic blues songs like Robert Johnson's "Malted Milk" and Big Bill Broonzy's "Hey Hey" along with some of his own compositions such a "Layla'" and "Tears in Heaven." The arrangements were stripped down to the bare minimum and he played with a passion and dignity that equaled and even surpassed his finest work in previous years. The show was an instant hit and when the CD of the concert was released a few months later, it sold millions of copies and earned a Grammy award for "Tears in Heaven." Clapton's *Unplugged* show didn't start the acoustic guitar revival, but it did turn it into a cultural phenomenon that reached beyond the guitar world. Artists saw how the show and CD had given Clapton's flagging career a boost and record executives saw how many units were sold. Before long practically every musician in the business was lining up to appear on *Unplugged*, and the guitar stores were full of players looking for acoustic guitars of their own.

Since handing over the job of selling guitars to T.J. Baden, Kurt Listug had essentially disappeared from the public eye. Kurt went to all of the trade shows along with his partner, but since Bob Taylor's name was on the headstock, Bob was the one people sought out. But even though Listug was something of an invisible man as far as the public was concerned, Bob Taylor considers him the reason the company was so successful. After all, Listug was the one who kept the company running smoothly, paid the bills, and made it possible for Bob Taylor to devote his time to designing guitars and the machines to build them.

Kurt's New Ad Campaign

Kurt Listug realized that he was going to have to come up with a way of letting the potential customers streaming into stores to buy the now trendy acoustic guitars know that Taylor guitars were different from the rest. He had already created a series of ads that extolled the features and benefits of Taylor guitars, but as good as the ads were, they didn't really differ that much from the ads of other builders at the time.

Guitar advertisements were still quite primitive in the early 1990s, and most could have run without change twenty years earlier. For the most part ads fell into one of three different categories: The Beauty Shot, The Celebrity Shot, and the Cheesecake Shot. The Beauty Shot basically consisted of a nice photograph of the guitar in question with a block of text that invariably described how the instrument was handcrafted to exacting standards from rare tonewoods by skilled artisans. The Celebrity Shot featured a famous musician holding a guitar with a quote about how this was the best instrument they had ever played. The Cheesecake Shot showed a scantily clad woman clutching a guitar, which was almost always an electric solid body, in a manner that suggested she was more interested in going out on a date with it than she was in playing a song on it.

Listug felt that one of the main problems with trying to advertise acoustic guitars was that even though they all have unique tones and varying degrees of playability, they tend to resemble one another in photographs. If it was well photographed, an inexpensive plywood guitar looked pretty much like the most expensive individually crafted instrument. Listug realized that he would have to come up with a way of creating awareness of the Taylor brand among

One of the *Trees* ads.

IN ITS SIMPLEST FORM, A GUITAR IS JUST A HOLLOW BOX MADE OF WOOD.

IT'S UP TO YOU TO DECIDE HOW TO FILL IT.

When you think about it, it's amazing that those sweet sounds can come from a wooden box. But quit thinking about it. And play. Write us at 1940 Gillespie Way, El Cajon, CA 92020 for the dealer near you.

The Taylor crew in the Santee factory just before the move to El Cajon.

guitarists. "Companies like Martin and Gibson have had decades to build up their brands," Listug says. "We just didn't have the luxury of waiting fifty years for musicians to figure out how good our guitars were and what a fine company Bob and I had created. I've always been fascinated by advertising so I began seriously looking at ads that helped create a strong brand identity for other products, that just didn't say, 'Our gizmo is better than the other guy's.'"

In 1990 Taylor and Listug both bought Harley-Davidson motorcycles, which led to an advertising epiphany for Listug. "After I got my bike, I subscribed to every motorcycle magazine out there," he says. "In one magazine there was an ad for Harleys that just showed a photo of the night sky with all the stars and a line that said something like, 'Did you ever look up in the sky and see a '57 Panhead?' There was no motorcycle in that ad at all, but I felt that it captured the experience of dreaming about and longing for a Harley, in a subtle way. It wasn't just another 'more horsepower and shinier chrome' ad. I kept thinking that I wanted to do something like that for our guitars, but I didn't really know how to achieve it."

In 1992 Listug was approached by John Vitro and John Robertson, two designers who worked for a San Diego ad agency called Franklin and Associates. The two men felt that they would be able to craft a series of ads that would help set Taylor apart from other guitar companies. "They said they had liked our ads up until then but felt they could do better," Listug says. "I remember John Vitro said that he wanted to do ads that were as good as our guitars. I was flattered by that, and when he used that Harley ad that had impressed me a couple of years earlier as an example of what we should be doing, I knew we were on the same wavelength."

The first ad campaign that Listug, Vitro, and Robertson created was called *Trees*, and in an homage to the Harley ad, it featured no photos of guitars at all. Instead, the ads, which were spread out over two pages, featured a beautiful photo of a lush forest superimposed with a variety of mock-Zen phases such as 'If a tree falls in the forest and you're not there to hear it, does it make a sound? Yes, it just might take 7 or 8 years.' "The *Trees* campaign was very inexpensive for us to produce." Listug says. "We used stock photos of trees and forests, so we didn't have to hire an expensive photographer. I think that the ads looked really good spread out over two pages and that they gave the impression that our company was really much larger than it was at the time." And since the ads were so different in format from what the other guitars companies were doing, it subtly reinforced the idea that Taylor was a company that did things in new and innovative ways.

When it came time to come up with the second ad campaign a couple of years later, Listug returned to Vitro and Robertson, who had since left Franklin and Associates and set up their own firm. The new campaign the trio came up with was called *Discovery*, and it featured evocative photos of music stores, musicians, and guitars that Vitro had taken on a cross-country tour. The text featured quotes from letters from actual Taylor customers explaining how they discovered their Taylor guitar.

At around the same time the *Discovery* campaign was being planned, Listug started working on a new catalog with Scott Mires, who had worked with VitroRobertson's clients on similar projects. Mires was also an expert on branding and he and Listug worked closely together to come up with a cohesive image for the company. Along with the catalogs, Mires also created the new Taylor logo, helped get the Taylor Ware clothing division up and running, and designed the Taylor website that went on-line in 1997.

The third VitroRobertson campaign was called *Storybook*, and like *Discovery*, it featured stories from real Taylor customers, but in this case they were retold as if they were old folktales. The images were also quite a bit different. "We wanted the ads to look like they were from

The new building at 1940 Gillespie Way.

old children's books," Listug explains. "We had artists do old-style illustrations and we printed the text on an old letter press, which we then bound into old books and photographed. We got a lot a flack for that because people didn't seem to get it. But that was my favorite campaign to date."

Bob Taylor is impressed with his partner's visionary marketing campaigns. "I get a real kick out of seeing what Kurt's going to come up with next," he says. "I am involved in the marketing and sales of our guitars, but I only try to be involved for as long as that particular meeting lasts. I leave it up to Kurt to be creative with our marketing. If it were left up to me I would probably just do ads with the clichéd photo of a guitar with text saying the usual 'crafted from all solid woods by skilled artisans' stuff you see in every other ad."

The ads that Listug and VitroRobertson created were noticed outside of the small world of music magazines and over the years their various campaigns have won many awards. Their ads have also been among the finalists for the Magazine Publishers of America Kelly Award, which is the most prestigious award for print advertising. Although they have never won first prize, Listug notes that their competition usually consists of giants like Nike, BMW, Porsche, Saab, and Chrysler/Daimler and that every consumer campaign he produced with Vitro-Robertson has made it to the finals.

Around the same time Listug was working on the *Trees* ads, he and Bob Taylor decided to cut back on custom options. Up until then customers could order a guitar with a variety of different inlays, styles of binding, finishes, and purfling. Now that the company was making more than 5000 guitars a year, the wide range of custom options had become a logistical nightmare. Taylor and Listug went through the custom orders and incorporated the most popular ones in the standard line. Now the entire line, except for the 400 series and the LKSM, came with abalone rosettes. Also, each model now had a unique inlay pattern. The 500s now came with pearl diamonds, the 600s with a three-piece abstract flower, the 700s with abalone dots, the 800s with large pearl diamonds, and the 900s with the Cindy inlay. Taylor also dropped the koa guitars from the line, as the supply of the Hawaiian hardwood was too sporadic.

In August 1992, the new factory building was ready. "When we did our first move from the tiny Lemon Grove shop to the Santee facility, we didn't miss one day of production," Bob Taylor says. "Our second move was a major, giant move. This time we were a company with around 45 employees, moving completely out of one building into another, and we only lost three days of production in that move. I think that was quite a little feat." As with the move from Lemon Grove to Santee, there was a transitional guitar for the move from Santee to El Cajon. This time they completed a 712 (ser.#16520) at the old factory and strung it up at the new factory.

A New Way of Finishing

Now that Bob Taylor had the factory of his dreams, he began to focus on solving the problem that had bedeviled him from the American Dream days: the finish. Spraying the finish was the final step in building a guitar, and it was the one most likely to fail. When Taylor, Listug, and Schemmer bought the American Dream in 1974 they finished their guitars with nitrocellulose lacquer, which had been the standard finish of the American guitar industry since the 1920s. Nitrocellulose (NC) lacquer was originally developed for the auto industry but guitar makers quickly discovered that it was durable, looked good, and was easier to apply than the shellac they had been using until then.

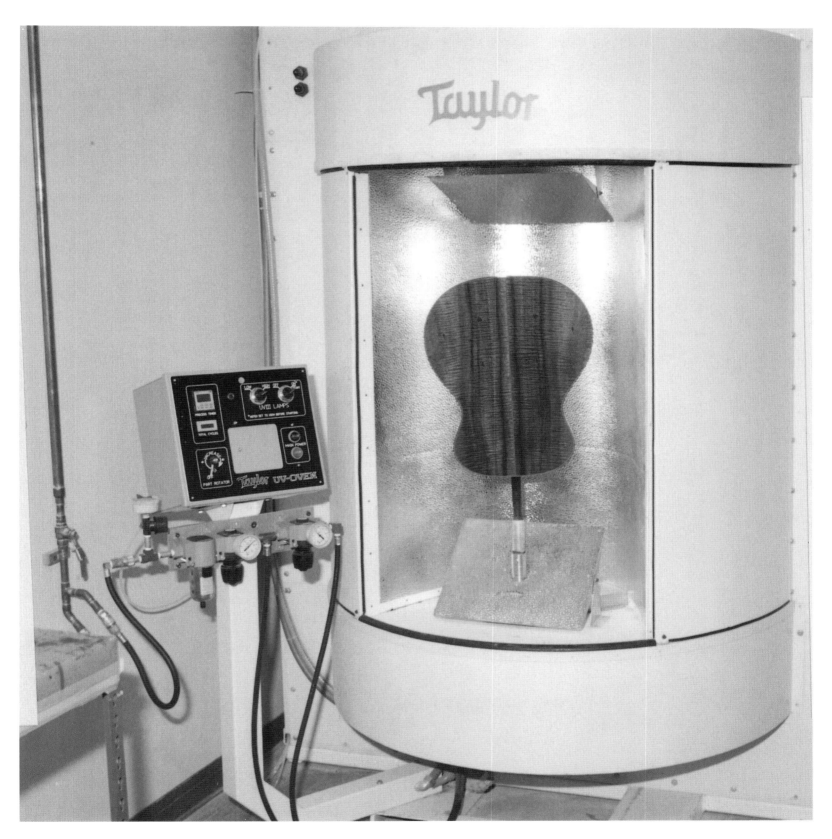

The UV oven that Matt Guzzetta built.

But NC lacquer had a number of problems as well, and the Taylor crew seemed to encounter all of them in their first few years. "We were using finish from a reputable, nationwide company and we did our best to make things work but it seemed that we could never really get the finish on the guitars done successfully," Bob Taylor recalls. "One time, in the early days, we finished our batch of guitars and the finish never dried. After curing for the normal week it was still very gummy. These guitars were our sole source of income and it almost destroyed our new business to lose them in the finish room."

In early 1976 their finish supplier suggested that a catalyzed lacquer might solve some of their problems. "This finish required a catalyst to be mixed in before spraying and that aided the drying process," Taylor says. "The finish was durable and had a good luster and so we began finishing our guitars with the stuff. Down the street, Stelling Banjos was using the same finish. We would talk about these things and share ideas and try out new things together. Finish went well for a bit, and then a guitar or two showed up with cracks in the finish after shipping them out to stores."

Taylor stopped using the catalyzed lacquer, but they knew that every guitar they had finished with it was likely to come back for warranty work. The lacquer company denied that the

The old, messy brown paste filler being applied to a guitar body.

problem was their fault and claimed that Taylor and Stelling must have been applying it incorrectly. The problem was finally resolved when Geoff Stelling hired a chemist and discovered that the lacquer company had left out the plasticizer, which made the finish more brittle than it should be.

Bob Taylor had figured out a way to improve nearly every technique used to build a guitar except for those used in the finishing process. "The thing about a finish on a guitar is that it requires so much effort to apply and takes so much time," he says. "We could make the body and neck in a few days, but then we'd be in the finishing process for two weeks or more. Then the guitar gets assembled and if something goes wrong with the finish you're sunk. The bridge has to come off, which can sometimes ruin the top. The neck needs to be removed and that's dangerous as well. Then all this thin wood needs to have the old finish stripped and sanded from its surface and you can't take any of the wood thickness off in the process or the guitar will be wrecked. So, you have this thousand dollar product with five dollars worth of finish on it, and if that fails you almost don't recover."

When Bob Taylor rehired Tim Luranc in 1983, he wanted to tap the finishing skills that Luranc learned from Geoff Stelling. "When I started at Taylor they were using nitro-cellulose,"

The new style clear filler.

Luranc recalls. "At Stelling we were using Fullerplast." Fullerplast is a catalyzed acrylic resin which when it cures is much harder and more durable than nitrocellulose lacquer. Fender used Fullerplast on their custom colored solid-body guitars in the 1950s and early 1960s, but no acoustic guitar builders had experimented with it yet.

"I think the first guitars we did were the colored finish instruments like the Prince guitar," Luranc says. " Since we weren't going to put pickguards on them and we thought the nitrocellulose wouldn't hold up very well, we used Fullerplast because it was so durable. It worked so well that we changed to it on the rest of the line." Even though the Fullerplast worked well, it still took a long time to cure. So over the next few years Taylor and Luranc experimented with different finishes. "After Fullerplast we went to conversion varnishes and then to polyurethane," Luranc says. "They all looked good, and they worked well, but they all took too long to cure. Then in 1991 Bob went to a seminar on using ultraviolet (UV) light in manufacturing, and he was particularly impressed with the idea of using UV to speed up the curing process."

When he got back from the seminar Bob Taylor and Matt Guzzetta designed and built an ultraviolet light curing booth and began experimenting with various finishes. "It was similar to the turning point we had reached earlier with the Fadal," Taylor says. "The magic dust had fallen on us and we no longer had a choice." Even though he knew that UV finishes were the future, it took him far longer to reach his goal than he anticipated. Bob Taylor and Steve Baldwin, the manager of the finish department, tried samples of just about every UV finish on the market, but most of the finishes were designed for metal and didn't work well on wood. As the Taylor Tech Sheet on UV finishes put it, "Either the stuff wouldn't spray or it wouldn't cure; or, it would spray and cure, but it would fall off of the rosewood; or it would stick to rosewood, but it would bubble; or it would go on like glass and it would stick and cure, but you couldn't sand it because it was so hard."

Bob Taylor was frustrated with the way the finishes he was getting off the shelf were working, so he began bypassing the salesmen and started talking directly to the chemists who formulated the products. The gambit paid off in 1994 when Taylor finally found a finish that worked as an undercoat. A few months later they found a formulation that worked as a topcoat. In May 1995 they started using UV finishes on the production line.

Tim Luranc remembers the problems that he had dealing with nitrocellulose finishes when he was rehired. "I would start the finish cycle by using paste filler to fill the pores," he says. "Then I'd let that cure for 24 hours. Then I'd spray the undercoat and let that cure. Then spray and cure, spray and cure again, and then the final buff and polish. That was a nine to ten day cycle. If you consider that we were starting maybe 25 or 30 guitars each day, there could be as many as 300 instruments in various stages of finishing. Keeping track of all of those instruments was a problem and storage was a nightmare because we had to make sure dust didn't land in the finish while it was still wet and tacky."

With the new UV system, the finish was sprayed on and the guitar was placed in Guzzetta's "oven" where the intense ultraviolet light completely cured the finish in about 30 seconds. Along with cutting the finishing cycle from days to hours, the new UV technique had some aesthetic advantages as well. "Typically, traditionally, a brown, oil-based paste filler is applied to all guitars, except maple, to fill the pores in preparation for finish spaying," Bob Taylor wrote in an article entitled "What UV Means to You." "This paste not only fills the pores, it also homogenizes the color variations in such woods as rosewood, walnut, and koa." Taylor and the UV finish team developed a clear pore filler, which allowed the natural variations in the color of the wood to show through. "Each finished rosewood guitar, for example, retains its unique character," Taylor continues, "Because there is no "shoe-polish-brown" filler wiped over the wood beforehand to mask its natural coloration."

Another advantage of the new UV finish was that it was much more durable than the older solvent-based finishes and could be applied in a much thinner "skin." "This thinner finish improves the sound of the guitar," Taylor states. "It's also more tolerant of weather, skin moistures, beer, solvents, etcetera, and it generally holds up better, making it more protective of the guitar."

Another New Body Shape

During this period Bob Taylor was so involved with working out the kinks in the new factory and getting the UV finish to work, he put most of his guitar design projects on hold. In 1993 one of those stalled projects was brought back to life thanks to an unexpected visitor. Country singer Kathy Mattea was performing in San Diego and stopped by the factory for a tour. She had been playing a custom black 612c since 1990 and had become friendly with T.J. Baden, who issued a standing invitation to visit if she was ever in the area. "It was my birthday, they had a cake waiting," Mattea recalls. "Everyone sang 'Happy Birthday' and it was so sweet. I was blown away. Then, Bob said, 'I have some real special wood I've been stashing away for years. Why don't you go out there and choose some, and let me make you a guitar.'"

Kurt Listug had been bugging his partner to finish designing a new body shape and realized that he might be able to enlist Mattea to help him get Taylor to finish up the guitar. "So, we're looking at wood, and Kurt gets in my ear," Mattea recalls. "He says, 'You should ask him about the guitar we can't get him to finish designing.' I said, 'What would that be?' And Kurt said, 'Oh, it's somewhere between a dreadnought and a grand concert, with the volume of one and the curves of the other.' Before I knew it, we'd chosen some Brazilian rosewood from trees

Kathy Mattea with her custom black 612c.

Special catalog for 1994 announcing the 20th Anniversary grand auditoriums.

that were older than me. We wound up at the computer with Bob drawing things, and me saying, 'Oh, I want one of those.'"

As Listug had predicted, Mattea's enthusiasm for the project rekindled Bob Taylor's interest in the project. After completing her guitar, Taylor and Listug suspected the new model, which they dubbed the grand auditorium, might fill a niche in the standard line. The dreadnoughts were well suited to flatpicking and the grand concerts were ideal for fingerpicking, but there really wasn't a guitar that worked for both styles. Rather than just add the grand auditorium to the standard line, they opted instead to offer it as a limited edition to mark the company's 20th anniversary in 1994.

Bob Taylor and Kurt Listug had spent the previous two decades creating a new kind of guitar company, so it made perfect sense to commemorate the 20th birthday of their company with a completely new guitar. The limited edition 20th Anniversary came in two styles, the rosewood and spruce XX-RS and the mahogany and cedar XX-MC. Taylor built 250 of each style, and were surprised to find that many customers bought them in pairs. The edition quickly sold out, and Bob Taylor got to work designing a new batch of limited edition grand auditoriums for 1995.

The 1995 series of limited edition grand auditoriums was announced at the Winter NAMM Show in Anaheim and included six different styles: the mahogany back and sides, cedar top GA-MC; the Indian rosewood back and sides, Sitka spruce top GA-RS; the black walnut back and sides, Sitka spruce top GA-WS; the koa back and sides, Sitka spruce top GA-KS; the koa back and sides, cedar top GA-KC; and the Brazilian rosewood back and sides, Englemann spruce top GA-BE. The bulk release of the different limited editions helped introduce the new body shape to a wider audience, and the different wood combinations allowed Taylor to test potential new model configurations.

New Ways of Building Guitars

That same NAMM Show saw the announcement of the Taylor Acoustic Bass, which was designed with the help of the innovative luthier Steve Klein. Bob Taylor had been familiar with Klein's radical acoustic guitars since the 1980s, but the two luthiers finally met in 1991 at the ASIA conference where Taylor had presented the lecture on his early experiences with Fadal to the guitar making community.

Steve Klein started building solid-body electric guitars in the late 1960s while he was still in high school. In 1969, he built his first acoustic guitar using, just as Sam Radding and Bob Taylor did on their early projects, Irving Sloane's *Classic Guitar Construction* as a guide. Not long after Klein built that instrument, his grandfather introduced him to Dr. Michael Kasha, a chemist who had a keen interest in the way acoustic guitars were built. Kasha felt that the traditional bridges and braces used by most luthiers were inefficient and didn't produce the best possible tone. At the time Kasha was working with various luthiers, most notably Richard Schneider, to put his theories into practice.

Although Kasha's work was primarily concerned with classical guitars, the young Klein felt that the designs could work with steel strings as well. After working on a few prototypes over the next few years, Klein finally came up with a basic design for a steel string guitar that fused Kasha's structural theories with Klein's own impeccable sense of visual design.

Klein's new guitar measured eighteen inches across the lower bout, which was one inch wider than Taylor's 17-inch jumbo, a guitar most players already considered to be quite large. In keeping with Kasha's ideas, the bridge was asymmetrical and was much wider on the bass side, which was supposed to drive the top more efficiently and increase both the treble and bass response. The most radical part of the guitar was the interior bracing that consisted of a series of braces that radiated out around the bridge in a starburst pattern. Other innovative interior features included a brace supporting the area around the soundhole that attached to the sides and a cross-braced back. Unfortunately for most guitarists, Klein's guitar were very expensive, and it seemed that only rich rock stars like Stephen Stills, Joni Mitchell, and Joe Walsh could afford them.

When Klein met Bob Taylor in 1991 Taylor mentioned that it might be fun to collaborate on a guitar together. Klein was intrigued with the idea and he suggested that it might be interesting to work on an acoustic bass. "I know that I'd been thinking, 'Boy, Steve sure knows how to do that low frequency stuff,'" Taylor recalls. "The things he does on his guitars would be perfect for bass. That style of bracing, those giant guitar bodies, that great bass response." Bob Taylor had reached a point in his career where he didn't feel the need to design every guitar himself and the chance to work with a creative builder like Klein was enticing.

Taylor and Klein worked together on coming up with a body shape that melded the aesthetic sense of the two builders. "I wanted something unusual, and yet somewhat Taylor-esque," Klein says. "We certainly achieved that with the Maccaferri-type cutaway, similar to the one used on the Leo Kottke model. The upper bout definitely has some Taylor lines. Bob, meanwhile, wanted it to look like something I would do, round and full of, as Bob put it, 'overpasses and freeways inside the guitar.' My stuff tends to be pretty elaborate and unusual, and, in that regard, is not easy to do."

Steve Klein carving braces on a miniature guitar.

After the two luthiers decided on a shape Klein returned to his workshop in Sonoma and began to work on the prototypes. Klein eventually came up with four models including two fretted four-string models, a fretless four-string, and a fretted five-string. Taylor exhibited the prototypes at the 1994 Winter NAMM Show where they drew an enthusiastic response from both players and dealers. Taylor and his crew spent the next few months refining Klein's designs and figuring out how to actually build the instruments using the Fadal.

Taylor finally settled on a large, 19-inch body with an unusual wedge shape that was a shallow 3 1/2 inches on the bass side and a deep 6 1/4 inches on the treble side. This design created the largest possible air chamber while maintaining playability. The soundhole was placed in an offset position, which allowed for a larger vibrating surface. The scale length was 34 inches long and the mahogany neck was bolted on using a variation of Klein's bolt-on neck design. The headstock was grafted on using an early version of the finger joint that would later become standard on Taylor guitars. The final production model was offered in two styles, the AB1, which had a spruce top and imbuia back and sides, and the AB2, which was built with imbuia for the top, back and sides. Both models had a satin finish. And, in tribute to the successful collaboration, the bass had Taylor's logo inlaid on the headstock and Klein's inlaid in the fretboard over the body.

Catalog photo showing the AB1 (left) and the AB2.

The bass was initially well-received by players and a few years later the bass series was expanded to include the AB3, which had a spruce top and maple back and sides and a gloss finish, and the AB4, which featured an all-maple body construction. The AB4 was available in a variety of sunburst finishes. But over time the original rush of enthusiasm for the bass subsided, and at the end of 2002 it was dropped from the line.

At the end of 1995 Taylor boasted a workforce of 136 employees who had built around 11,000 instruments that year. In 21 years they had gone from being a tiny workshop to one of the largest builders of acoustic guitars in America. Not only that, Bob Taylor's production methods had become the envy of the industry. When he got his first Fadal in 1989, many luthiers thought he was somehow betraying the ancient craft of guitar making. But now they were constantly stopping by the factory to see how he did it. To Bob Taylor's credit, he was always glad to offer advice and help with suggestions. "I realize that these guys are my competition," Taylor says. "But they are also the only people I can talk to about this stuff. When I rode motorcycles I talked to other guys who rode motorcycles. Now that I'm making guitars I find that I have the most interesting conversations with guys like Jean Larrivée, James Olsen, and Bill Collings. Only a guitar maker knows the problems associated with being a guitar maker."

A red custom AB3.

"As much as I like the high-tech methods Taylor's been using for ten years to speed things up, we are essentially using CNC to replicate hand maneuvers, to mimic the way the guitar was designed to be put together a long, long time ago." Bob Taylor

Taylor
Turns 30

The Taylor Baby. A fancy new series. Walnut and koa guitars. Redesigning the old body shapes. The 25th Anniversary. Yet another new building. The New Technology Neck. The Nylon String Series. A totally new pickup system. The future.

A Baby in the House

1996 was an especially productive year for Taylor. To start with, they added the grand auditorium to the standard line after offering it as a limited edition for two years. Then they introduced a new ultra-deluxe line of guitars they dubbed the Presentation Series. They offered a slew of limited edition models including a variety of rosewood 400s, a 412 and a 512 with mahogany top, back, and sides, a Nanci Griffith Signature Model, and a six-string version of the Leo Kottke Signature Model. And perhaps most interestingly, they brought out a 3/4-size guitar they called the Baby Taylor.

Page from the 1996 catalog announcing the introduction of the Baby Taylor.

Baby Taylor.

Taylor decided to give the new grand auditoriums a 4 designation, and they offered them in every series from the 500s on up. All of the new 4s were built to the same specs as the rest of the series they were part of, except for the 514, which had a cedar top rather than the spruce top that was standard for the 500s. The new body size was an immediate hit with guitarists, and by the end of the year grand auditoriums were outselling every shape but the dreadnoughts.

The Presentation Series was based on the limited edition GA-BE from 1995. The series included the PS-12 grand concert, the PS-14 grand auditorium, the PS-10 dreadnought, and the PS-15 jumbo. As with the GA-BEs, the tops were made of Englemann spruce and the fretboards were inlaid with a magnificent abalone tree-of-life pattern designed by Larry Breedlove and Bob Taylor. The back and sides were made from Brazilian rosewood that came from Bob Taylor's personal stash of wood, and rather than plastic, the instruments were bound in rosewood.

And then there was the Baby Taylor. At first glance it appeared to be a modest little instrument. It had a satin finish, no binding, laminated mahogany sides, and an arched, laminated mahogany back. The top was made of solid spruce and the neck was attached by screws that went through the tongue of the ebony fretboard. "For the entire 21 years of Taylor's existence," Bob Taylor says, "I've had people approach me with some variation of, 'I have a kid, and I want to get him or her a "starter" guitar — something good, but affordable.'"

The idea sat on the back burner until Bob Taylor was spurred into action by an unusual conversation. "I had gone to a NAMM Show and talked to Stan Werbin of Elderly Instruments about ukuleles," Taylor says. "I had this sense that ukuleles were coming back around, which, it turns out, was correct. But when I sat down and started tooling and sketching an outline of how I'd make a ukulele, I kept saying, 'This should be a travel guitar.' So, I changed the design, and I started wondering, 'How can I do this? What should I do? How can I make it different?'"

Bob Taylor and his team started working on a design that could be easily built, sounded good, played well, and was still affordable. The CAD/CAM programs helped them come up with workable designs quickly and the Fadals were able to produce the parts efficiently. They opted to use a scaled down dreadnought silhouette for the body shape and it was available with two different size necks, a normal 1-11/16-inch width, and a narrower 1-1/2-inch width that would be more suitable for the smaller hands of children. The price was $398 with a case.

Taylor thought the primary market for the Baby Taylor would be children and that it would be a good idea to offer the guitar with some sort of instructional material geared to younger players. Before the marketing crew could research what was already available on the market, an intriguing opportunity dropped right in their laps. Rick Turner, one of the founders of Alembic guitars who had kept in touch with Bob Taylor since the days when they were both represented by Rothchild, called Bob to talk about the new UV finish process. Taylor invited Turner and his wife Jessica Baron Turner to come down to El Cajon to see how the process worked and to check out the new Baby Taylor guitars they were starting to build. While the Turners were touring the factory, they mentioned in passing that Jessica had developed a new method for teaching children to play guitar that was based on an open D tuning.

Although Jessica Turner had published another book on guitar instruction, she wasn't able to interest her publisher in her new Smart Start method, as she called it. Bob Taylor on the other hand, liked the idea and offered to order 3000 copies to package with the new Baby Taylor model. "That initial order was enough to get Jessica's publisher, Hal Leonard, interested in the project," Turner recalls. "The proposed cover art wasn't very good so Bob Taylor had his graphics people design a new cover, which featured the Baby Taylor, of course, but it looked so much better than the original design." Taylor also loaned the Turners some Baby Taylors to use in the Smart Start video that was produced by Homespun Videos.

The Smart Start program was announced at the 1997 Winter NAMM Show in Anaheim. Bob Taylor invited Jessica to give a presentation about the Smart Start program at a concert the company arranged for their dealers. "It was an incredible show with Michael Hedges, Jackson Browne, Leo Kottke, Dan Crary, Doyle Dykes, Laurence Juber, Karla Bonoff, and Kenny Edwards," Turner says. "Jessica was put on in the middle of all this to talk about the Baby Taylors, the Smart Start program and how to inspire future generations of guitar players. I was standing at the back of the hall with our one-and-half-year-old son Elias, who noticed his mom on stage and suddenly realized that his dinner was up there. He started making a fuss and I figured that since we were talking about families and music that it would be fine to put Elias onstage so he could be with his mom. He crawled across the stage and she put down the Baby Taylor to pick him up. He then grabbed a flatpick that was on the stage and started strumming the guitar, which was tuned to open D, and began singing "Kumbaya." The place just went wild. We couldn't have scripted such a moment if we tried. Years later people still walk up to her at trade shows and talk about that moment and how Elias proved to them that little kids can learn to play guitar using her method. The Smart Start series has gone on to sell more than 110,000 copies. That success probably never would have happened without Bob initially saying yes and really getting behind the project."

The cover of the book and video for the Smart Start program.

The Baby Taylor was an immediate hit with players. "We had certain uses in mind when we started to design the Baby Taylor," Bob Taylor says. "But as we showed it to people, it became obvious that this guitar served more purposes than even we could have imagined. We'd get different comments, like, 'It sounds and feels so good — when can I get one?' Or, 'You're going to be selling these to more than just kids. I could play slide guitar on this.' Or, 'I want one of these by my bed, so when I get an idea in the middle of the night, I don't have to go get my guitar out of its case.' Or, 'I want one of these for my grandchild.' 'I want four of these — one for every kid.' 'I want one for my daughter and one for me.'"

The Baby Taylor sold so well that in 2000 Taylor opened a new 8000 square foot factory devoted to building just that one series. That same year they started making a larger version of the Baby, which was dubbed the Big Baby. This new guitar was a 15/16th size dreadnought with a solid spruce top and laminated sides and laminated arched back. By 2003, the Baby Taylor came in a variety of styles including the Baby-M, which featured a solid mahogany top, as well as Baby Taylors that had solid spruce tops and different laminates for the back and sides such as rosewood, sapele, koa, maple, and bubinga.

Redesigning the Old Models

The 1997 Winter NAMM Show was also the place were Taylor announced that the six-string Leo Kottke Signature Model, which was introduced as a limited edition the previous year, was being added to the standard line. The company also introduced the limited edition Kathy Mattea 612KM, which featured a black stain, a custom inlay, and a sharp, Florentine cutaway. The 612KM also marked the return of colored finishes to the Taylor line. Along with that particular limited edition, the options for the standard 600 Series were expanded to include red, black, and amber finishes.

Along with the new models, Taylor debuted a redesigned version of their most venerable model, the dreadnought. The shape of the new dreadnought was a subtle but elegant upgrade of the silhouette they had been using since 1974, when Taylor, Listug, and Schemmer bought the American Dream from Sam Radding. "The dreadnought and jumbo shapes we inherited had a nice, 'Industrial Revolution' sort of design aesthetic to their curves," Taylor explained in the spring 1997 issue of *Wood&Steel*. "They've been great guitars, and very popular, but for years I've wanted to create bodies that were uniquely, identifiably 'Taylor.'"

The inspiration for the redesigned dreadnought came from Bob Taylor's newest model. "The grand auditorium truly embodies my design sense," he says. "At some point it hit me that there is a particular nature to the shape of the grand auditorium that could be worked into the designs of our other guitars. In other words, a dreadnought could be specifically "dreadnought" in character, yet at the same time look like a cousin to the grand auditorium." The new dreadnought was very slightly smaller across the upper and lower bouts, with a more curved, less boxy look overall. The changes didn't affect the tone, and the more graceful appearance was immediately hailed as an aesthetic success.

The six-string version of the Leo Kottke Signature Model.

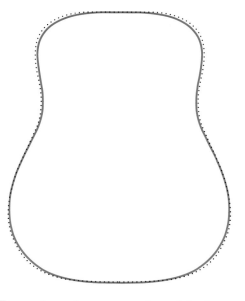

Illustration showing the difference in shape between the new and old dreadnought body shapes.

Dotted outlines are the old shapes

New Dreadnought shape is solid green

The top, back, and sides of the W65 are made of solid claro walnut.

Lots of New Models

In 1998 Taylor expanded the line from 38 models to 61. The company was able to find a fairly reliable source of koa, so they reintroduced the Koa Series, this time with five different models. Each new instrument in the Koa Series featured tortoiseshell colored plastic binding, an abalone rosette, and the same inlays that were used on the 1995 Limited Edition Grand Auditoriums. The resurrected Koa Series included two dreadnoughts, the K10 which had an Englemann spruce top, and the K20c, a koa top, back, and sides guitar with a cutaway, and the K22, a koa top, back and sides grand concert. The new series also featured the K14c, a cutaway grand auditorium with a cedar top, and the K65, a jumbo 12-string with a koa top. Taylor had almost run out of Brazilian rosewood, so they started making the top-of-the–line Presentation Series out of extremely fancy AAA-grade koa.

Another new group of guitars introduced that year was the Walnut Series, which included the W10, a dreadnought with a Sitka spruce top, the W12c, a grand concert cutaway with a cedar top, the W14c, a grand auditorium cutaway with a cedar top, the spruce top W15 jumbo, and the W65, a jumbo 12-string with walnut top, back and sides. In some ways the Walnut Series guitars were a tribute to the company's earliest days. Walnut was used on the shallow body dreadnoughts that Tim Luranc used to build during the American Dream days and the inlay pattern was resurrected from the first version of the 900 Series. The abalone top border recalled the days before the 810 was codified, and most of the guitars that Taylor built had the same level of fancy trim.

Bob Taylor had always liked the sound of walnut, which he felt split the difference between the brightness of mahogany and the warm, bassy tones of rosewood. Another advantage of walnut is that it is a domestic American hardwood, which means that supply will be more stable than tropical tonewoods like rosewood, mahogany, and koa. Kurt Listug liked the idea of being able to offer an instrument that was made of a tonewood that wasn't used by every other guitar maker.

The growing scarcity and rising prices of favored tonewoods drove Taylor to experiment with alternatives for their less expensive models. Throughout its brief history the 400 Series had been made from a variety of tonewoods including mahogany, maple, rosewood, and even a limited run of koa. In 1998 Taylor settled on using ovangkol for the back and sides. Ovangkol was an African hardwood that looked a bit like walnut and had a similar tone to rosewood. Taylor also changed the cosmetic specifications on the 400 Series. The old style pinless bridge was swapped out for a pin-style bridge that was identical to the bridges used on the more expensive guitars. Also, the top was sprayed with a gloss finish while the back and sides retained the satin finish. The body was bound in white plastic.

The choice of offering a guitar with just a gloss top was an unusual choice, but Taylor felt that the instruments with an all-satin finish didn't stand out when displayed next to an instrument with a gloss finish. "It turned out that it wasn't that much more expensive to do a gloss finish on the top of a guitar," Listug says. "And we felt that our new UV finish looked so good that it gave our guitars a competitive advantages over the other builders. Now, our less expensive instruments looked the same from the front as our more expensive models."

That same year Taylor introduced the 300 Series, which was less expensive than the 400 Series. The backs and sides of the 300s were made of sapele, an African hardwood that was similar in tone and appearance to mahogany. As with the 400s, the top had a gloss finish and the back and sides were sprayed with a satin finish. The body was bound in black plastic.

The 700 Series also got a makeover. Ever since it was introduced in the late 1970s, customers saw the series as a poor man's version of the more popular 800 Series. But even though they cost less and sounded about the same as the 800s, sales always lagged behind the fancier models. Bob Taylor and Kurt Listug decided to switch the top wood from spruce to cedar, which gave the 700s a brighter, crisper tone than before. The darker cedar also gave the redesigned model a distinct look that set it apart from the 800s. Taylor also expanded the color palette on the 600 Series, which now included red, black, green, purple, and amber.

Perhaps the most sweeping change was the addition of pickups as a standard feature on almost every model in the standard line with a cutaway. The only cutaway models offered without pickups were in the 900 Series, the Presentation Series, the Koa Series, the Walnut Series, as well as the Dan Crary and Leo Kottke Signature Models. Taylor had offered pickups as a custom option since the early 1980s, but since the mid-1990s they realized they were making more cutaways with pickups than without. It was something of a paradox that as more and more people were inspired to play acoustic guitar because of MTV's *Unplugged* television show, they insisted that their new acoustic guitars come with a pickup so they could plug them in.

The groundbreaking ceremony for the new building at 1980 Gillespie Way.

On the 300 and 400 Series guitars Taylor used the Fishman Prefix System, which included an under-the-saddle piezo transducer and a preamp with EQ that was mounted in the guitar's waist on the bass side. The 500, 600, 700, and 800 Series had the same Fishman pickup along with an internal microphone. The preamp and EQ, which was mounted in the side, also included a blender control that allowed the musician to mix the amount of microphone to pickup signal.

On January 27, Windham Hill records released *Sounds of Wood&Steel*, a CD compilation that was masterminded by T.J. Baden, who was now vice-president of sales and marketing, and produced by Windham Hill's Larry Hamby. The CD featured an eclectic mix of players including country stars like Clint Black, Vince Gill, and Kathy Mattea; fingerpicking legends like Leo Kottke, Will Ackerman, Doyle Dykes, and Michael Hedges; and rockers Steve Stevens, Stuart Smith, and Joe Lynn Turner. All of the recordings were acoustic and all were made using Taylor guitars.

Baden felt that a CD of great musicians playing Taylors would help introduce the guitars to a new audience, but he also realized that the recording would have to be a music collection first and foremost. All of the musicians were intrigued by the idea, and they each turned in excellent performances. Some of the highlights included Clint Black's version of Jerry Reed's infamous fingerpicking workout "The Claw," Russ Freeman's jazzy "Larry's World," and Steve Stevens's "Sadhana," which he played on a prototype Taylor nylon-string guitar. Baden con-

The completed building at 1980 Gillespie Way.

The 25th Anniversary Grand Auditorium.

tributed a track of his own, and showed himself to be an able guitarist. The CD also included a song called "Java Man," that sadly turned out to be the last recording made by Michael Hedges before he was killed in car accident. The CD sold well enough that it spawned two follow-up discs in 1999 and 2003.

Getting Bigger

In August 1998 Taylor began moving into a new 44,000 square foot building next to the 25,000 square foot building they had occupied since 1992. The new building was two stories tall and the top floor, all 14,436 square feet of it, was devoted to the company's administrative functions and included offices for the accounting, personnel, purchasing, customer service, and public relations departments.

As with the older building, Bob Taylor designed the new facility from scratch. It was designed to house the UV finishing department; the rough-milling department; the final assembly department; and the tooling department. It also boasted a humidity controlled wood storage area as well as the shipping department. All of the other departments remained behind in the smaller building.

At the end of 1998 Taylor occupied four buildings, the original 25,000 square feet at 1940 Gillespie Way, an 8000 square foot factory at 1900 Gillespie Way, an 8000 square foot case factory at 1725 Gillespie Way, and the new 44,000 square foot building. Altogether the complex covered around 85,000 square feet. The company finished the year with 250 employees who built 21,000 guitars.

1999 marked the 25th anniversary for Taylor Guitars. Just as they did five years earlier, Taylor released a Limited Edition to honor the occasion. The Limited Edition came in two body styles the XXV-GA grand auditorium and the XXV-DR dreadnought. Both models were made with quilted sapele that was stained an attractive caramel color. The tops were Sitka spruce and the bodies, necks, and headstocks were bound in cream-colored celluloid. They built 500 of each style.

The choice of sapele for the commemorative models was unusual, but Bob Taylor came up with the idea after a great deal of thought. "We sat there trying to come up with an idea for the 25th Anniversary guitars," Bob Taylor recalls. "I didn't want to take an 810 or a 615 and put an inlay on it that says '25 Years' and sell it as an 'anniversary model.' We raised the bar with our 20th Anniversary models in 1994, for which we created the grand auditorium—a new shape, a new bracing concept, a totally new tone for us. With the 25th Anniversary guitar I just couldn't get excited about decorating something we were already making and calling it an "anniversary model."

The only part of the guitar that looked back to previous designs was the fancy fretboard inlay, which Bob Taylor designed for the 20th Anniversary model five years earlier. "It was my intention to use it as a hallmark 'anniversary' pattern," Taylor says. "I plan to use it on the 30th and 50th anniversary models. Anytime you see that, you know it's a Taylor anniversary guitars; the only change will be the Roman numerals engraved in it."

Many guitar companies use a major anniversary as an occasion to look back at past glories. It's common practice for them to reissue models that include cosmetic or structural features from previous decades. Bob Taylor and Kurt Listug decided to use anniversaries as a way to look to the future rather than to the past and to use the opportunity to introduce new products. On the 20th anniversary they brought out the grand auditorium body shape, which was added to the standard line a couple of years later. They continued their tradition of innovation

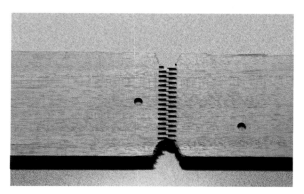

The finger-jointed neck and headstock.

A batch of necks and headstocks after they have been jointed together.

on their sapele 25th Anniversary model, which may have looked like a cosmetic variation of a standard model guitar, but it was the first model to feature Bob Taylor's latest innovation, the New Technology neck.

The New Technology Neck

Bob Taylor's first 20 or so years as a guitar maker were devoted to honing his building techniques, learning to use his increasingly complex tools, and refining his designs. His guitar innovations, such as making slimmer necks or using bolt-on necks, were evolutionary rather than revolutionary. That is, they were just refinements of components that already existed. But the New Technology neck, or NT neck as it came to be called, was a completely new approach to attaching the neck to the body.

A batch of necks getting their three-piece heels clamped up.

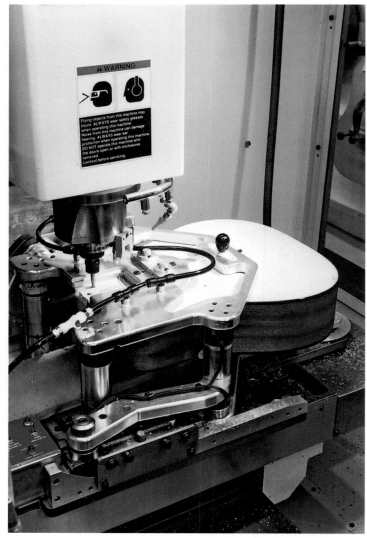

Fadal cutting neck pocket into the body of a guitar.

Fitting the NT neck
into the body pocket.

The standard method of attaching a neck to a flattop guitar required that the fretboard extension be glued to the top of the instrument. This was true whether the neck was attached using bolts or a dovetail. "That means the neck attaches to the body at two places," Bob Taylor explains. "At the heel joint and, by extension, via the upper part of the fingerboard. Thus, the neck shares some of the tension support duties with the body, which is ill-equipped for the task."

On the NT neck, the fretboard extension is actually supported by the end of the neck, and the whole assembly is now set into a pocket cut into the body and top. "According to our new design, you actually inlay the fingerboard into the top of the guitar, leaving a virtually undetectable 3 or 4/1000ths-of-an-inch gap all the was around it. Underneath the fingerboard is a half-inch of the neck mahogany, so we have special blocks that go in there. It's radically different; you're fitting the neck into the body both ways, like a neck is dovetailed into the body of a violin, or an archtop guitar. But instead of the support being up on top of the guitar, now it's down and flush with the guitar. So, when you look at the guitar, it looks exactly the same as acoustic steel-string flattops have always looked."

Another innovation on the NT necks was a high-tech twist on an ancient building technique: making a three-piece neck with a grafted on headstock and stacked heel. In the 19th Century most guitars were made in this fashion, but in the early part of the 20th Century builders in America began to switch over to one-piece necks, which held up better under the extra tension of the newly popular steel strings. "Our new three-piece neck has a heel that's stacked on, instead of being one, big wasteful piece of wood cut all the way up the neck," Taylor explains. "Also, the headstock is grafted-on, which is a technique that classical guitar builders have used forever. The big difference is that we use a new finger-joint and they used a simple scarf joint." The complex finger-joint Taylor came up with is actually stronger than a solid piece of wood, and it uses much less material.

It took about three years to work out all of the kinks on the NT necks, and the entire effort would not have been possible without the power and precision provided by the CNC mills Taylor had been working with for the past decade. "When people designed guitars 100-plus years ago, they had a workbench with chisels and hand planes and molding planes and hammers, and their thinking process was, to a certain extent, determined by those tools. They weren't thinking, 'this guitar is going to be anything I want it to be,' because they weren't able to separate their understanding of the guitar from their knowledge of how to make things. In other words, they couldn't conceive of a design we'd think of today that would require a laser to cut an 8/1000th wide slot, because they didn't have lasers and they couldn't cut that slot.

"Well, we're capable of doing that and many other technological things that weren't dreamed of decades ago. We bought our first Fadal in 1989 and we started carving necks and cutting inlay patterns, and we'd improve the quality of what we had been able to do by hand. But as much as I like the high-tech methods Taylor's been using for ten years to speed things up, we are essentially using CNC to replicate hand maneuvers, to mimic the way the guitar was designed to be put together a long, long time ago."

The NT neck was more complicated to make than the bolt-on neck Taylor had been constructing up until that point, but it solved a number of structural issues that had been annoying Bob Taylor for years. And the combination of the three-piece neck and the precision of the CNC machines meant that Taylor was able to waste much less wood than before. "We want to consume less of a tree every time we make a guitar," Taylor explains. "Why cut down a tree to make 50 guitars when you can figure out a way to get 100 guitars from that same tree? Well, some people might say, 'well that's just an economic move on their part.' Well, no it isn't. It's a determination to be less wasteful. We're nearing the end of the resources. There's enough of

The award winning catalog put together by Mires Design.

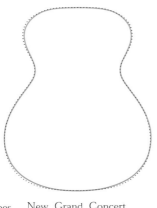 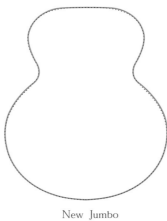

Illustration showing the
difference between the
new and old jumbo and
grand concert shapes.

Dotted outlines are the old shapes   New Grand Concert   New Jumbo
shape is solid blue   shape is solid red

it now, it's renewable, so let's not waste it." Over the next couple of years Taylor phased the NT necks into the entire line.

Most of the news about the Taylor's 25th anniversary dealt with the guitars and Bob Taylor's innovations in design and building techniques. But Taylor's long-time partner Kurt Listug got some well-deserved recognition from his peers in the advertising world. On April 30 the San Diego Ad Club awarded the "Best of Show" honor for the 1998 Taylor catalog, which he designed with the help of Mires Design. Listug had been content to stay out of the limelight, but Bob Taylor always cites him as the main reason their company has been as successful as it became. "I never would've gotten this far without Kurt as partner," Taylor stated in an interview in the fall 1999 issue of *Wood&Steel*.

In that same interview Listug reflected on why the two fledgling guitar builders were able to grow such a flourishing company. "Although Bob and I were both making guitars at the American Dream, I was never that interested in that part of business. I was interested in the guitars themselves, but I branched off to handle the business side of things and over time I realized I had an aptitude for that. It also made it easier on Bob because he didn't have to keep showing me how to do something on a guitar that he'd shown me a hundred times before and I still didn't get it."

The combination of Listug's business sense and Taylor's genius for guitar and tool design proved to be explosive. In their 25 years together Taylor and Listug estimated their company had built over 100,000 guitars, which is a remarkable total when you consider it took Gibson 44 years to build the same number of instruments and it took Martin 114 years to reach a similar figure.

Taylor's output was impressive and at the end of 1999, in his annual speech at the company's holiday party, Bob Taylor delivered a list of figures that put an unusual spin on the previous year's production totals. He estimated his workers used 24 miles of fret wire, 141.8 miles of guitar strings, and 571,200 sheets of sandpaper. They spent $59,888 on glue for the case factory, they bought 54,200 ebony fretboards, and they made 48,000 sales calls. He also figured that they brewed 13,500 pots of coffee that took 1,680,000 minutes to drink and caused 267,000 trips to the toilet that had to be cleaned 26,700 times.

With their 25th anniversary behind them, Taylor approached the new millennium with their usual optimistic outlook. Since they expanded the standard line to 61 models in 1998, the 2000 NAMM Show in January was a showcase for a wide variety of Limited Editions. They introduced the magnificent Gallery Series, which was inaugurated with a model called Living Jewels a blue guitar that featured multicolored koi inlaid into the top and fretboard. Taylor also announced a series of Limited Edition Signature Models that included instruments designed for Jewel, Kenny Loggins, Richie Sambora, Doyle Dykes, John Cephas, Chris Proctor, and Clint Black. They also introduced the 15/16ths size Big Baby and began offering the smaller-sized Baby Taylor in a variety of woods including maple, rosewood, and bubinga.

Headstock of a Taylor
nylon-string guitar.

Later that year Bob Taylor was awarded US Patent Number 6,051,766 for the NT neck design. It was his first patent. Around the same time Taylor and Listug signed a five-year lease on a 22,000 square foot building in Tecate, Mexico, which was to be the new home for the case factory. The partners had been talking about opening a case facility in Mexico for years, and were quite pleased they were finally able to get the opportunity to do it. "The big picture is that the company wants to grow," Listug said at the time. "And there's an opportunity in Mexico with the lower costs there. With our own factory we can hire and train our own people, which will be good for us. We don't intend to build guitars there, but in the future we may start making parts such as bridges there. "

In 2000 Bob Taylor also redesigned the jumbo and grand concert body shapes to bring them in line with the grand auditorium and the redesigned dreadnoughts. The new body shapes had been worked out prior to the introduction of the NT neck, but Taylor decided to wait until the production kinks had been worked out before committing to the new shapes. "To change the shape of a guitar even a little bit requires entirely new tools," Taylor explains. "It makes no difference if you're redesigning an existing shape, or creating an entirely new one; it's the same amount of work and time. In order to make the NT necks we had to change everything, from the aluminum body molds to the side-benders we use. There was no sense in retooling first to build new body shapes for our old method of constructing guitars and then retooling a year later to implement the new neck technology."

"The difference is subtle but striking," Taylor says. "You change a couple of little curves, take a 16th of an inch away here, take something that was flat for five inches and put a slight curve in it, droop a little section and make another curve tighter, and suddenly you have the same basic guitar shape, but it's way more pleasing to my eye. It's well worth the effort."

Rather than introduce a batch of new models in 2001, Taylor decided to concentrate of refining the current line of guitars. They switched the plastic binding on the 300 and 400 Series guitars to a new fiber binding, which gave the instruments a softer, less hard-edged look. In keeping with his stated goals of conserving wood whenever possible, Bob Taylor started switching from abalone to koa wood rosettes on the 500 and 700 Series. The pieces for the new rosettes were salvaged from the cut-offs that were leftover from the Koa Series and were previously discarded as scrap.

The maple 600 Series was expanded to include three new sunburst patterns: a reddish Cherry Sunburst, a brownish Tobacco Sunburst, and a golden Honey Sunburst. The 800 Series was left unchanged, but the 900 Series fretboard, which previously featured the Cindy pattern that Bob Taylor designed for his wife, was redesigned with a sleeker, more modern design. Because of the way the NT neck was inlaid into the top, Taylor stopped inlaying abalone around the tongue of the fretboard. The Walnut Series got a new Celtic motif fretboard inlay and the Koa Series was now bound in agoya shell. After being made of ultra-fancy koa for three years, the Presentation Series was being made of Brazilian rosewood again. The Acoustic Bass Series now included four models: the AB-1, with a spruce top and imbuia back and sides, the all imbuia

NS72ce with a cedar top and rose-wood sides and back. The sound-hole rosette was etched with a laser.

The new 110 (left)
and the 214.

AB-2, the AB-3, with spruce top and maple back and sides, the AB-3, and the new AB-4, which featured a maple top, back and sides.

The Doyle Dykes Signature Model, which was offered as a limited edition in 2000, was added to the standard line. The new model had maple back and sides and a spruce top. It had a grand auditorium silhouette with a grand concert depth. The model also sported a sharp, Florentine cutaway and L.L. Baggs pickup that was built to Dykes's specifications.

The Nylon String Guitars

If 2001 was a conservative year, 2002 saw the introduction of Bob Taylor's most audacious guitar yet: the Nylon Series. Bob Taylor had been toying with the idea of making a nylon string guitar as early as 1995. He built a number of prototypes and showed them at various trade shows. Taylor showed his early versions to a number of classical guitar players, including Christopher Parkening, but their reactions were decidedly lukewarm. Surprisingly, the prototypes found favor with electric guitarists and steel string guitarists who were looking for a different sound. In 1998 Steve Stevens, Billy Idol's guitarist played one of the prototypes at the Taylor NAMM booth and sparked interest in the guitar among other non-classical guitarists.

> "It took a little while to gain the confidence to trust my ear on this project, but once that happened, we got there really quickly."

Unfortunately, Taylor was unable to immediate capitalize on the buzz as building the new factory and NT neck project took precedence. But the extra time allowed Bob Taylor and his staff to rethink the nylon-string guitar project and allowed them to create an instrument that was more suited to Taylor's customers. So an instrument that started out as a guitar designed to appeal to classical players slowly evolved into a crossover guitar, one that was designed to bridge the gap between traditional steel string guitars and nylon string classical guitars.

Building a nylon-string guitar required Bob Taylor to learn a whole new set of guitar making skills. Because nylon strings exert much less tension than steel strings the tops are generally much thinner. Also, the bracing tends to be of a fan pattern rather than the cross bracing Taylor had been working with for decades. Taylor experimented with a variety of bracing patterns similar to those used by the great Spanish builders Ramirez and Rodriguez, but he soon started tweaking them. "It took a little while to gain the confidence to trust my ear on this project, but once that happened, we got there really quickly," Taylor says. "I like guitars that have clear treble, bright notes, and sustain. So I started looking for a tone that is open and clear." Bob Taylor eventually settled on an asymmetrical fan pattern that incorporated a ladder brace under that top that was situated below the soundhole and above the bridge.

He and his team believed that most people who bought the new nylon string guitar were likely to be steel string players, so they borrowed a few features that were commonplace in the steel string world, but unusual in the classical guitar world. The fretboards were slightly arched like steel string guitars and all four of the initial models had cutaways and pickups. The body shape was based on the grand concert but it had the depth of a dreadnought. And unlike the standard line, which was grouped by wood, the new guitars were grouped by string type. The new name started with NS, which stood for Nylon Series, followed by a two-digit number that designated the wood choice. On the NS32ce, for example, the 3 showed the back and sides were made of sapele, just like the 300 Series, the 2 was the designation for the grand concert size, and the 'ce' meant the guitar had a cutaway and an electric pickup.

The four models were the Sitka spruce top, sapele back and sides NS32ce, the Sitka spruce top, ovangkol back and sides NS42ce, the Englemann spruce top, maple back and sides NS62ce, and the cedar top, Indian rosewood back and sides NS72ce. Bob Taylor was excited about how the nylon string guitars turned out and he is interested to find out how musicians will utilize them in the future. "If we could fast forward 20 years, I have a feeling there will be people who will have found a bridge to classical guitar playing, who'll bring their body of knowledge and playing style with them, whether it's fingerstyle or rock and roll," he says. "Maybe that makes these guitars sound more significant than they'll really be, but I do believe in the power of manufacturing to create new musical opportunities."

Later that same year Taylor added the mahogany back and sides, cedar top cutaway NS52ce to the Nylon Series. The Fall LTDs included a number of grand auditorium nylon strings. The larger bodied guitars were offered without cutaways, but they did have a Fishman transducer mounted under the saddle. The new models included the Sitka spruce top, sapele back and sides NS34; the Sitka spruce top, ovangkol back and sides NS44; the cedar top, mahogany back and sides NS54; the Englemann spruce top, maple back and sides NS64; and the cedar top, Indian rosewood back and sides NS74. The larger guitars had a much warmer tone with more acoustic volume that the smaller instruments.

In 2003 Taylor announced two new mid-priced guitars, the 110 and the 214. They were designed to sell for well below the 300 Series and to compete with instruments imported from Asia. The 110 was a full size dreadnought with a laminated arched back and solid spruce top. The neck joint was a simplified version of the NT neck, which cut down on construction time. The 214 was a grand auditorium with a solid sapele back and sides and a solid spruce top. It had the same simplified neck joint as the 110. Both instruments had a satin finish.

Also in 2003 Bob Taylor revoiced the dreadnoughts, giving them a richer, bassier tone. Over the last few years players had commented that the dreadnoughts and the grand auditoriums sounded too similar, with both having a brighter, crisper tone. After extensive testing and building a dozen prototypes, the Taylor design crew decided to slim down the top bracing, reduce the size of the bridge plate, and move the X-brace closer to the soundhole.

The Expression System Pickup

The 110 and the 214 were immediately popular with dealers, but the big buzz at the 2003 Winter NAMM Show was the release of the new Taylor designed and built Expression System pickup. The Expression System, or ES, was designed by long-time Taylor employee David Hosler with help from Matt Guzzetta and repair technician David Judd. The internal preamp for the ES was designed by the sound engineering legend Rupert Neve. The entire project took three years to bring to fruition.

Hosler had played guitar since he was a teenager and had owned and operated his own custom guitar building and repair shop for a dozen years, so he was well aware of the issues facing acoustic guitarists who wanted to amplify their instruments. He was familiar with the advantages and disadvantages of the piezo and magnetic pickups on the market, and he was confident that he could come up with something better.

The first thing Hosler had to do was to figure out how an acoustic guitar actually produced sound. Hosler understood the basic principles of how a guitar top worked, but he realized he would have to gain a deeper knowledge of the subtle interplay between the top, back, sides, strings, and bridge. He began searching the Internet for institutions and companies that were involved in testing moving parts and the effects of vibration on various types of structures, which

The Taylor Expression Pickup System. >

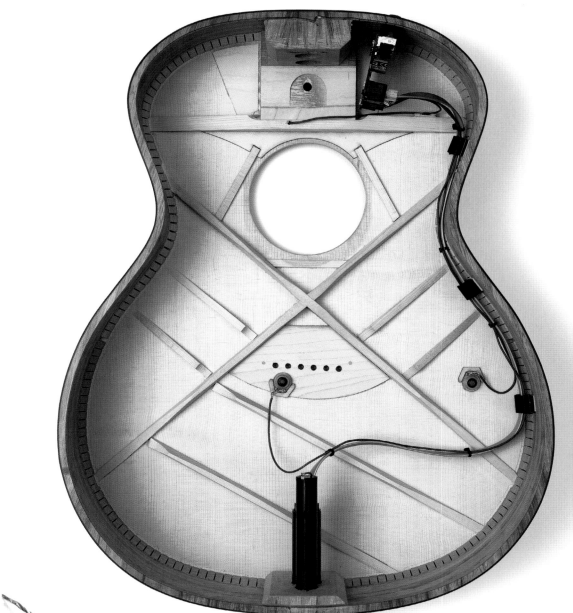

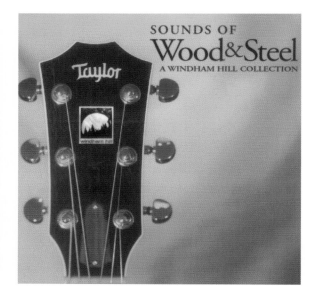

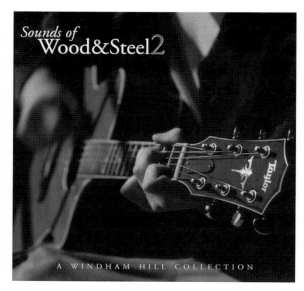

The three CDs that TJ Baden produced. Bob Taylor made his recording debut on Volume 2.

eventually led him to Mark French, who was an adjunct professor of structural dynamics at the University of Michigan, Dearborn. French had also worked as an engineer in the automotive industry, but most importantly, he was also an amateur guitar builder.

Hosler and French measured the top vibrations of a Taylor guitar using an optical measuring system known as 3-D laser interferometry and then translated that data into animated videos. This allowed them to see how the entire top was moving and revealed some surprising results. "One of the interesting things we learned is that the bass doesn't come off the bass side of the top," Hosler said in an interview in the Winter 2003 issue of *Wood&Steel*. "Another is how much the neck contributes to the sound. The bottom line in this whole process is that very little of what we thought we knew about the guitar was true."

They discovered that the top vibrations and the interactions of the top with the back, sides, and necks were much more complex than they had anticipated. As Jim Kirlin described it in *Wood&Steel*, the two men found "the entire guitar top never moves in the same direction. There is a constant seesaw effect, in which the soundboard undulates along the top and bottom, and back and forth, and between left and right." To add to the complexity, they also found that the back moved in a series of waves.

Hosler felt that piezo pickups that mounted under the saddle, such as those built by Fishman and L.R. Baggs, and pickups that mounted an element under the top like the one made by Barcus-Berry were only amplifying a small part of the sound. He finally settled on a system that used three elements, two Dynamic Body Sensors that were mounted under the top, and a Dynamic String Sensor that was mounted in a channel underneath the fretboard. The sensor under the fretboard was a magnetic pickup that picked up the vibration of the string in the same manner as any other magnetic pickup. But the two top sensors, which were also magnetic, picked up the top's vibration in a way that was more akin to a phonograph cartridge picked up the vibrations in a record's grooves.

The preamp for this trio of sensors was designed by audio engineering legend Mr. Rupert Neve. "Rupert's coming on board gave us horsepower," Bob Taylor says. "He knows a lot about magnets, audio transformers, and a few real basic technologies that have gotten recording and public-address systems all the way up to where they are now. He also inspired us along the way, unlocked a lot of secrets about how magnetic pickups work, and really was able to take David Hosler's inventive fervor down this long path of experimentation."

Mr. Rupert Neve's preamp was an extremely high-quality unit that, when the tone controls were set flat, was designed to amplify the signal from the sensors with as little tone coloration as possible. The onboard controls were set in the shoulder of the guitar and were set almost flush with the side. A guitar equipped with an Expression System could be connected to an amplifier via an XLR cable or a standard 1/4 inch phone plug. Mr. Rupert Neve also designed the K4 Equalizer, which was a stand-alone device. The unit, which was capped with a piece of koa, gave the ES a greater degree of flexibility in connecting to mixing boards, recording consoles, and amplifiers.

2003 was an unusual year for the Taylor company. "We started the year by not knowing if our country was going to go to war or not," Listug says. "The uncertainty about that, combined with the generally sluggish economy really depressed guitar sales. Then I had heart bypass surgery that kept me out of the office for two months. When I got back to work, Bob and I spent some serious time deciding what to do next. One of the things we did was put the mid-priced 110 and 214 into production. I think that Bob and his crew did a tremendous job with that. They took the 110 from prototype to production and to shipping them to stores in five weeks."

At the Summer NAMM Show Taylor announced they were going to make more than 130 different LTDs that fall. "It sounds like a lot when you put it that way, but when you consider that each series contains eight or nine different models, and that there are more than ten different series, it's not that overwhelming," Listug says. "Our designers had come up with so many different cool designs it seemed a shame to let them go unbuilt."

Even with all of the uncertainty at the beginning of the year, Taylor managed to increase their sales once again. By the end of the year they had made a little over 72,000 instruments, their highest total yet. They also began to look forward to their 30th anniversary in 2004. "Our 30th Anniversary model is going to be a deeper bodied grand concert with a slotted peghead like our nylon-string guitar," Bob Taylor says. "But the most important feature is going to be that 24 7/8 inch short-scale neck. Up until now all of our guitars have had a 25.5-inch scale length, which gives the guitar excellent projection and volume. But we've found that more and more players have been asking for a shorter scale instrument. On this style of guitar the strings aren't as tight, which makes the instrument a little easier to play. Surprisingly, Doyle Dykes, who is one of the best players I have ever heard, has been one of the guys really pushing us to do this. He feels that the shorter scale puts less strain on his hands, which will let him play longer without injuring himself."

Looking Forward

Bob Taylor and Kurt Listug took a tiny custom guitar shop and over three decades transformed it into one of the most successful guitar companies in the world. "I've been asked countless times about why I think we've done so well," Taylor says. "People always expect me to say something like, 'It's the quality of our guitars' or 'It's the building techniques we've developed' or 'It's the excellence of our employees.' Those are all important factors, but I always say the real reason for Taylor's success is the quality of my relationship with Kurt. We really need each other to make this company happen."

Kurt concurs. "I discovered early on that even though I loved guitars, I wasn't cut out to be a luthier," he says. "It turned out that I was as good at managing a business as Bob was at building guitars. It was extremely fortunate for both of us that our skills and interests complemented each other so well. I know that Bob would have been successful at whatever he chose to do, because he is such a brilliant engineer and builder, but I like to think that together we created something that no one else could have done."

"I give Kurt most of the credit for the success of the company," Taylor says. "I think I was probably destined to be a guitar maker, and I like to think I would have succeeded on my own if I had happened to buy the American Dream by myself. You know, I tend to get the lion's share of the attention because it's my name on the headstock, but if it wasn't for Kurt in the background keeping the company running smoothly, we wouldn't have had the time or money or tools to develop things like the NT neck or the Expression System pickup."

And what does Bob Taylor see as his legacy? "I think we've built some really nice guitars over the years, which I hope people will play long after I'm gone. On the technical end of things I pioneered the use of CNC machines in the building of acoustic guitars and there are some tools we designed that I'm proud of. But I think I'd be content to know that after I've gone, people said, 'He left the world of guitars better off than when he found it.' I think that would be a good way to be remembered."

"Taylor makes great guitars because we know how. And to prove it, we can even make one out of a junky, old, discarded pallet." Bob Taylor

Taylor Custom Shop and Limited Editions

Early custom guitars. Almost a rainbow of finishes. The Pallet Guitar. The Cujo Guitar. Lots of limited editions and signature models. The custom shop reopens. Liberty Tree. The Gallery Series. More than 130 limited editions for 2003.

Taylor's Origins as a Custom Shop

Over the years, Bob Taylor and his design crew have treated custom orders as a fertile source of ideas to enhance the standard line. From the early days of the American Dream, Bob Taylor realized that designing and building custom guitars for clients was the most direct way of learning what players wanted. So even as he developed new methods to build the standard line of guitars, he kept in touch with what musicians wanted by building a number of custom guitars. After all, if enough people began ordering similar custom features that was a good sign that those features might be successfully integrated into the standard line.

The Taylor Guitar company started out as a custom shop. When Bob Taylor, Kurt Listug, and Steve Schemmer bought the American Dream in 1974, all of the instruments they built were made to order. They offered two stock body shapes—the dreadnought and the jumbo—but the wood choice and the selection of cosmetic appointments like the fretboard inlays and the body trim were left up to the customer. In 1975 they combined some of the most popular features such as a dreadnought body shape, rosewood sides and back, spruce top, and white binding and came up with the 810, their first distinct model. In a way, the creation of the 810 was a collaboration between the guitar builders and their customers.

It took a while for the features of the rest of the standard line to get sorted out. In 1975 and 1976 Taylor, Listug, and Schemmer experimented with a variety of woods and trim styles to add to the line of guitars. Confusingly for historians and collectors, some of their experiments were given model designations that contradict the current naming system. "Around 1975 or 1976, we made a few of our fancy bird's-eye maple guitars and called them our 700 series," Listug explains. "We didn't make many of them, and later we introduced them as our premium guitars, the 900 series. I think we even made a few bird's-eye maple dreadnoughts, and called them 715's. The same guitar today would be known as a '910 Maple.'"

Another naming anomaly from the early days was the way they designated abalone-bordered guitars. "Back then, the trick was to load up the guitar with tons of abalone inlay," Listug recalls. "It took us forever to make a guitar, anyway, so why not take another day or two to add a bunch of inlay, which would enable us to sell it for more. We even came up with a model designation for an 'abalone boat' guitar: Just add 30." Under that naming system, which only lasted a few months in 1976, an 810 with abalone bordering became an 840, while a 12-string 855 became an 885, and so on. Today, models with similar features would probably be part of the 900 Series.

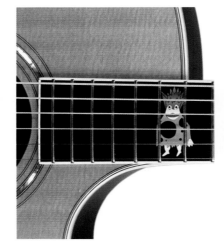
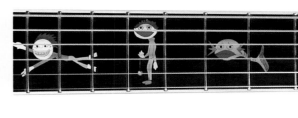

From 1977 through 1980, Taylor, Listug, and Schemmer worked on codifying the line and added the rosewood 700 Series, the 900 Series, and the 500 Series. They also introduced the 600 Series, which was initially built with mahogany sides and back, then dropped from the line in 1979, and reintroduced as a maple guitar in 1981. By the early 1980s, Taylor offered a variety of custom options such as sharp, Florentine cutaways, three different neck widths, and factory installed Barcus-Berry pickups.

Throughout the 1980s, the acoustic guitar business was sluggish and Taylor, like every other guitar company was scrambling for business. They began to take custom orders for instruments they probably would have passed on if times weren't quite so desperate. As luck would have it, some of those guitars turned up in the hands of some of the most visible musicians of the era, which in turn put the Taylor company in the public eye.

The Colored Finishes

The most striking custom orders were for maple guitars with the stained, multi-colored finish developed by Larry Breedlove. In 1984 Prince took delivery of his purple 12-string, which launched a brief vogue for colored finishes. Kenny Loggins ordered a sky-blue jumbo 12-string, Harvey Reid ordered a ruby-red 12-string, Jeff Cook of the country band Alabama had a green dreadnought, which he was pictured holding on his band's Christmas album.

In 1987 Steve Stevens, the guitarist for Billy Idol ordered a black Jumbo cutaway with "atomic energy" symbols inlaid in the fretboard and around the soundhole. Stevens liked his guitar so much that he custom ordered a Taylor for his partner that featured the stylized planet Saturn graphic from the cover of Idol's *Whiplash Smile* album. Other interesting custom guitars from this time included a black 612-C that was built for the country singer Kathy Mattea and a guitar for Edie Brickell that featured colorful fretboard inlays that were cut by Larry Breedlove.

In the 1980s, the custom shop also gave birth to the Dan Crary Signature Model and the Leo Kottke Signature Model, two guitars that were designed with the direct input of the artists. Unlike the other guitars that Taylor built for recording stars, these two models both became part of the standard line. The success of these two models inspired the Taylor design team to work closely with other prominent artists to develop other signature models.

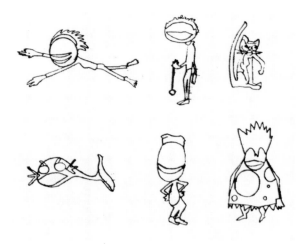

Concept drawings by Larry Breedlove based on Edie Brickell's hand-drawn cartoons.

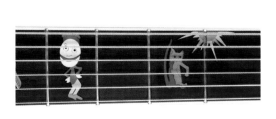

The final inlay job on Edie Brickell's custom Taylor guitar.

One of only ten limited edition Pallet Guitars. Like the original, these guitars were made from oak shipping pallets and2X4s.

In 1993 the growing popularity of custom orders led to Taylor temporarily suspending production of them. As the slump in acoustic guitar sales throughout the 1980s gave way to a boom in the 1990s, Taylor found they were getting more custom orders than they could handle. The sales department was having difficulty keeping track of the orders while at the same time the builders were still learning to work with the new Fadals. At that time Taylor and Listug decided to take the most popular custom features and make them part of the standard line.

In the 1980s Taylor began offering limited runs of various guitars. These instruments, which were essentially custom orders generated by the Taylor company itself, ranged from completely new guitars like the grand auditorium to the brightly stained Artists Series to more whimsical guitars like the Cujo model, which was inspired by the movie based in Stephen King's novel.

The total number of each limited edition was set by various criteria. The anniversary models and certain signature models were limited to a predetermined quantity. Those made with particularly rare wood were limited by the supply of the material in question. And some models, particularly the cosmetic variations on the standard line, were limited to the number of instruments ordered during a set period of time.

The Design Studio

Although Taylor wasn't taking custom orders from the public, they were still generating them in-house. Without a doubt the most successful of these was the Limited Edition 20th Anniversary grand auditorium, which was the first version of the shape that has become Taylor's most popular body style. In 1995 Taylor opened the Design Studio, which became their R&D center. Bob Taylor and his staff used this area of the factory to experiment with new bracing patterns, different body shapes, new wood combinations, and new building techniques. They also began producing a very few special guitars built from the particularly fine pieces of wood that came through the factory.

Most of these instruments were made of the rarest, most beautiful pieces of exotic tonewoods and inlaid with highly figured pieces of pearl and abalone. But the most interesting guitar to come out of the Design Shop's early days was made from an oak shipping pallet that was pulled out of a garbage can. "The whole point of the Pallet Guitar is to return the emphasis to the guitar maker," Bob Taylor explained in an interview in the Spring 1995 issue of *Wood&Steel*. "By now a lot of people think that Taylor makes great guitars because we have a stock of exceptional wood. Even salesmen use that as a selling point. But that's not what makes our guitars so good. Taylor makes great guitars because we know how. And to prove it, we can even make one out of a junky, old, discarded pallet."

The back and sides of the Pallet Guitar were made of oak, while the top was made from a 2x4 that

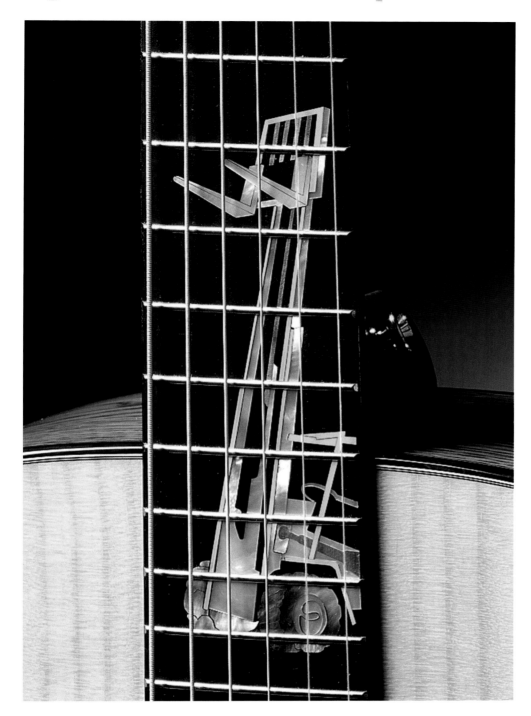

Close-up of forklift inlay.

Larry Breedlove's original sketch for the forklift inlay.

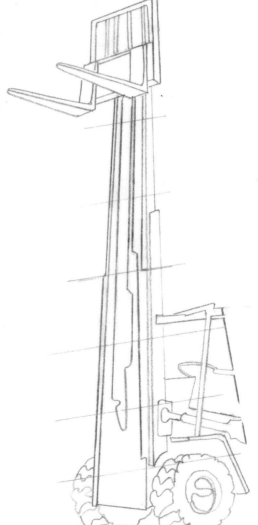

was so nondescript it was impossible to guess its species. "We did the back in a three-piece configuration, although it actually took five pieces of oak," Taylor explains. The top was made of six pieces of wood, although it was so skillfully joined it was nearly impossible to tell. Rather than try to hide the nail holes that covered the back and sides, Taylor decided to draw attention to them by inlaying aluminum dots that resemble nail heads in them. The fretboard featured an inlay designed by Larry Breedlove of a forklift done in Formica and pearl.

The Pallet Guitar was whimsical in appearance but it did prove an important point. Although it didn't sound as good as a rosewood or mahogany guitar, it did sound better than anyone expected. Bob Taylor set out to demonstrate that a talented luthier could take just about any piece of wood and make a good guitar out of it. And if he could take inferior wood and turn it into a good instrument like the Pallet Guitar, just imagine what he could do with a great piece of wood. The Pallet Guitar was one of the most talked about guitars at the Winter NAMM Show and over the next few years it was a prominent part of Taylor's show booth.

The original 512c that inspired the
Nanci Griffith Signature Model.

Limited Editions

Also in 1995, Taylor introduced two limited edition models: the 612-Cotten and the 810 Brazilian/Englemann. The 612-Cotten was built to honor Richard Cotten, a Nashville guitarist and music storeowner who had recently died of leukemia. Cotten was one of Taylor's first dealers in the South and he was a big fan of the 612 model. The Limited Edition featured a sharp, Florentine cutaway, unstained maple sides and back, and a special "cotton-ball" inlay that was a visual pun on Cotten's last name.

The 810 Brazilian/Englemann was built from wood that wasn't up to the cosmetic standards of the 900 Series, but was still functionally and acoustically sound. The 810 Limited Edition cost quite a bit less than its fancier counterpart, and made it a good value for a guitarist who wanted the sound of Brazilian rosewood, but didn't want to pay a premium for a pretty piece of wood. This model was also a tribute to the first 810s built in the 1970s, which were made of Brazilian rosewood.

The 612-Cotten and the 810 Brazilian/Englemann sold quite well so in 1996 Taylor increased the number of limited editions they planned to release. There were eight distinct models altogether and rather than put them all out at once, they decided to release some during the spring and some during the fall. This was the start of what became something of an annual tradition. Every January, at the Winter NAMM Show, Taylor would announce the special guitars that would be released that spring. Then at the Summer NAMM Show, which was in Nashville, they would announce the guitars that would be released that fall.

The spring LTDs for 1996 consisted of six models. There were four new variations of the 400 Series, including the 410ce, which was basically a standard 410 with a cutaway and pickup; the 422-R and the 420-R, which were 400s but with rosewood sides and back; and the 412-M, which was a grand concert 400 with a mahogany top.

The other spring LTDs included a six-string version of the Leo Kottke Signature Model. This limited run was so popular that the model was added to the standard line in 1997. Also released that year was the Nanci Griffith Signature Model, which was produced in a numbered series of 100 guitars. The Nanci Griffith model was a 512c with a sunburst, which was essentially a replica of the Taylor guitar she had been playing for years.

In the fall of 1996 Taylor brought out two limited editions: the mahogany top, back and sides 512-M and the cedar topped 714. Although the mahogany topped guitar had a rich tone and a lovely appearance it only sold a few units. But the cedar topped 714 sold so well that it became part of the standard line a couple of years later.

Reopening the Custom Shop

In 1997 Taylor reopened the custom shop. Bob Taylor felt that his various departments were now running smoothly and that he and his crew could take on just about any job. Most of the new customs they began making tended to mix and match the various features from the different series they currently made with the occasional discontinued design elements from the past. But every now and then they would take on an unusual job such as a double-neck guitar for Richie Sambora or a baritone guitar for Dave Matthews.

In 1997 Taylor introduced the limited edition 612-KM, which was based in part on the 612c that Kathy Mattea custom ordered in 1991. The new signature model, which was built in a series of 100 units, was stained black like Mattea's original guitar, but it had a new inlay in the fretboard and headstock that was designed specially for her. "I remember when Taylor came out with the Nanci Griffith model and the Kottke model," Mattea said. "I thought, 'Man, what a milestone for them.' I'm thrilled to think that I might see someone playing 'my' model Taylor out there. And I hope they grow to love their guitar as much as I love mine."

That summer Taylor released five limited editions. The 510-LTD was based on a variation of the standard 510 that Bob Taylor had built for himself. The new model featured a Sitka spruce top instead of the Englemann spruce top that was standard on the 500 series at the time. It also had ivoroid binding on the body, neck and headstock and small pearl dots in the fretboard. The cosmetic features were a subtle change, but they gave the guitar a look that recalled guitars built in the 1930s. Taylor also released the 514-CW, a cutaway grand auditorium with a cedar top and wood binding. The 714-Cedar was brought back due to popular demand. And Taylor built a small number of 710kce's, a koa, cutaway version of the standard 710.

Perhaps the most interesting model was the 810-WMB. This model was essentially a standard 810 with slightly lighter top braces, which gave the guitar a bassier response. (The W stood for Wood binding and the MB for More Bass,

Richie Sambora's custom Koa double neck.

One of the 125 Cujo dreadnoughts
and a closeup of the fretboard inlay
on the Cujo guitar.

Taylor Custom Shop and Limited Editions

although a few wags claimed it stood for With Martin Bass, a reference to the booming bass tone associated with Martin guitars.) The 810-WMB marked the first time that Bob Taylor tried to create a guitar with a different sound than the bright, clear tone that his instruments had become known for. The tweaked version of the 810 sold fairly well, but Bob Taylor continued to experiment with the bracing patterns under the top for the next few years.

The Cujo Guitar

That fall Taylor only introduced one limited edition, but it was a very special guitar. In 1995 Bob Taylor bought some figured walnut from a wood dealer named Skyler Phelps. The tree was cut down on a farm in Northern California, and Phelps mentioned in passing that the tree was used in scene in *Cujo*, the movie about a rabid St. Bernard based on the novel by Stephen King. The Taylor crew began to jokingly refer to the walnut as being "*Cujo* wood." At some point someone at Taylor decided to turn the joke into reality and approached Stephen King and asked if he would allow them to base a guitar design on a scene from the movie. King, who was an avid guitarist himself, was tickled by the idea and quickly said yes.

Over the next few months the Taylor design shop worked on a fretboard design and finally settled on an inlay that featured the rabid dog, a bat silhouetted against the moon, and part of the barn from the film. The inlay was made up of pieces of agoya shell, abalone, black oyster shell, mahogany, maple, and Formica. The inlay was the most complex design that the Taylor team had done up to that point. They only made 250 *Cujo* instruments—125 grand auditoriums and 125 dreadnoughts—and each one included a label hand signed by Stephen King, who got the first *Cujo* model off the line.

In 1998 Taylor expanded the line from 36 models to 61 so, not surprisingly, they didn't offer any special models that year. 1999 marked their 25th anniversary, which they celebrated by releasing a limited run of 25th Anniversary guitars made of quilted sapele. They also created a series of 18 commemorative models based on the 300, 400, 500, 600, 700, and 800 series from the standard line.

The three models in the 300 Series all had mahogany tops and included two dreadnoughts--the 310-M, the 310-MCE—and the 314-MCE grand auditorium. The 400 and 500 commemoratives, which also included a standard dreadnought, a cutaway dreadnought, and a grand auditorium, were essentially identical to those in the standard line except for the addition of an abalone top border. The 600 series commemoratives also featured an abalone top border, but substituted a 612 grand concert for the non-cutaway dreadnought. The 700 and 800 series commemoratives were both built with Brazilian rosewood for the sides and back.

The Gallery Series

In 2000 Taylor introduced the Gallery Series, which was designed to showcase the artistic ability and technological prowess of his crew. "For some time, we design guys at Taylor have been talking about how much fun it would be to utilize our current technological capabilities, and our comfort with cutting all these different materials with lasers," Bob Taylor explained in the Winter 2000 issue of *Wood&Steel*. " Now, I realized a long time ago that there are people out there who are better artists than we are, and I'd been thinking about collaborating with some inlay-

The 25th Anniversary Dreadnought

One of the 100 Living
Jewels models and
some details of koi .

art specialists. But one day it occurred to me we didn't need an inlay artist, we just needed some fresh art, some new ideas."

Bob Taylor's first artist was a young man named Pete Davies, whose father worked as a master machinist at Taylor for years and whose mother managed the Taylor Ware line of clothing and accessories. "Pete's a good artist, and right away he demonstrated a knack for being able to change his art so that it would be 'inlayable,'" Taylor continued. "What kind of art is inlayable? Think of coloring book art, cartoon art, certain kinds of tattoo art. In its simplest form, it has to fit together like a jigsaw puzzle or a paint-by-numbers pattern—a bunch of colorful little shapes that don't look like much individually, but when you put them together they form a unique image."

Davies immediately grasped the potential of what could be done by treating the guitar as canvas and for his first guitar he came up with the idea of using brightly colored koi fish as the subject. Rather than use the traditional pearl and abalone, Davies used synthetic materials like Color Core Formica, faux-pearl, and material that was made of ground up turquoise, coral and stone mixed with resin. The first Gallery Series guitar, which was dubbed "Living Jewels," was stained blue and the multi-colored fish appeared to swim off the fretboard and onto the top. It was offered in a limited edition of 100.

Front and back of the Sea Turtle Gallery Series model, showing the turtle and jellyfish detail.

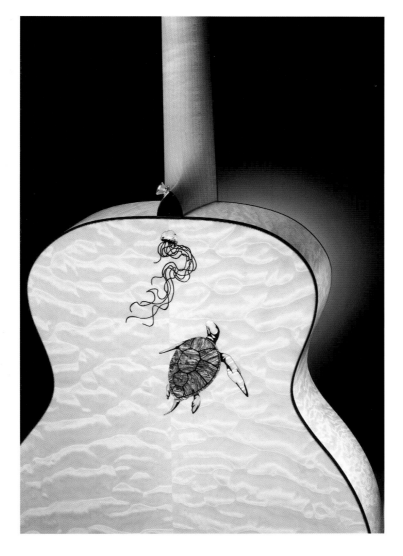

The second guitar in the Gallery Series was dubbed the Sea Turtle and featured two turtles swimming along the fretboard and a turtle and jellyfish swimming on the back. This model was subtler than the Living Jewels guitar, but the curly maple on the back that made it look as if the sea creatures were swimming through the waves was a particularly clever use of material. That same year Taylor released a series of 25 limited edition Pallet Guitars. As with the original, these instruments were made from oak shipping pallets and mystery wood 2x4s.

Lots of New Signature Models

Also in 2000 Taylor released a slew of signature models, which were designed with the input of Kenny Loggins, Jewel, Richie Sambora, Doyle Dykes, John Cephas, Chris Proctor, and Clint

Front view of the Jewel Kilcher Model.

Rear view of the Jewel Kilcher Model.

Front view of the Richie Sambora Model.

Black. Loggins had been playing Taylor guitars for years and had almost a dozen in his collection including a custom blue 12-string, an AB-1 bass, a handful of standard models and a bunch of Baby Taylors. The Kenny Loggins Signature Model (KLSM) was based on the K-15c, which was a koa cutaway. The top, back and sides of the KLSM were built with figured koa and a fretboard inlay that featured flowers cut from maple and koa. The Richie Sambora Signature Model (RSSM) also featured an all-koa construction, but it was based on the smaller grand auditorium size. The custom fretboard inlays were cut from bloodwood and maple.

The Jewel Kilcher Signature Model (JKSM) was based on the 314 and featured a spruce top and satinwood back and sides. The JKSM also boasted an inlay of her signature in the fretboard and an inlay in the back of an emblem that Jewel called the 'flower of life." The John Cephas Signature Model (JCSM) was an austere version of the 914. It featured the premium Indian rosewood, Englemann spruce top, and wood bindings of the 900 series but not the fan-

Front view of
the John
Cephas Model.

Rear view of the
John Cephas
Model.

Front view of
the Kenny Log-
gins Model.

Front view of
the Clint Black
Model.

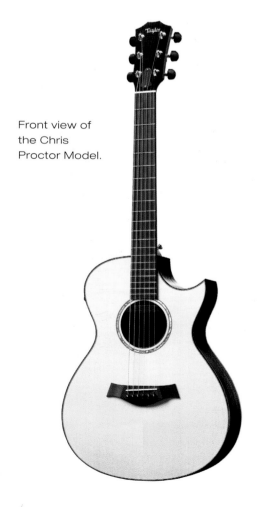

Front view of
the Chris
Proctor Model.

cy fretboard inlays and abalone top borders. The JCSM included a subtle inlay of a bluesman walking down the road.

The Clint Black Signature Model (CBSM) was the most difficult of the 2000 signature editions to bring to fruition. Black was involved in every step of the design process and he re-worked the fretboard illustration a number of times before everyone was satisfied that it would look good as an inlay . The fretboard featured a musical staff in pearl and agoya shell that appeared to weave in and out of the frets. The guitar itself was based on Black's favorite Taylor, the 912. "Clint really made us work for this one," Larry Breedlove recalls. "But in the end it was worth it. It's a really beautiful guitar."

The Chris Proctor Signature Model (CPSM) paid tribute to the musician who helped Bob Taylor get the grand concert body style off the drawing board and into the hands of players. As with the John Cephas model, the CPSM is based on a stripped down version of the 912. The CPSM had no fretboard inlay at all and a wide, 1 7/8ths inch nut width. Proctor had long been an advocate of the wide fretboard/small body set up, and this version captured his aesthetic perfectly.

The Doyle Dykes Signature Model (DDSM) was the one guitar in the 2000 signature series that featured more than just a cosmetic re-working of an existing instrument. Dykes had been playing a custom 614c grand auditorium that had been built with the shallower body depth of the grand concert. Dykes felt that this combination gave him the volume of the larger guitar, with the projection and treble response of the smaller instrument. The DDSM had maple sides and back, a spruce top, and a sharp, Florentine cutaway. It was also available in a black finish or a natural finish. The model proved to be so popular that it was added to the standard line the following year.

Not all of the limited edition guitars in 2000 were expensive showpieces. That fall Taylor brought out a koa version of the 300 series and a maple version of the 400 series. The 300 LTDs included the 310k dreadnought, the 310kce cutaway dreadnought with Fishman pickup, the 314k grand auditorium, and the 314kce grand auditorium with a cutaway and pickup. The 400 series LTDs featured the same model breakdown. That year Taylor also built a number of limited edition 800 series instruments out of Brazilian rosewood and Englemann spruce.

In 2001 Taylor brought out the third instrument in the Gallery series. Like the two previous Gallery guitars, this one also featured a nautical theme. Dubbed the Gray Whales, this guitar included a pod of gray whales swimming up the fretboard and a sailing ship that appeared to be sailing out of the soundhole. The soundhole itself was ringed by a complex image of a rope that included a variety of sailor's knots. The back and sides were made of zircote, a Mexican hardwood that resembles Brazilian rosewood.

Many of the other limited editions in 2001 featured unusual tonewoods as well. The 300 series LTDs were made of imbuia, which had been used on the acoustic basses since 1995. Over the years Bob Taylor had saved up enough sets of imbuia that were too small for the basses, but large enough for a run of 400 guitars. "I'd love to use imbuia all the time for guitars," Taylor explained. "The only thing preventing me is the scarcity." The limited edition 700 Series guitars for that same year were made of cocobolo, a very dense tonewood that has a tone and appearance that is often compared to Brazilian rosewood.

Once again Taylor built a small run of limited edition 800s in Brazilian rosewood. He also earmarked fifty sets of particularly fine Brazilian to make into limited edition 910s and 914s. And he was able to score enough koa to build 500 limited edition 400 series guitars. The 600 Series LTDs for 2001 featured the same Artist Series inlays that first appeared on the multi-colored guitars from the late 1980s. They also had abalone-bordered tops and a choice of sunburst finishes.

Front view of the
Doyle Dykes Model
with black finish.

Front view of
Liberty Tree Guitar.

Rear view of
Liberty Tree Guitar.

Close-up of
Liberty Tree Guitar.

The Liberty Tree Guitar

In 2002 Taylor released the Liberty Tree Guitar, which was built using wood from a 400-year-old tulip poplar that had been designated as a gathering place for patriots in Annapolis, Maryland in the years leading up to the American Revolution in 1776. Each of the original thirteen American colonies had such trees, but over the last two hundred years they had each died off, leaving the Maryland Liberty Tree as the last survivor. It grew on the grounds of St. John's College until it was severely damaged by Hurricane Floyd in 1999. Prior to that, it had seemed to be indestructible and had survived fires, lightning strikes, and major storms.

In the 1840s it suffered extensive damage from fungus and a worm infestation. Some schoolboys filled a hollow in the trunk with gunpowder and set it off as a prank. The blast knocked off all of the tree's leaves and appeared to have killed it. But the next spring the tree burst back into life. The gunpowder seemed to have killed only the fungus and the worms. By 1907 the tree was in very bad shape and the trunk was reinforced with concrete, which held it together until September 1999 when Hurricane Floyd damaged the tree beyond repair.

On October 25, 1999 officials at St. John's College finally bowed to the inevitable and ordered the damaged old tree to be cut down. They had the workers save a few choice pieces of wood and had the rest of the tree hauled to the dump. At that point a landscaper named Mark Mehnert realized there was still quite a bit of usable wood left and followed the trucks to the landfill and rescued as much of the stump and larger branches as he could. He stored the wood in a climate-controlled warehouse at his own expense while he tried to find a buyer who recognized the importance of the wood. In May 2000 he finally hooked up with Bob Taylor, who jumped at the chance to own this important piece of American history.

"I would've given anything to get my hands on the wood from the Liberty Tree," Taylor says. "But I figured the tree had been there for hundreds of years and everyone there knew about it. There must have been far more important people than me trying to get that wood. But then Mark called and offered it to me after all these people turned him down." Taylor eventually bought 30,000 pounds of wood and had it trucked to Pacific Rim Tonewoods in Washington, where it was cut, sawn into sets and dried. The wood arrived in El Cajon in late 2000, where Bob Taylor and his design team set about creating the inlay design for the guitar.

They finally settled on a grand concert body size and with an abalone-bordered top. The headstock was inlaid with a depiction of the first post-revolution version of the American flag that was made of bloodwood and dyed maple. The fretboard inlay extended onto the top and featured a laser etched maple rendition of a rolled copy of the Declaration of Independence. The rosette featured thirteen stars, one for each of the original colonies.

The Liberty Tree Guitar looked beautiful, but everyone at Taylor was nervous about how it would sound because no one had ever made a guitar out of tulip poplar before. "The wood on those guitars has a weight and density that's real similar to walnut," Bob Taylor says. "The sound was somewhere between walnut and mahogany. I'm really glad that the wood turned out to sound good."

Taylor eventually made around 400 full-size Liberty Tree guitars, which sold out quite rapidly. When they had completed the run of full-size guitars, they realized that they had enough small pieces of wood left over to make a run of around 400 Baby Taylor size Liberty Tree guitars. Bob Taylor has said that of all the guitars he has designed and built over the years, he is proudest of the Liberty Tree Guitar.

The Fall LTDs for 2002 featured some interesting new variations. In a reversal of 2001's models, the 300 series was made of maple and the 400 was made of imbuia. Each series included a version of the new grand auditorium 12-string, which was Taylor's first new 12-string mod-

Front view of a
Rick Nielsen Signa-
ture Model.

el in years. The 500 and 700 series were each represented by a single dreadnought. Each model included a larger, vintage style V-shaped neck. Then there were four limited edition 600 series models, which were all built of "white maple," which had a creamy color as the result of a quick wood-curing process. The models included a dreadnought, a grand auditorium, and grand auditorium with a cutaway and pickup, and grand auditorium 12-string.

The 800 series LTDs were made of figured cocobolo and included a dreadnought, a cutaway dreadnought with pickup, a grand auditorium, a grand auditorium with cutaway and pickup, and a grand auditorium 12-string. Taylor also released the Doyle Dykes "Desert Rose" Signature Model, which was a cosmetic variation of the DDSM from 2001. The new version featured an orange colored finish that recalled the finish on the Gretsch Tennessean that Dykes's hero Chet Atkins used to play. The headstock was inlaid with a desert rose and there was a desert scene inlaid around the 12th fret.

At the 2003 Winter NAMM Show in January they announced four new Signature Models, two Commemorative Models, and six NAMM Show Special Editions. At the Summer NAMM Show in Nashville, Taylor announced more than 130 fall LTDs. It almost seemed as if Taylor were actually building more limited editions than standard models. As part of the value-added thinking behind the limited and special editions, every cutaway model included the new Expression System pickup.

Even More Signature Models

The four signature models included instruments inspired by the Christian rock band Jars of Clay, Cheap Trick's lead guitarist Rick Nielsen, smooth jazz pioneer Russ Freeman, and Susanna Hoffs, who was the lead singer for Bangles. The Jars of Clay Signature Model (JCSM) was available as a dreadnought and as a grand auditorium. The top was made of cedar and the back and sides were made of sapele. Both models came with a rounded, Venetian cutaway and the new Expression System acoustic pickup. The Rick Nielsen Signature Model (RNSM) was based on a jumbo maple cutaway and came stock with an emerald green finish. The fretboard inlays were an imaginative reworking of the checkerboard motif that has graced Nielsen's guitars, straps, trousers and sneakers since the 1970s. It also came standard with an Expression system pickup.

The Russ Freeman Signature Model (RFSM) was based on the rosewood and spruce 814ce. The RFSM featured a close-up of a grinning jazz cat inlay on the headstock and an inlay of the same cool cat slinking off to a gig inlaid on the fretboard. The Susanna Hoffs Signature Model (SHSM) was based on an all-koa grand concert and featured the Bangles logo inlaid in the headstock.

The two commemorative models included the John Denver Commemorative Model (JDCM) and the Windham Hill Commemorative Model (WHCM). John Denver bought his first Taylor in 1994 and within a few months he bought a half a dozen more. The JDCM was based on one of his favorites, an all-koa

Detail of a green RNSM showing the exploding checker-board inlay pattern.

Front view of a Russ Freeman Signature Model.

K22. This model was built to honor the singer who died in 1997 in a tragic airplane crash. The fretboard inlay was based on a statute of Denver that was created by Sue DiCicco and now stands on the grounds of the Windstar Land Conservancy in Snowmass, Colorado. Taylor donated a percentage of the profits from each JDCM to the Windstar Foundation, which was co-founded by Denver and Tom Crum.

The Windham Hill Commemorative Model was designed to celebrate the famous record label that first came to prominence in the 1970s with a series of ground breaking acoustic guitar recordings. Windham Hill was the label that released the three *Sounds of Wood&Steel* CDs that were produced by Taylor's own TJ Baden. The WHCM was based on a dreadnought body with an Englemann spruce top and Indian rosewood sides and back. The headstock was adorned with the Windham Hill Logo and the body, neck and headstock were bound with ivoroid.

The NAMM Show Specials showcased some of the design shop's coolest ideas. Two of the instruments, the Pelican Guitar (PG-LTD) and the Running Horses Guitar (RH-LTD) featured inlays designed by Pete Davies Jr. The back and sides of the PG-LTD were made of myrtle wood, which is a wood that grows on the Pacific coast. The pelican inlays were laser cut from koa, walnut, satin wood, and myrtle. The RH-LTD was made of maple and featured a delicate, golden honey sunburst. The fretboard inlays of three running horses were laser cut from koa and maple. Both models featured the grand auditorium body shape.

The other NAMM models included the "Ruby Red" Presentation Series (PS-LTD), which was built with a AAA grade maple back and sides with and an Englemann spruce top that was colored a beautiful, translucent red; the Cowboy Sunburst (CS-LTD), which was a sunburst maple dreadnought with checkerboard binding; and the NC72ce-LTD, which was a Brazilian rosewood 700 series nylon string guitar.

Perhaps the most striking NAMM Special was the Hot Rod Guitar (HR-LTD), which was designed by Pete Davies with input from a long-time customer named Jared Rogers. As the story goes Rogers was taking a tour of the factory and he met Davies. It turned out that Davies and Rogers both shared a passion for hot rod cars. Davies showed Rogers some designs he had come up with a couple of years ago for a guitar based on a hot rod theme. Bob Taylor liked the design but felt at the time that it would have been too difficult to build. But Rogers fell in love with the design and convinced Taylor to accept a custom order for one. After seeing how well the guitar turned out, Bob Taylor changed his mind and authorized a limited edition based on the design.

The HR-LTD came in two versions; a black maple jumbo and a red back and sides, natural top grand auditorium. Both versions featured wooden flames inlaid in the fretboard and around the soundhole.

Lots and Lots and Lots of LTDs for 2003

The Fall LTDs for 2003 included so many different models that Taylor had to create a new numbering system to keep them straight. Each series included up to six variations and each variation was given a letter and number suffix. Each variation within a particular series was designated by the suffix L1, L2, L3, and so on. So, for example, a 2003 Limited Edition dreadnought 900 series in maple would have the designation 910-L2, while the rosewood version would be designated 910-L1.

The 300 series was available in koa, which was given the suffix L1 and maple, which was given the suffix L2. There were nine models altogether in the koa 300 series including cutaway and non-cutaway dreadnoughts, jumbo 12-strings, and grand auditoriums, a cutaway grand concert, a cutaway jumbo, and a grand auditorium 12-string. The maple 300 series featured the same mix of models. The 400 series came in imbuia (L1) and Indian rosewood (L2) and featured the same combination of models as the 300 series.

The 600 series was available with a cherry red to black sunburst (L1) or a dark blue to light blue sunburst (L2). Each version was available in seven styles including cutaway dreadnoughts, grand auditoriums, grand concerts, jumbos, jumbo 12-string, and grand auditorium 12-strings. There was also a non-cutaway jumbo 12-string offered in the 600 series.

The 700 series only featured one style, but in keeping with the general 2003 theme of confusion, they were built with different top woods depending on the body shape. The back and sides were made of grafted walnut, which was a wood that was created when a farmer grafted English walnut tree trunks, which had great tasting walnuts, to the disease resistant claro walnut root stocks. The graft line is still visible when the trees were cut down and gives the wood a remarkable grain pattern. The 700 series was available in cutaway and non-cutaway grand auditoriums, with Western red cedar tops, cutaway and non-cutaway dreadnoughts and grand concerts, which came with Englemann spruce tops, and a grand auditorium 12-string, which came with a Sitka spruce top.

The 800 series was remarkably straightforward and featured eight different styles built from Brazilian rosewood and Sitka spruce. The eight styles included a mix of dreadnoughts, jumbos, grand concerts and grand auditoriums.

The 900 series came in Indian rosewood (L1) or maple (L2). In an interesting twist each version came with a different fretboard inlay. The rosewood series featured the "Cindy Inlay" that Bob Taylor designed for his wife years ago, while the maple series featured the original 900 series inlay. Each series was offered in seven different models including a dreadnought, a jumbo 12-string and cutaway versions of the grand concert, grand auditorium, grand auditorium 12-string, and jumbo.

The most varied limited edition series were the Presentations, which came in six different styles. These included guitars made of Brazilian rosewood (LI), fancy koa (L2), grafted walnut (L3), cocobolo (L4), and maple, which came in a blue-burst finish (L5) and red-burst finish (L6). Each model in the Presentation series was bound around the top, back, and sides and around the soundhole with heart of abalone. The Brazilian and koa models also included abalone trim around the fretboard and around the headstock.

The Maranatha! series of guitars marked a departure from the standard Taylor grouping system. These instruments were designed with the input of worship leaders affiliated with the Calvary Chapel church, which is based in Southern California and the Maranatha! record label, which was on of the pioneer labels in Contemporary Christian music. The Maranatha! Worship Leader series was available in three degrees of fanciness. The least expensive was the 214-L3, which featured sapele sides and back and a spruce top. The next most expensive models were the 410ce-L3 and the 414ce-L3, both of which featured mahogany sides and backs and spruce tops. The most expensive versions were the 910ce-L3 which were made with Indian rosewood back and sides and an Engelmann

Front view of Ruby Red Presentation PS10ce.

A small selection of the one-of-a-kind inlays that the Taylor crew has designed for customers over the years.

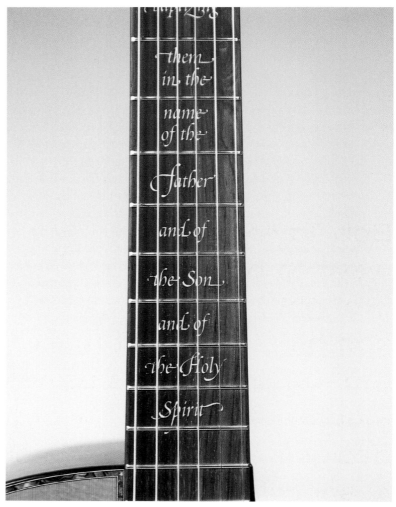

spruce top and the and the 954ce-L3, which substituted a Sitka spruce top for the Englemann top. All three levels of guitar featured a dove inlay on the headstock, although the fancier the guitar, the fancier the inlay.

And finally the 2003 limited editions included a number of nylon string guitars. The most intriguing one was the Doyle Dykes Nylon String (NS-DDSM), which featured a 14-fret neck and a custom L.R. Baggs pickup system. The other models were four grand auditorium cutaways including the sapele NS34ce, the rosewood NS74ce, the blue-burst maple NS64ce-L1 and the black-burst/cherry finished maple NS64ce-L2. Because one of the three sensors in the Expression System pickups require steel strings to work, the nylon string guitars were equipped with Fishman pickups.

2003 marked a turning point in the way Taylor marketed guitars. Prior to that year, the bulk of the guitars that the company made were part of the standard line and the special orders and limited edition instruments were just the icing on the cake. But in 2003, the limited editions almost became the standard line. Bob Taylor's genius for creating new ways to build guitars had unexpectedly brought him full circle. Three decades ago he started out making guitars to order. Now he was using sophisticated CNC machines and a crew of talented builders, designers and programmers to do essentially the same thing. Bob Taylor just spent thirty years turning a small custom guitar making shop into a giant custom guitar making shop. As the old saying goes, the more things change, the more they stay the same.

Bob Taylor's genius for creating new ways to build guitars had unexpectedly brought him full circle. Three decades ago he started out making guitars to order. Now he was using sophisticated machines and a crew of talented builders, designers and programmers to do essentially the same thing.

Thank You

The Author

I would like to thank Bob Taylor and Kurt Listug for giving so freely of their time and for allowing me to tell the story of their guitars. It goes without saying that this book would not have happened without their support. John D'Agostino and Amy DeGroot also offered valuable assistance, as did Rita Hoffman, who did an excellent job tracking down and processing most of the photos in the book. I also want to thank those people who allowed me to interview them over the course of this project. There are too many to mention individually, but you know who you are. Other people I want to thank include Frank Ford and Richard Johnston of Gryphon Stringed Instruments, who answered countless questions about the history of guitars and the music industry; John Morton and David Giulietti, who helped explain the mysteries of machine tools to me; Teja Gerken and Jason Verlinde, who offered their support as friends and as fellow writers; and Jürgen Sandhop and Alexander Schmidt who took my words and turned them into a book. And I want to thank my wife Leanne for putting up with me throughout the process of writing this book.

Michael Simmons, December 2003

The Publishing House

PPVMEDIEN would like to thank all staff at Taylor Guitars that have helped producing this book with great patience and commitment. We would particularly like to thank Bob Taylor and Kurt Listug for their trust, openness and support as well as Rita Hofmann, John D'Agostino, and Jonathan Forstot for supporting the project with unfailing good humor and interest. We would like to thank Robert Wilson for developing the idea of this book and for his kind provision of suggestions, information and help. Many thanks for her commitment and cooperation go to our graphic designer Saskia Kölliker.

U V W

X Y Z

1 2 3